Returning to the Source

# Returning to the Source

## The Final Stage of the Caribbean Migration Circuit

*Edited by*

DWAINE E. PLAZA *and* FRANCES HENRY

University of the West Indies Press

Jamaica ● Barbados ● Trinidad and Tobago

University of the West Indies Press
1A Aqueduct Flats   Mona
Kingston 7   Jamaica
www.uwipress.com

10 09 08 07 06     5 4 3 2 1


CATALOGUING IN PUBLICATION DATA

Returning to the source: the final stage of the Caribbean
migration circuit / edited by Dwaine E. Plaza and Frances Henry
p. cm.
Includes bibliographic references.

ISBN: 976-640-174-8

1. Return migration – Caribbean, English-speaking. 2. Caribbean,
English-speaking – Emigration and immigration. I. Plaza, Dwaine E.
II. Henry, Frances.


JV7321.R48 2006     304.8'729041



Book and cover design by Robert Harris.
E-mail: roberth@cwjamaica.com
Set in Tiasco 11/14 x 24

Printed in the United States of America.

For the millions of sojourners who left the Caribbean for North America and Europe in pursuit of a better life. Most aspired to return to the source and live out their lives in the only place they felt that they belonged and were at "home". Few will ever see their return dream materialize.

*In memory of Frank Gonzales and Tommy Plaza – two who never made it "home".*

# Contents

# Foreword

## Always on the Move

| Anton Allahar |

The English-speaking Caribbean is closely associated with the movement of people. All the way from the indigenous sea-going Caribs to the African slaves brought through the Middle Passage to the East Indian indentured servants who crossed the "dark waters" to the modern period, Caribbean people are noted for their movement. Whether it is to the beat of their lively music, to visit friends, to take on new adventures in new lands or to make the journey back "home", they are constantly on the move, and that constant movement has fitted them for most social encounters. This is why George Lamming sees the creolized Caribbean person as possessed of great cultural capital and as more than the sum of national groupings that went into her or his making: "No Indian from India, no European, no African can adjust with greater ease and naturalness to new situations" (Lamming 1960, 34).

The themes of travel, departure and return define much of Caribbean history and literature; they are linked with the above-mentioned ideas of both home and movement. These are recurrent motifs that reflect the post-colonial condition where the forced migrations associated with slavery and indentureship are the backdrops against which post-colonial Caribbean peoples now seek to establish diasporic existences and to fashion a new "way in the world" (Naipaul 1995), and also, more recently, to contemplate a return to their Caribbean homes. These twice-migrants (first from Africa and India and then from the Caribbean) are today reacting to the initial trauma of forced removal from their ancestral lands and have embraced a form of identity politics informed by a spiritual yearning for rootedness and symbolic return to "home".

Facing economic hardships, racism and general social exclusion in the new country, the migrants often find it comforting to think of "home" as a paradise that is free from the social malaises of their adopted countries. Thus, it is common for such immigrants to develop and propagate myths of the Caribbean as a place with economic and racial equality, with a deep sense of community caring and civic pride where everyone knows everyone and where everybody looks out for everybody. And as is well known, for a variety of social and psychological reasons, immigrants can come to believe these myths are true and even base decisions to return on those beliefs. The difficulty is that they seek to return with new baggage acquired in their years of "exile" (in Lamming's thinking), with new ideas and with hopes of reclaiming a "home" that is no longer there. In many cases, this has led to great disillusionment, at times even anger, as the comforting myths that were created to buffer the harsher aspects of a life of voluntary exile are quickly shattered.

## Diasporic Community and Identity

Given the earlier arrival and greater numbers of Africans, African-Caribbean sensibilities and sensitivities have come to define most of the region's identity politics. There are Middle Eastern-, Chinese-, European- and East Indian-descended populations in both the Caribbean and the Caribbean diasporas across the world, but it is to the African element that most attention is paid, and when independence came to these English-speaking countries, it was said to be "black" in complexion. Hence, those immigrants who claim African ancestry see the Caribbean as both "home" and an African diasporic "home away from home".

However, any talk of return migration must take into account the racial differentiation of Caribbean populations, the considerable racialization of popular political consciousness today, and the attempts of those non-African peoples to carve a space for their own Caribbean-derived identities within the Caribbean itself and in the diaspora (Allahar 1998). Here the politics of diaspora are increasingly tied to the politics of home, for whether in "exile" abroad or at "home" in the Caribbean, the connection to an African homeland is the centrepiece of much contemporary Afrocentric politics (Allahar 2004). For this reason, the concept of "diaspora" has come to figure so prominently in the common political parlance of today.

In Caribbean diasporic communities around the world, those first generation immigrants, who opted some four or five decades ago for a sort of voluntary "exile", have managed to make their marks on their host societies. For cultural change is a two-way process, and as Edwin Carrington has pointed out in the case of Europe, "the Caribbean's economic and cultural influence on Europe also needs to be created frontally. Their wealth may no longer fuel the advancement of Europe but they continue to provide significant political/cultural dimensions to Europe's own way of life and represent vital linkages in Europe's outreach for international influence" (Carrington 1991, xi–xii). Obviously, however, it is not just in Europe, for the Caribbean immigrant in New York, Boston, Toronto, Montreal, and so on, has had a clear economic, political and cultural impact on those cities and societies, and these are the points of departure for return migration among first-generation immigrants.

## Return to the Source

As is well documented, the most significant out-migration of Caribbean peoples began in the post–World War II period when largely unskilled jobs in the various European and North American capitals were plentiful. Facing the trauma of uprooting in the early years and not yet having the comfort and security of a critical mass of like-cultured compatriots, those immigrants faced all kinds of problems associated with racial discrimination, cultural misunderstanding, police harassment, unemployment and inadequate housing. By the late 1950s and early 1960s, as their numbers began to grow, West Indians in such cities as London, Birmingham, New York, Boston, Toronto and Montreal began to establish the first institutions of diasporic communities: a home away from home. These usually assumed the form of popular cultural institutions such as churches, restaurants, barber shops, hair dressing salons, cultural festivals like carnivals (notably in Notting Hill, Brooklyn and Toronto), sporting clubs and some professional associations.

With the passage of time, many members of that first generation became more culturally settled and more financially secure. By the 1970s they began to marry and produce a second-generation Trinidadian Canadian, Jamaican American, Barbadian English. Now at or nearing retirement years, they find themselves with sufficient accumulated resources to contemplate a return to "home" to spend those years in freedom: free from want, free of the winter, free of the hustle and bustle of having to work for a living, free of racism, and free of the sense of being an "other". They can be whole people once more, and for many this is very compelling.

Owing to post-war affluence and the heavy emphasis that Caribbean people have traditionally placed on education, this immigrant cohort has done quite well, which afforded them the opportunity to make more frequent trips back "home". Their children, on the other hand, still facing racial discrimination and exclusion in their countries of birth, began to identify with and embrace their parents' home as their home, and they came to adopt their parents' cultural icons as theirs. This was given a great boost with the simultaneous rise to world prominence of Bob Marley and the reggae craze that swept Europe and North America, followed by the successful export of soca music, the appearance of outstanding sportsmen like Brian Lara and Dwight Yorke, and even the pride in Nobel laureates Arthur Lewis, Derek Walcott and V.S. Naipaul. That first generation, who, in the early days, used to have to pay as much as ten dollars per minute to call the Caribbean, were aided by technological advances in the 1980s and onward that saw the phenomenon of the overseas phone call at less than a dollar a minute and the evolution of email (and, of course, the Internet) that put them in daily contact with news and developments back "home". Suddenly, coupled with cheaper air fares, "home" was a great deal closer, and the initial alienation that accompanied their immigration to foreign lands began to dissolve.

Added to this is the fact that, whether through the remittance of money, the cultural impact of multiple vacation trips or even the Caribbean person's penchant for travel abroad to visit friends and family, diasporas have exercised a decided impact on "home" matters. Indeed, owing to the forces of globalization, much of the Caribbean's popular culture, for example, is now produced and packaged in the diasporas (New York, Toronto and London). Recording studios based in the imperialist centres do the music, foreign factories fabricate most of the textiles and other materials for the carnival costumes, and in the Trinidad carnival, whole bands of masqueraders are known to travel "home" for the festival. Interestingly, too, because one soca or reggae performance in the New York, Miami or Toronto diaspora will net performers far more money than they would make at home, the promoters of Caribbean concerts outside the region can get performers to forgo significant Caribbean gigs in favour of foreign engagements.

## Conclusion

Now that migration is understood as a circular process, it implies not only leaving home but also a return to home. "Return" is seen as tied to a yearning for reconnection with family, friends and all that is familiar and suggests comfort. For, as noted earlier, in the modern globalized world, alienation and rootlessness associated with living in huge, impersonal, fast-paced, industrial megalopolises have served to isolate people from traditional communities of meaning and acceptance. These are the motivating forces behind the modern search for, maybe even preoccupation with, identity and belonging (identity politics of race, ethnicity, sex, sexual orientation, nationalism and so on), which also speak to the Caribbean immigrant and her or his urge to "return to the source".

In sum, then, for the individual in the diaspora, a Caribbean identity usually implies a crisis of belonging commonly experienced by the minority ethnic migrant, uprooted from the familiarity of home, cut adrift and all alone in a new land, feeling insecure and sometimes scared. The human condition, both today and in earlier times, is such that humans prefer to imagine a time when life was better, simpler and more predictable. Especially for those who, for whatever reasons, will feel physically, emotionally and psychologically displaced (for example, migrants and refugees), it is important and comforting to remember or even to invent the idea of the "good old days". That memory or invention is what lies behind much return migration, for as the challenges of migrant living mount, migrants can always harbour the idea of "going back home". It is like having a psychological escape valve, and just knowing it is there and can be activated whenever one wishes, gives one the strength to persevere and to give "exile" one more shot. Nostalgic recollections and even invention of what "home" was like provide cures for feelings of homelessness and alienation. It gives migrants security and familiarity about home and kinship, and it also tells them who they are and where they came from, all in an unbroken chain of generations. This provides a sense of continuity and comfort that guides migrants in their daily quest for meaning and belonging in life and can, eventually, play a key role in any decision to return *home* (Smith 1984).

# References

Allahar, A.L. 1998. Popular Culture and the Racialisation of Political Consciousness in Trinidad. *Wadabagei: Journal of the Caribbean and Its Diaspora* 1 (2): 1–41.

———. 2004. Ethnic Entrepreneurship and Nationalism in Trinidad: Afrocentrism and Hindutva. *Social and Economic Studies* 53 (2): 117–54.

Carrington, E. 1991. Foreword. *Europe and the Caribbean,* ed. P. Sutton. London: Macmillan.

Lamming, G. 1960. *The Pleasures of Exile.* London: Michael Joseph.

Naipaul, V.S. 1995. *A Way in the World: A Novel.* New York: Vintage.

Smith, A.D. 1984. National Identity and Myths of Ethnic Descent. *Research in Social Movements, Conflict and Change* 7: 9–130.

# An Overview of Return Migration to the English-Speaking Caribbean

| Dwaine E. Plaza *and* Frances Henry |

## Introduction

This book has two major objectives. First, it problematizes the concept of return migration. Second, it provides new data on the returning phenomenon from several perspectives within the English-speaking Caribbean region. The book brings together the results of research conducted by ten scholars on the returnee phenomenon that has dramatically increased since the 1990s. The increase is primarily due to the fact that the earlier waves of "pioneer" migrants who left for Britain in the late 1950s and the United States and Canada in the 1960s began reaching retirement age. In their attempt to fulfil the migration cycle, many of these men and women contemplated and acted on their desire to return to their place of birth to build a big home and display their success to those family, kin and friends who did not move. Many of the returnees have had difficult lives abroad working, often for only minimum wage, at jobs that were menial and hazardous to their long-term health. Most kept their hardships and lifestyles in the metropolitan countries a secret from family and kin in the Caribbean, because they feared losing admiration for their decision to migrate.

Prior to the return "home" of these pioneers, many had made return visits to rekindle family ties and linkages. Most would return to their villages laden with gifts, sporting fancy clothes and possessing a large amount of foreign dollars. The ritual of showering gifts on relatives and displaying wealth is partly imposed by the expectations of the people "back home". The transnational pressure to succeed has been strong enough to prevent some migrants from visiting "home" until they can do so in style. This same pressure often delays the permanent "return" because migrants must wait until they have sufficient resources for a grandiose return to impress family and friends.

Migration research is especially important today because of the massive movement of people in a world characterized by globalized transportation and communication systems as well as an integrated capitalistic economy. The pressure on people to move, especially from less-developed areas of the world, is therefore substantial. As well, their movement back to their countries of origin is also facilitated by the same globalized mechanisms that make that movement easily possible.

This introduction provides a brief summary of various traditional theoretical models developed to explain migration processes and how they relate to Caribbean people on the move. Our main intention, however, is to introduce the concept of transnationalism which we and many of the contributors to this volume understand to be the main driving force behind the current trends in the choices migrants make both in immigrating and in emigrating. This introduction also includes a summary review of relevant literature, much of which focuses on the factors responsible for both migration and return migration.

The Caribbean has been incorporated into the global system of capitalism since the fifteenth century, and the region has experienced successive waves of immigration, emigration and circulation. Most of the early flow was part of a system of coerced one-way immigration from Africa. Later movements included voluntary immigration from places like India, Syria, Portugal, China and various parts of Europe. Over time, migrations of all descriptions have been a fundamental force in the creation and maintenance of Caribbean societies (Conway 1988). Common to the migration traditions that have become part of the culture of the region has been the development of a desire on behalf of Caribbean people to circulate, but ultimately to return to their place of birth as a result of either wealth or old age (Thomas-Hope 1985, 1992, 1999; Byron 1994, 1999, 2000; Marshall 1982, 1983, 1987; Gmelch 1980, 1987, 1992).

A return to home is to be expected in any long-distance movement and concurs with Ravenstein's (1885) view that every migration flow has its counter-flow. One of the issues problematized in this book is the definition of what constitutes return migration to the English-speaking Caribbean. Eldridge (1965) was one of the first researchers to develop a typology of migrants that included return migration. He defined a primary migrant as anyone leaving a home region for the first time; a secondary migrant as anyone moving, subsequent to the first move, to any place other than the place of birth; and a return migrant as anyone returning to a place of birth. This definition is of course limited because it does not consider the many variations on the theme of "returning" to a place of birth particularly as this relates to the English-speaking Caribbean.

Bovenkerk defines two types of returnees in his typology of migration: "intended permanent emigration with return" and "intended temporary migration with return" (1974, 15). In addition, Bovenkerk notes that "the shorter the distance of emigration, the higher the incidence of return migration; . . . the longer the emigrants stay away the less chance they will return" (17). Changes in the economic balance between the place of origin and the place of destination also directly affect the volume of return migration.

Sill (2000) notes that contemporary scholars have incorporated more variations in their returnee classifications. These include the following: labour migrants who have returned to live in the country of origin as a result of successfully earning enough money; individuals who have left the labour market and returned to retire in their native land; individuals who have returned to their country of origin in order to take advantage of improved social, economic or political conditions; and migrants who failed to obtain work and returned shortly after arriving in the destination country. Also included in an expanded definition of returnee migrants are the related categories of circular or cyclical migration. These newer categories include such individuals as short-term guest workers, forced repatriations of refugees, deportees, transnational seasonal returnees, second-generation professionals who may have been born abroad but who decide to migrate to their parents' birth place and other non-voluntary migrants.

## Part 1: Theoretical Perspectives on Return Migration

Traditional sociological approaches have considered the migration process to be static in that people leave their countries in response to economic opportunities abroad. This has been given the name "push-pull". Having achieved their objectives, or not, migrants are often pulled back to their countries of birth because this is often the location where they feel a cultural affiliation and a level of comfort. This is the phenomenon of return migration. Several theories have emerged to explain return migration. These include the disappointment theory, the circular migration theory, the target income theory and the social network theory.

## The Disappointment Theory

The disappointment theory of migration maintains that people engage in return migration because they "failed" (that is, could not find employment or could earn only low wages) at the target location (Herzog and Schottman 1982). People move with the intention of settling in the new location but with limited information before migration, some may miscalculate the benefits of migration and then decide to return. It is difficult to know what information prospective migrants have before migrating; hence, supporters of this hypothesis use measures of distance and the immigrants' education as proxies for available information. They believe that the greater the distance between origin and destination, the sparser the information about a new location and thus the greater the chance of making a mistake. This theory does not apply well to migrants from the English-speaking Caribbean because of geographical proximity to receiving countries in North America. In addition, the improvements in communication technology and low-cost airfares have provided an avenue for real-time information sharing for family and kin in both the sending and receiving countries.

## The Circular Migration Theory

The circular migration theory refers to "a great variety of movement, usually short term, repetitive or cyclical in nature, but all having in common the lack of any declared intention of a permanent or long lasting change of residence" (Zelinsky 1971, 225–26). Land shortages, pressures on agricultural resources, and the temporary and unstable quality of migrant employment in the home country make it difficult for people to earn sufficient income to support themselves and their families. Under these conditions, circular migration provides the means to maximize family income and keep the mover's options open for both the origin and destination, reducing the risk of not being able to support the family (Elkan 1959; Hugo 1981). As the constant shuttling back and forth becomes more difficult to sustain, the migrant is likely to bring his or her family to settle permanently in the new "home" country (Durand and Massey 1992). In general, this theory does explain the movement of seasonal farm workers circulating between the Caribbean and North America. It also explains the newer phenomenon of transnational seasonal returnees who live between their "home" country and the place where they originally migrated to. These individuals have typically retired and are enjoying the benefits of a good pension that allows them to live in two places. They can maintain a home in North America while at the same time having a winter residence in the Caribbean. This new generation of "snowbirds" is able to take advantage of cheaper airfares and access to better health care and social services. They can also continue to stay in touch with transnational family and kin spread throughout the diaspora. This advantage is mainly available to those men and women from North America, Europe and Britain who migrated in the 1960s.

## The Target Income Theory

According to the target income theory, immigrants move to accumulate savings to invest in better technologies or to buy more land in their home community (Borjas 1994; Hill 1987; Lindstrom 1996; Massey et al. 1993). This theory assumes that immigrants have a strong preference for remaining in their home community rather than relocating to a new country, but they must resort to international migration because of limited opportunities at home (Berg 1961). This cohort of immigrants plan to stay in the new country for as long as it takes to accumulate enough savings to reach a particular level of income: they then return to their place of origin. The higher their income, the faster they are able to accumulate their target income and the sooner they return. This theory seems to best apply to migrants from the English-speaking Caribbean. The flow of migration from the region in the post-emancipation period has followed this circulatory flow (Marshall 1982). Many of these individuals move to another place but maintain contact with family and kin left behind and, in retirement or old age, attempt to return to their place of birth.

## The Social Network Theory

Social network theory regards immigration as a social process that involves networking as well as an economic process. As proposed by Massey (1987, 68), "Immigration is far more dynamic than standard economic analysis suggests because it tends to feed back on itself through social channels.... Once a critical takeoff stage is reached, migration alters social structures in a way that increases the likelihood of subsequent migration.... It relies on a variety of social-structural mechanisms, the most important of which is network formation." In addition to increasing the probability of migration by reducing its cost, social networks may increase the probability of permanent settlement (Greenwood 1969; Taylor 1976). Prospective immigrants can count on earlier migrants for information, transportation, housing and, in some cases, even employment. Every new migrant expands the social network and reduces the risk for all other potential migrants (Lomnitz 1977). According to this model, return migration to the Caribbean could work in the other direction. Once away, the Caribbean migrant could be receiving feedback from family and kin left behind, hence making the decision to return much more likely if the information is positive.

## Part 2: Transnationalism

More recent research, including many of the chapters in this volume, demonstrates that the return process is in fact more complex. Until recently, migration was understood in terms of two opposing outcomes: permanent settlement or permanent return. Return migration especially was thought of as the final outcome of the migration process. This relatively static bipolar model is a simplistic depiction of unilinear flows as well as return migration and is not consistent with the realities of population movements in an increasingly transnational world. These complexities, which characterize migration and the return migrant, are more aptly encompassed within a framework of migration processes.

Migration processes can best be understood in terms of the transnational movement of people. This term can be defined as referring to the multiple ties and interactions that link people and their institutions across the borders of nation-states. Transnationalism is now understood to have many elements including "social morphology, as a type of consciousness, as a mode of cultural reproduction, as an avenue of capital, as a site of political engagement, and as a reconstruction of place" (Vertovec 1999). As a descriptive category or social morphology, transnational groups are those that are globally dispersed but still identify in terms of their original ethnicity and relate to both the host states in which they reside and the home countries from which they or their ancestors originated. They are tied together transglobally through a variety of social relationships or networks. Transnational diaspora communities are therefore characterized by combinations of ties: positions in networks and organizations that reach across the international borders to link people together. These communities are formed on the basis of dynamic social processes – not static notions of ties and positions. Cultural, political and economic processes in transnational social spaces involve the accumulation, use and effects of various sorts of capital. Migration and re-migration may not be definite, irrevocable and irreversible decisions; transnational lives in themselves may become a strategy of survival and betterment. Transnational webs may also include relatively immobile persons and collectives. Even those migrants and refugees who have settled for a considerable time outside their country of origin frequently maintain strong transnational links. These links can be of a more informal nature, such as intra-household or family ties, or they can be institutionalized, such as political parties maintaining branches in various countries, both of immigration and emigration.

Transnational diaspora communities can perhaps best be understood as part of the processes of global integration and time-space compression. This is partly a technological issue: improved transport and accessible real-time electronic communication is the material basis of globalization. But above all, it is a social and cultural issue. Globalization is closely linked to changes in social structures and relationships as well as shifts in cultural values concerned with place, mobility and belonging. This is likely to have important consequences, which we are only just beginning to understand (Bauman 1998; Castells 1996).

One of the most intriguing features of transnational communities is the role that personal identity plays in the consciousness of its members. Some

identify more with one society or another while others assume multiple identities. Hall (1988) has noted that the condition of the transnational provides
for ever-changing representations or identities. Robin Cohen observes that
to a certain degree "a diaspora can be held together or re-created through the
mind, through cultural artefacts and through a shared imagination" (1987).
Cultural products are important in maintaining identity – and such forms as
music, religious practices, fashion, visual arts, films, language (accent and
colloquial adages) and ways of cooking food are some of the most conspicu-
ous areas in which such processes are observed.

## Origins of the Transnational Caribbean Diaspora

When slavery ended in the Commonwealth Caribbean (following the legal
proclamation of 1834), former slaves were eager to establish their own communities away from the plantations. Many moved to free lands on neighbouring islands or at least off the plantation property but discovered that they
could not survive without part-time or seasonal work on the plantations or at
other places of employment. Circulation – a form of migration in which the
migrant families live year-round in the home community while the migrant
members of the family move away seasonally for work – became a part of the
wider culture.

Gradually over time, local circulation expanded to include regional circulation and longer periods of migrant residence away from home. Circulation
within the Caribbean region expanded further over time to include longer-
distance movement to Panama in the late nineteenth century, the United
States in the period of 1900 to 1930, Britain in the 1950s, and Canada and the
United States again from the late 1960s to the present. The longer-distance
moves were associated with longer-term residence abroad and in some cases
led to permanent settlement abroad. Over this long period up to the 1960s,
the genesis of a Caribbean diaspora in some major cities in the eastern United
States (New York, Boston and Baltimore), Canada (Toronto and Montreal),
and in the United Kingdom (London, Manchester and Birmingham) can be
observed. The formation of large Caribbean-origin migrant communities in
these cities and the resources that such immigrant communities provided to
new migrants strengthened and transformed the Caribbean culture of
migration. Caribbean peoples began to see themselves as both "here" and

"there" – with the "here" being wherever they were living (in the Caribbean, Britain, Canada or the United States) and the "there" being any of the Caribbean communities in another country to which they were connected through family ties, friendships and community linkages. "Home" began to be viewed not just as the place where one was born or just where one lived, but more generally where friends, relatives and members of the cultural community were to be found. In effect, what began as a Caribbean culture of migration expanded over time to become a diasporic Caribbean transnational cultural community.

Caribbean people in the international diaspora are quite diverse – they originate from different islands, ethnic groups, social classes and cultures within the Caribbean region, and many are now part of a second if not third generation in the metropolitan countries where they have settled. Despite this diversity, they form a cultural and social community based on their identification with the music, history, traditions and achievements of people from the Caribbean region and their participation in Caribbean community organizations, cultural events, churches and temples.

The Caribbean-origin communities in New York, Toronto or London are clearly transnational, drawing on strong links and support from Caribbean family and friends in the Caribbean and other countries. Most Caribbean migrants who have legal immigrant status move about quite freely. Many make return trips to the Caribbean to vacation and to see friends and kin. They receive visits from relatives living in the Caribbean, Canada, the United Kingdom and the United States. Family members in the metropolitan countries send large amounts of cash and gifts (often in the form of "barrels" of clothing and household items) to support relatives in their respective home countries.

An impressive body of relevant research exists on diasporas (Clifford 1994), "transnational social networks" (Fawcett 1989; Boyd 1989; Massey 1987), "transnational communities" (Basch et al. 1994; Vertovec 2001) and global migration patterns (Castles and Miller 1993). Studies of Caribbean migrants and their communities in Britain, the United States and Canada have contributed in important ways to this large body of research. Previous studies have addressed such matters as the history of the black diaspora in the North Atlantic (Gilroy 1993) and its cultural politics in Britain (Gilroy 1991, 2000). They have examined the evolution of the Caribbean culture and practice of migration from colonial times until the late twentieth century

(Simmons and Guegant 1992). These and other studies draw attention to the role of political, cultural and social economic forces from colonial times to the present in the formation of the Caribbean diaspora and the development of Caribbean transnational communities.

The pioneering study of transnational process among various Caribbean communities in New York by Basch et al. (1994, 12) provided important new insights on the role of transnational migrants "who develop and maintain multiple relationships (familial, economic, social, organizational, religious and political) that span borders". Various studies have examined how Caribbean transnational migrants forge a complex matrix of intense social relationships that connect localities – Kingston, Miami, London, New York, Toronto, Montreal – in different nation-states – Jamaica, the United States, the United Kingdom, Canada (for example, see Olwig 1993; Portes 1996; Glick-Schiller 1998; Foner 1997; Ho 1999; Plaza 2000; Goulbourne 2002). Previous researchers also point to the importance of occupations and activities that require regular and sustained social contacts over time, and across national borders for their implementation (Guarnizo 1997).

These studies find that migrants do not forget their home communities, nor do they lose contact with families, community organizations and political movements in their countries of origin, as they become part of a new society (Ho 1993; Goldring 2001; Olwig 2002). Rather, the migrants take advantage of new opportunities, through travel and inexpensive telecommunications, to be simultaneously part of their home society as well as the society to which they have moved (Glick-Schiller et al. 1992; Portes 1996; Vertovec 2001). Both the home and migrants' newly settled societies are in turn simultaneously transformed by these transnational links.

Much of the research on transnational social networks and communities assumes that these societies are particularly strong when they arise as part of an effort to overcome oppression. Transnational social networks and communities among formerly colonized and still racialized minorities are understood to be part of their effort to resist marginalization, discrimination, exploitation and segregation in the countries to which they have moved, in their home nations and in the international system generally. From this perspective, Caribbean carnival parades in New York, Miami and Toronto are perceived to be more than simply efforts by a cultural minority to feel "at home" in a new place and to maintain cultural traditions. Such public displays of culture and other actions by the minority transnational community members serve to generate community solidarity, recognition and resources for social action and transformation.

Transnationalism plays a major part in the return migrants' reintegration and mobilization for social development. Faist (2000) highlights the bridging function of social capital. This function occurs not only when groups are formed at home and overseas, but also when there is an active transnational exchange between these groups; that is, between migrants who are abroad and their families, kin and advocates who are in the origin country. Such transnational exchanges help the development of the origin community, even as these exchanges allow migrants to prepare for their eventual return and retain contacts with their hometowns. On the other hand, as migrants abroad plan for their eventual return, they pool their economic and social resources to offer assistance to the origin community.

## Part 3: Literature on Return Migration to the Caribbean

Although return migration on a global scale has been the subject of considerable study in places like Italy, Greece, Mexico, Ireland and Turkey, only a handful of studies have been done on return migration to the English-speaking Caribbean (Bovenkerk 1974; King 1986). Most research on the phenomenon of return migration to the Caribbean region has focused on Puerto Rico and the Dominican Republic – primarily because these Spanish-speaking territories have sent larger numbers of their population to the United States – more than any other country in the region. As a result of their substantial numbers of migrants, these two locations have the largest number of individual potential returnee migrants (Pessar 1997; Muschkin 1993; Grasmuck and Pessar 1992; Guarnizo 1997).

Return migration to the English-speaking Caribbean only began to receive serious attention from research scholars in the early 1970s. Most of the early studies concentrated either on the returnees' adjustment problems (Patterson 1968; Davidson 1969; Taylor 1976; Nutter 1985) or the development implications of return migrants and retirees (Gmelch 1987; Stinner 1982; Thomas-Hope 1985; Byron 1994). There have also been a few studies of return migration from Britain to the Caribbean that indicate the significance of the social and economic aspects of the return phenomenon. Peach

(1968) points out how each wave of returnees fluctuated depending on the booms and busts in the British economy. Davidson (1969) found that the returnees to Jamaica experienced a shock upon return due to the realization that the cost of living had risen alarmingly and there was neither work nor housing. Philpott (1968) reported similar results of disillusionment for return migrants from Montserrat who ultimately went back to England after a short return period. Studying the social adjustment aspect of return to the region, Taylor (1976) notes that there were differences in happiness and success between retiring returnees to rural versus urban areas in Jamaica. Returnees to the rural areas indicated much higher levels of satisfaction than individuals returning to the urban areas.

Another limitation of the existing return migration literature to the English-speaking Caribbean is the fact that it has been focused on the experiences of the returnees, who are typically around retirement age (Rubenstein 1982; Thomas-Hope 1985, 1999; Gmelch 1980, 1987; Gmelch and Gmelch 1995; Byron 1994). In looking at the economic impact of returnees on the host society, Gmelch (1980) found that retirees brought with them innovations and investments which benefited the Barbadian economy and society. Thomas-Hope (1999) noted a similar phenomenon in Jamaica whereby retiring return migrants had a dramatic impact in jump-starting the poor economy through the influx of foreign currency and, by hiring builders and other trades people, they also aided the local labour market. Abenaty (2000) also points out a similar pattern among seniors returning to St Lucia. Many continued to be economically active by starting small entrepreneurial enterprises, many of which employed locals. Abenaty also notes that senior returnees experienced problems in terms of disappointment on their return to St Lucia. Many had high expectations for being welcomed back to the island of their birth. Most found, however, a great deal of resentment towards them for what the local population regarded as ostentatious displays of their wealth.

More recently, Thomas-Hope (2002) notes a similar disillusionment with the decision to return among a group of skilled returnees to Jamaica. During their stay abroad, the highly skilled group tended to develop livelihood expectations that could not easily be met in Jamaica, their country of origin. After living in their place of origin for more than a year, many continued to maintain close economic and social links with their former country of residence. Many of the skilled returnees in the sample continued to maintain a foreign citizenship, thus suggesting that their return to Jamaica may not be the final move in the migration cycle.

Goulbourne's (2002) study of returning migrants to Jamaica in the 1990s further highlights new issues and problems for families and governments in areas that both receive and send migrants. The return of elderly men and women has a number of negative effects, starting with the absence of grandparents in the upbringing and development of the young who remain behind in Britain. The impact of the returnees on the local housing stock, the local communities and the medical facilities was seen as detrimental and resulted in driving up costs for local governments, particularly those hard hit by structural adjustment policies over the last ten years. The added drain on the system by these newly returned local-foreigners resulted in disillusionment among both the returnees and the local population.

Nutter (1985), Byron (2000) and Plaza's (2002) work has captured the most recent phenomenon of second-generation return migration to the Caribbean. Nutter's sample of return migrants in Kingston, Jamaica represents a significantly skilled minority with respect to the national workforce, and their success appeared to be related to their education and work experience obtained overseas. Byron's (2000) research finds that some young, economically active returnees to the region have tended to invest in small cluster business categories linked to the tourism industry. Others have sought jobs as employees within hotels. Most, however, have become self-employed, providing accommodation, transportation, boutiques and bars to serve the tourism industry and, more generally, the service sector. More recently, Plaza (2002) identified a growing trend of "return" migration to the Caribbean among second-generation British-Caribbean persons. Second-generation "returnees" from Britain do not fit the typical profile of elder retired migrants returning to their place of birth. These individuals typically have a university degree or a specialized professional qualification and a desire to work once they move back to the Caribbean. The findings from Plaza's (2002) research suggest that a hoped for idyllic reconnection with the Caribbean has not taken place for second-generation returnees because the issues of race, gender, skin colour and class politics prevent their smooth transition into their "home" societies.

More recently there has been an increased interest in the return migration phenomenon by government officials in the English-speaking Caribbean because the circulation of these individuals appears to have an impact on the local economy in terms of the growth of self-employed businesses, tourism and service sector industries (De Souza 1998; Thomas-Hope 1999; Potter 2001). The future cohorts of returnees do represent a potential resource for local Caribbean governments since they often bring savings, skills and an entrepreneurial fervour that might be used to help kick start economies depleted by years of structural adjustment.

Despite the existence of some important research on return migration to the English-speaking Caribbean, much still needs to be done, especially with respect to new trends and developments. This is the primary focus of this collection – to provide more information on the returnee phenomenon to the Caribbean. The topics covered in this book are important for policy makers because of the increasing number of Caribbean-born retirees from North America and Europe who could potentially choose to return "home" in the next ten years. Most of these would be elder returnees since many of the migrants who left in the late 1960s have now reached pensionable age. Having as much information about the social, cultural, political and economic adjustments is important for families, government officials, individual sojourners and those contemplating the move back.

## Part 4: Factors Involved in Making the Decision to Return

The decision to return to one's place of birth is very complex and depends on a set of facts about a migrant's life, cultural references and values. It is also a strategic choice made at a particular time in an individual's life. The path leading from *intention* to return (professed by the majority of migrants) to *actual* return is difficult to predict. Economic theory offers two different perspectives on return migration. Neoclassical economic theory views return migration as a cost-benefit decision, with actors deciding to stay or return in order to maximize expected net lifetime earnings (Todaro 1976). In the neoclassical model, social attachments generally operate on the cost side of the equation. Attachments to people and institutions in the origin country lower the costs of going "home", both psychologically and monetarily, and they raise the costs of remaining abroad. In contrast, attachments (to grandchildren, family or kin) at the place of destination operate in precisely the opposite direction, raising the costs of return migration while decreasing the costs of staying.

Migrant motives for return to the English-speaking Caribbean have included strong family ties in the home country, dissatisfaction with present social status or conditions (typically in Canada, the United States or Britain), obligation to relatives, feelings of loyalty, guilt for living abroad, patriotism, perception of better opportunities opening up in the Caribbean and nostalgia (Sill 2000). Some intervening factors that influence return include the following: changes in the social or political conditions in either homeland or receiving context (such as recession or political opposition to migration); marriage while in the destination country; marriage or relationship breakdown while abroad; having children in the new country of residence and the need to socialize them in the Caribbean; the number of family members who have migrated; ownership of property in the receiving country; the distance between the source and destination country; the number of return visits over the period of migration; the form of government in the home country; inequality in the source country; the acquisition of citizenship in the host country; length of stay in the host country; and the age at the time of migration.

Among the most important factors that encourage return are lasting ties with family and local society, and the education of migrant children. Among the conditions that prompt return include the maintenance of affective ties with the home country through frequent trips home, close relations with fellow absent compatriots, listening to local music, participation in traditional cultural events, the maintenance of the local language (dialects) and reading both newspapers and Internet websites from home. But these factors are only determinant when they compound a low degree of host country satisfaction.

Reagan and Olsen (2000), using data from the National Longitudinal Survey of Youth, compared patterns of return migration among both male and female immigrants. They did not find a gender differential but they did uncover lower probabilities of return migration among those who had arrived at younger ages, those with higher potential wages, those with more years in the United States and those participating in welfare programs. Duleep and Regets (1999, 186) characterize the emigration of foreigners either as "mistaken migration", whereby disillusioned immigrants return home soon after arrival or "retirement migration", where immigrants return home after withdrawl from the labour force at an older age.

An observation on length of stay in the country of immigration implies that the process of integration is an evolutionary one that transforms the aspiration, ways of thinking, and interests of the émigrés. This realization enables Cerase (1974) to refine his observations and to outline three types of returns: failure returnees (return before two years), innovative returnees (returning after six to ten years), and retirement returns (return after eleven to twenty years). Failure returns are frequently prompted by disappointment and often follow short stays overseas. Failure is not an abstract notion, and many empirical studies have sought to determine its characteristics. Difficulty in adjusting to the host country is found to be the primary cause of failure. There are many facets to adjustment including migrant age: the older a migrant is at the time of departure, the shorter the stay abroad. The manifestation of racism in host countries constrains or limits access and opportunity for migrants of colour and is a strong factor in lack of adjustment.

Others, while recognizing the impact of racism, are able to accommodate themselves in the new, yet discriminatory society. Returns are also promoted by cataclysmic events such as loss of employment or housing, illness, divorce, death, and so on. These difficulties play the role of catalyst, transforming a potential choice into a positive decision. (See figure 1.1 for an illustration of the return migration phenomenon to the English-speaking Caribbean using the typologies of Cerase [1974] and Sill [2000].) The new model presented adds a different timescale and some new cohorts of returnees which include young professionals and deportees.

Most return migrants in the English-speaking Caribbean cannot be viewed as failures, but as "successes". That is, most returnees have met their income goals and are returning home to enjoy the fruits of their success. Therefore, unlike neoclassical economics, the new economics of labour migration predicts that return migrants will be negatively selected with respect to work effort – those migrants who work fewer hours per week will have to remain abroad longer to meet a given income target. Factors of attraction, although difficult to measure, are clearly determined and appear to be a stronger motivation than factors of dissuasion. This does not mean that dissuading factors are unimportant. On the contrary, they are often more mentioned in the literature and include racism, difficulty in integration, difficulty in finding work and difficulty in coping with climate.

The decision to return to one's country of origin is essentially an affective one, tempered by a strategy for a higher socio-professional status. At the two extremes, failure returns and structural returns (when chances and opportunities are either positively or negatively comparable in the two countries, emotional factors take precedence in the decision to return). Between failure and structural return, the decision to move back is the result of a strategy that has social ascension as its goal. Migrants negotiate between the affective nature of their decision for themselves, their family and the receiving society.

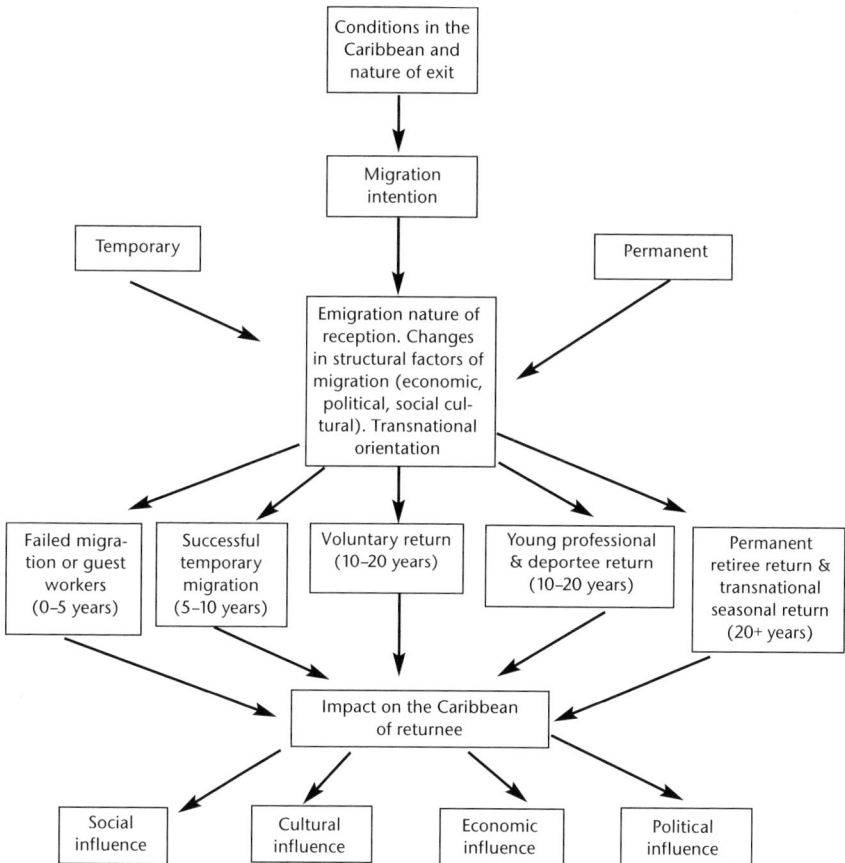

**Figure 1.1** A Model of Return Migration to the English-Speaking Caribbean

*Source:* Modified for the Caribbean context from Cerase's (1974) and Sill's (2002) general models of return.

## Part 5: Factors That Increase Successful Reintegration to the Home Country

Return migration and reintegration present a significant challenge to the English-speaking Caribbean territories. For return migration to work, the social and economic conditions for the migrants' smooth and dignified return must be in place. Crucial to reintegration and return migration is the role of financial capital. If earning more abroad is a primary reason for emigration, then the bringing home of significant savings and investment from abroad is important to sustain a migrant's intention of return and successful reintegration.

The return and readjustment for migrants are influenced by many factors that can make the re-entry difficult or relatively easy:

1.  Length of stays abroad, the returnees' stage in the life cycle, their socio-economic status and their access to resources on return all affect re-entry. Those who have stayed abroad a long time without making return visits in between find it difficult to reintegrate.
2.  Socio-economic status and available resources – brought back, previously invested or mobilized on return – have a strong bearing on the degree and speed of reintegration to the home country.
3.  Reintegration hinges on the capacity of the society of return to accommodate the returnees. Much depends on that society's security and stability, the state of its economy and its capacity to mobilize resources to assist or facilitate reintegration of the sojourner.
4.  Return migrants who have not been alienated from the culture and practices of their origin communities will have a greater chance to become reintegrated.
5.  Maintaining a transnational connection over the period they were away plays a major part in reintegration into a migrant's birthplace. Such transnational exchanges help in the development of the origin community, even as they allow migrants to retain contacts with their hometowns and prepare them for their eventual return.
6.  Reintegration often hinges on the presence of extended families, kin or co-ethnics in communities receiving returnees.
7.  Sojourners who have stayed abroad a long time without making return visits may find it difficult to reintegrate. This is especially true for the

children of returnees or those born and raised abroad. This may raise issues of what constitutes "home" for these so-called returnees.

## Conclusion

Return migration and circulation has long been an integral part of the social and economic fabric of the English-speaking Caribbean region. Returnees in the past as well as the present play an extremely significant role in the region's development. Returnee groups, as a result of their lifetime of work overseas, are able to contribute to the region's experience and skill base. Many returnees are also parents and grandparents who add to the human and social capital of their "home" nations in myriad ways, and they add to the transnational reciprocal linkages which serve to bind members of the diaspora together.

Several opportunities and problems are generated by the process of return and resettlement to the English-speaking Caribbean. These include both practical and psychological difficulties involved in the decision to move from one place to another, and these are often compounded by the returnees' memories and expectations of the idealized homeland that they departed from some ten or more years ago.

By including ten case studies concerned with various types of return migration to different locations, this book seeks to develop a broader and more encompassing approach to the study of return migration by locating it in the context of the transnational pursuit of mobility, happiness and success for men and women originally from the English-speaking Caribbean.

The long-term future of return migration to the Caribbean is still very unpredictable. Demographically, there is a growing number of second- and third-generation Caribbean men and women living in the international diaspora. These are individuals who do not know the Caribbean as their place of birth or idealized paradise. Some of these men and women are the product of inter-ethnic non-Caribbean/Caribbean relationships. Most, however, know the Caribbean as a region where they can visit distant family and kin. Their connection to the Caribbean region may be primarily based on their parents' or grandparents' experiences and reminisces. It may also be based on their love of Caribbean foods or music: both of which they have come to equate with being authentically Caribbean. As a consequence of the shifting

demographic realities, the current phenomenon of return migration may
diminish in the future because the pool of traditional "returnees" will
become fewer and fewer.

One factor that might continue to fuel the desire for return among the
future third and fourth generations in the international diaspora is the continued existence of racism and alienation in metropolitan countries where
Caribbean people have settled. Faced with these sad realities, in future many
may continue to hold onto the same dreams as their ancestors – to return to
the "source" where they will be accepted and feel at home regardless of skin
colour or ethnicity. This naïve desire does not, of course, take into consideration the realities of Caribbean societies that are also stratified based on
"race", gender, social class and sexual orientation. They are also societies
which have had to weather the harsh realties of structural adjustment economic policies which have helped to create a more individualistic society
where it is "everyone for him or her self".

During the most recent period, a new phenomenon of transnationalism
has emerged among older retired migrants moving back from the Caribbean
to North America. These are typically individuals who went abroad for
schooling or who spent a long enough time living abroad to get their citizenship status for Canada or the United States. These "successful" temporary
migrants likely spent less than ten years in the metropolitan countries before
returning to their place of birth. As legal citizens of both their countries of
origin and the host migrant countries, these people are free to live in any part
of the world and still enjoy the protections of being a Canadian or American.
These migrants returned to the Caribbean in the late 1970s and 1980s and
started their own businesses or worked in high profile positions within the
government. In the late 1990s, some of them reached retirement age in the
Caribbean and have now begun to return to North America in search of better medical care, to be reunited with children and grandchildren, or to escape
the rising levels of crime and social instability in the Caribbean. The pattern
of migration – to-ing and fro-ing – include people who are moving in
response to conditions in both locations. They are the new transnationalists
whose legal movement out and back is likely to increase over the years as
more individuals are desirous of taking advantage of the benefits offered in
both locations.

The research question that is still very much open – even after the completion of this book – is as follows: how long will the return migration phenom-

enon sustain itself among Caribbean-origin men and women now living in the international diaspora?

## The Contributions

This book contains ten contributors who are leading experts in the English-speaking Caribbean on the return migration phenomenon. The chapters are broadly focused on the bigger territories like Jamaica, Barbados and Trinidad, but we also have significant contributions from the smaller islands such as St Lucia and Tobago. The chapters in this collection are primarily qualitative in nature because very little accurate data currently exist on the number of English-speaking Caribbean migrants who return either temporarily or permanently. The governments in these countries excel in documenting the exit of Caribbean migrants, but these same governments struggle to document those who have actually returned. Some of this difficulty in tracking individuals returning is that many are actually living more transnational returnee lifestyles whereby they will spend many months in the Caribbean but then return to their place of migration to reconnect with family and kin still living abroad or to seek out medical or other social services more readily available outside the region. Hence the new waves of returnees are more transnational than previous waves who returned to the Caribbean back in the 1970s and 1980s; those who returned with the intention of never leaving again.

### *Dennis A.V. Brown*

The central theme of this chapter is a broad overview of the history of Caribbean migration/circulation from the period of post-emancipation to the present. Brown notes that the character of the return migration process to the region is a dynamic one that has evolved in accordance with the changing character of Caribbean society and its relationship to global society. The presumption is made that this interface between processes at the local, regional and global levels is fundamental to what happens within Caribbean society.

## George Gmelch

This chapter examines the emigration and return of Barbadians from Britain and North America. While both ends of the migration cycle are described, Gmelch's focus is on the experiences of Barbadians returning to the Caribbean, and what it means to come home, for both the individual and the society.

## Roger-Mark De Souza

This chapter examines the attachments, socio-cultural connections, kinship bonds and interpersonal relations involved in the return migration process. Using one hundred life stories from interviews with Trinidadian long-term returnees, De Souza examines the saliency of socio-cultural factors that influence return movement, particularly the sense of belonging. He finds that while social attachments are the main reason for return, it is the area where returnees experience the most problems.

## Francis K. Abenaty

This chapter examines the return of St Lucians to their place of birth. Abenaty is particularly concerned with comparing the return experiences from a group of British-born, or British-reared, respondents, to those of some St Lucian returnees who had migrated to Britain in the 1950s and 1960s.

## Heather A. Horst

This chapter examines the relationship between building a home and becoming a returned migrant in Jamaica throughout the 1990s. In particular, it examines how returnees use their newly constructed house as conduit for gaining a sense of belonging at "home". Focusing upon the processes of rebuilding a life at "home", the chapter examines the ways in which returning migrants utilize material culture to transgress the sense of alienation from land and people in Jamaica and explores the relationship between particular objects of material culture. Returnees seek to construct lifestyles which counteract the years of hard work endured in order to allow return and retirement in Jamaica. Large houses and consumer goods both assert and assist in the creation of a lifestyle of leisure and enjoyment.

## Dwaine E. Plaza

This chapter examines the trend of "return" migration to Jamaica and Barbados among second-generation British-Caribbean people. Second-generation "returnees" from Britain do not fit the typical profile of elder retired migrants returning to their place of birth. These individuals typically have a university degree or a specialized professional qualification and a desire to work once they move to the Caribbean. The desire, on behalf of the young returnees, for an idyllic reconnection with the Caribbean has not manifested itself because the issues of race, gender, skin colour and class politics prevent their smooth transition.

## Elizabeth Thomas-Hope

This chapter illustrates the nature of return migration as an essential aspect of circulation. Using a transnational theoretical framework, this chapter highlights the ways in which this space is constructed and "politicized" in the sense that it is negotiated by migrants in an effort to maximize the value of their migration. Who returns is determined by factors of selectivity that originate in international and national relationships and, at the same time, in community, family and individual livelihood strategies. Neither the outward nor the return moves are confined to one type of person or carried out for a single purpose. On the contrary, persons in all professions, the unemployed, dependents and students, as well as persons of all ages, be they male or female, have been and continue to be engaged in the migration process – outward movement and return.

## Godfrey C. St Bernard

This chapter uses a phenomenological approach to examine the experience of return for Tobagonians. Using a case-study approach, the meanings and experience of return migration are examined from the perspective of both the retirees and of others actively participating in the island's labour force as entrepreneurs. The chapter examines the nature of return and the extent to which returnees are likely to foster or hamper social development prospects for Tobago.

## John Small

This chapter examines the interlocking dynamics of emigration and the causes for the flow of Caribbean people to the United Kingdom, Canada and the United States in general, and the return flows to Jamaica in particular. The chapter construes the experiences of the migrant and adjustment issues in the receiving country as critical variables in the decision to return. Data on return migration to Jamaica is presented with particular emphasis on the return flow from the United Kingdom. The chapter also examines the activities of returnees and the process of readaptation to the homeland.

## Harry Goulbourne

This final chapter examines the return phenomenon from Britain to Jamaica in the 1990s. Goulbourne highlights the impact of age and gender in the return migration process and resettlement; reassessment of the present and potential skills and financial contribution of returnees to Caribbean economies; the impact of returnees on family members who remain in the United Kingdom, in particular the absence of grandparents. From this overview, Goulbourne makes policy suggestions for both the sending and receiving countries and highlights areas for future research on the phenomenon.

# References

Abenaty, F.K. 2000. St Lucians and Migration: Migrant Returnees, their Families and St Lucian Society. PhD diss., South Bank University.

Basch, L., et al. 1994. *Nations Unbounded: Transnational Projects Post-Colonial Predicaments and Deterritorialized Nation-States.* Amsterdam: Gordon and Breach.

Bauman, Z. 1998. On Glocalization: Or Globalization for Some, Localization for Some Others. *Thesis Eleven* 54: 37–49.

Berg, E.J. 1961. Backward-Sloping Labor Supply Functions in Dual Economies: The Africa Case. *Quarterly Journal of Economics* 75: 468–92.

Borjas, G.J. 1994. The Economics of Immigration. *Journal of Economic Literature* 32: 1667–1717.

Bovenkerk, F. 1974. *The Sociology of Return Migration: A Bibliographic Essay.* The Hague: Martinus Nijoff.

Boyd, M. 1989. Families and Personal Networks in International Migration: Recent Developments and New Agendas. *International Migration Review* 23 (3): 606–30.

Byron, M. 1994. *Post-War Caribbean Migration to Britain: The Unfinished Cycle.* London: Avebury Press.

———. 1999. The Caribbean-Born Population in 1990s Britain: Who Will Return? *Journal of Ethnic and Migration Studies* 25 (2): 285–301.

———. 2000. Return Migration to the Eastern Caribbean: Comparative Experiences and Policy Implications. *Social and Economic Studies* 49 (4): 155–88.

Castells, M. 1996. *The Rise of the Network Society.* Oxford: Blackwell.

Castles, S., and M. Miller. 1993. *The Age of Migration: International Population Movements in the Modern World.* New York: Guilford Press.

Cerase, F. 1974. Migration and Social Change: Expectations and Reality – A Study of Return Migration from the United States to Italy. *International Migration Review* 8 (2): 36–50.

Clifford, J. 1994. Diasporas. *Cultural Anthropology* 9 (3): 302–38.

Cohen, R. 1987. *The New Helots: Migrants in the International Division of Labour.* Aldershot: Grower Publishing.

Conway, D. 1988. Conceptualizing Contemporary Patterns of Caribbean International Mobility. *Caribbean Geography* 2 (3): 145–63.

Davidson, B. 1969. No Place Back Home: A Study of Jamaicans Returning to Kingston. *Race* 9 (4): 499–509.

De Souza, R.M. 1998. The Spell of the Cascadura: West Indian Return Migration. In *Globalization and Neoliberalism: The Caribbean Context,* ed. T. Klak, 227–53. Lanham, MD: Rowman and Littlefield.

Duleep, H., and M. Regets. 1999. Immigrants and Human-Capital Investments. *American Economic Review* 82: 186–91.

Durand J., and D.S. Massey. 1992. Mexican Migration to the United States: A Critical Review. *Latin American Research Review* 27: 3–43.

Eldridge, H.T. 1965. Primary, Secondary, and Return Migration in the United States, 1955–60. *Demography* 2: 444–55.

Elkan, W. 1959. Migrant Labor in Africa: An Economist's Approach. *American Economic Review* 49: 188–97.

Faist, T. 2000. Transnationalization in International Migration: Implications for the Study of Citizenship and Culture. *Ethnic and Racial Studies* 23 (2): 189–222.

Fawcett, J. 1989. Networks, Linkages, and Migration Systems. *International Migration Review* 23 (3): 671–80.

Foner, N. 1997. The Immigrant Family: Cultural Legacies and Cultural Changes. *International Migration Review* 31 (4): 961–74.

Gilroy, P. 1991. *There Ain't No Black in the Union Jack: the Cultural Politics of Race and Nation.* Chicago: University of Chicago Press.

———. 1993. *The Black Atlantic: Modernity and Double Consciousness.* Cambridge: Harvard University Press.

———. 2000. *Against Race: Imagining Political Culture Beyond the Color Line.* Cambridge, Mass: Belknap Press of Harvard University Press.

Glick-Schiller, N. 1998. The Situation of Transnational Studies. *Global Studies in Culture and Power* 4 (2): 155–66.

Glick-Schiller, N., et al. 1992. *Towards a Transnational Perspective on Migration.* New York: New York Academy of Sciences.

Gmelch, George. 1980. Return Migration. *Anthropol* 9 (1): 135–59.

———. 1987. Work, Innovation and Investment: The Impact of Return Migrants in Barbados. *Human Organization* 46 (2): 131–40.

———. 1992. *Double Passage: The Lives of Caribbean Migrants Abroad and Back Home.* Ann Arbor: University of Michigan Press.

Gmelch, G., and S.B. Gmelch. 1995. Gender and Migration: The Readjustment of Women Migrants in Barbados, Ireland and Newfoundland. *Human Organization* 54 (4): 470–73.

Goldring, L. 2001. The Gender and Geography of Citizenship in Mexico–US Transnational Spaces. *Identities: Global Studies in Culture and Power* 7 (4): 501–37.

Goulbourne, H. 2002. *Caribbean Transnational Experience.* London: Pluto Press.

Grasmuck, S., and P. Pessar. 1992. *Between Two Islands: Dominican Migration.* Berkeley and Los Angeles: University of California Press.

Greenwood, M.J. 1969. An Analysis of the Determinants of Geographic Labor Mobility in the United States. *Review of Economics and Statistics* 59: 189–94.

Guarnizo, L.E. 1997. The Emergence of a Transnational Social Formation and the Mirage of Return Migration among Dominicans. *Identities: Global Studies in Culture and Power* 4 (2): 281–322.

Hall, S. 1988. Migration from the English-Speaking Caribbean to the United Kingdom, 1950–1980. In *International Migration Today,* vol. 1, ed. R. Appleyard. Paris: UNESCO.

Herzog, H., and A.M. Schottman. 1982. Migration Information, Job Search and the Remigration Decision. *Southern Economic Journal* 50 (1): 43–56.

Hill, J.K. 1987. Immigrant Decisions Concerning Duration of Stay and Migratory Frequency. *Journal of Development Economics* 25: 221–34.

Ho, C. 1993. The Internationalization of Kinship and the Feminization of Caribbean Migration: The Case of Afro-Trinidadian Immigrants in Los Angeles. *Human Organization* 52 (1): 32–40.

———. 1999. Caribbean Transnationalism as a Gendered Process. *Latin American Perspectives* 26 (5): 34–54.

Hugo, G.J. 1981. Village-Community Ties, Village Norms, and Ethnic and Social Networks: A Review of Evidence from the Third World. In *Migration Decision Making: Multidisciplinary Approaches to Microlevel Studies in Development and Developing Countries,* ed. G.F. DeJong and R.W. Gardner, 180–201. New York: Pergamon.

King, R. 1986. Return Migration and Regional Economic Development: An Overview. In *Return Migration and Regional Economic Problems,* ed. R. King, 1–37. London: Croom Helm.

Lindstrom, D.P. 1996. Economic Opportunity in Mexico and Return Migration from the United States. *Demography* 33 (3): 357–74.

Lomnitz, L. 1977. *Networks and Marginality.* New York: Academic Press.

Marshall, D. 1982. The History of Caribbean Migrations. *Caribbean Review* 11 (1): 6–9.

———. 1983. Toward an Understanding of Caribbean Migration. In *US Immigration and Refugee Policy: Global and Domestic Issues,* ed. M. Kritz, 152–69. Lexington, Mass: Lexington Books.

———. 1987. The History of West Indian Migrations: Overseas Opportunities and Safety-Valve Policies. In *The Caribbean Exodus,* ed. B. Levine. New York: Praeger.

Massey, D. 1987. *Return to Aztlan: The Social Process of International Migration From Western Mexico.* Berkeley and Los Angeles: University of California Press.

Massey, D., et al. 1993. Theories of International Migration: A Review and Appraisal. *Population and Development Review* 19 (3): 180–210.

Muschkin, C. 1993. Consequences of Return Migrants Status for Employment in Puerto Rico. *International Migration Review* 27 (1): 79–102.

Nutter, R. 1985. Implications of Return Migration for Economic Development in

Kingston, Jamaica. In *Return Migration and Economic Development,* ed. R. King. London: Croom Helm.

Olwig, K.F. 1993. *Global Culture, Island Identity Continuity and Change in the Afro-Caribbean Community of Nevis.* Reading, UK: Harwood Academic Publishers.

———. 2002. A Wedding in the Family: Home Making in a Global Kin Network. *Global Networks* 2 (3): 205–18.

Patterson, H. 1968. West Indian Migrants Returning Home. *Race* 10 (1): 69–77.

Peach, C. 1968. *West Indian Migration to Britain.* London: Oxford University Press.

Pessar, P. 1997. *Caribbean Circuits: New Directions in the Study of Caribbean Migration.* New York: Center for Migration Studies.

Philpott, S.B. 1968. Remittance Obligations, Social Networks and Choice Among Montserrat Migrants in Britain. *Man* 3 (3): 465–76.

Plaza, D. 2000. Transnational Grannies: The Changing Family Responsibilities of Elderly African Caribbean-Born Women Resident in Britain. *Social Indicators Research* 1 (1): 75–105.

———. 2002. In Pursuit of the Mobility Dream: Second Generation British/Caribbeans Returning to Jamaica and Barbados. *Journal of Eastern Caribbean Studies* 27 (4): 135–60.

Portes, A. 1996. Transnational Communities: Their Emergence and Significance in the Contemporary World-System. In *Latin America in the World Economy,* ed. R.P. Korzeniewicz and W.C. Smith, 120–43. West Port Connecticut: Greenwood Press.

Potter R.B. 2001. *Tales of Two Societies: A Pilot Study of foreign-born returning nationals to Barbados and St Lucia.* Final Report to the British Academy on Grant APN 29771.

Ravenstein, E. 1885. The Laws of Migration: I. *Journal of the Royal Statistical Society* 48 (2): 167–235.

Reagan, P.B., and R.J. Olsen. 2000. You Can Go Home Again: Evidence from Longitudinal Data. *Demography* 37: 339–50.

Rubenstein, H. 1982. Return Migration to the English-Speaking Caribbean: Review and Commentary. In *Return Migration and Remittances: Developing a Caribbean Perspective,* ed. W.F. Stinner, K. de Albuquerque and R.S. Bryce-Laporte, 3–34. Washington, DC: Smithsonian Institution.

Sill, S. 2000. Return Migration. Unpublished article.

Simmons, A., and J.P. Guengant. 1992. Caribbean Exodus and the World System. In *International Migration Systems: A Global Approach,* ed. M. Kritz, L. Lim and H. Zlotnik, 210–45. Oxford: Oxford University Press.

Stinner, W. 1982. *Return Migration and Remittances: Developing a Caribbean Perspective.* Washington, DC: Praeger.

Taylor, E. 1976. The Social Adjustment of Returned Migrants to Jamaica. In *Ethnicity in the Americas,* ed. F. Henry, 115–25. The Hague: Mouton.

Thomas-Hope, E.M. 1985. Return Migration and its Implications for Caribbean

Development: The Unexplored Connection. In *Migration and Development in the Caribbean: The Unexplored Connection,* ed. R. Pastor, 145–68. Boulder: Westview.

———. 1992. *Explanation in Caribbean Migration.* London: Macmillan Press.

———. 1999. Return Migration to Jamaica and Its Development Potential. *International Migration* 37 (1): 183–205.

———. 2002. Transnational Livelihoods and Identities in Return Migration to the Caribbean: The Case of Skilled Returnees to Jamaica. In *Work and Migration: Life and Livelihoods in a Globalizing World,* ed. N. Nybergg Sorensen and K.F. Olwig, 187–201. London: Routledge.

Todaro, M.P. 1976. *Internal* Migration *in Developing Countries.* Geneva: International Labor Office.

Vertovec, Steven. 1999. Conceiving and Researching Transnationalism. *Racial and Ethnic Studies* 22 (2): 447–62.

———. 2001. Transnationalism and Identity. *Journal of Ethnic and Migration Studies* 27 (4): 573–82.

Zelinsky, W. 1971. The Hypothesis of the Mobility Transition. *Geographical Review* 61: 219–49.

# Return Migration to the Caribbean

## Locating the Concept in Historical Space

| Dennis A.V. Brown |

The nexus between society and migration is often alluded to in the study of the latter phenomenon. However, the ways in which changes in society are mirrored in migration are not always given the centrality of place that they deserve. The recent literature on return migration to the region tends to either herald the existence of a pattern that is related to the most recent historical epoch (Pessar 1997), or point to the existence of distinctive patterns without reference to the socio-historical formations that have led to their existence (De Souza 1998). The integral connection between migration and the evolution of Caribbean society lends a dynamic character to the ways in which people move into and out of the region. If it is accepted that the regions' history can be divided into individual epochs characterized by distinctive political, economic and social configurations locally and internationally, then it is understandable that the character of the migration process associated with these arrangements would evince qualitatively different expressions over time.

The notion of return migration to the region has its material basis in the historical tendency of Caribbean people to venture beyond the regions' shores. Its historical genesis can be associated with the phase of migration that began in the middle to late nineteenth century. The process, however, is best understood to be related to the character of the society and economy of the region. Given that these are subject to change and tend to be greatly influenced by the wider global setting, the character of return migration will be historically specific. This makes it possible to conceive of this phenomenon in mutative or historically sequential terms rather than as an unchanging process with general features that can be understood by being studied at any given point in time.

The central theme of this chapter is that the character of the return migration process to the region is a dynamic one that has evolved in accordance with the changing character of Caribbean society and its relationship to global society. The presumption is made that this interface between processes at the local, regional and global levels is fundamental to what happens within Caribbean society (Brown 2000). Global historical epochs, it is argued, are given form by cycles of technological innovation and diffusion that affect production arrangements in very fundamental ways, leading in turn to a restructuring of socio-economic life within industrial societies and the wider world. This Schumpeterian interpretation of the Kondratiev long waves suggests that there are junctures between historical epochs in which changes in the productive capacities of industrial societies are translated into social change and dislocation throughout the world (Schumpeter 1939; Kondratiev 1935). According to this conceptualization, societies are in a constant state of change in which the features associated with one set of technological innovations begin to dissolve no sooner than they are established, making way for the new institutional forms and arrangements associated with the next wave (Perez 1985).

This means that there will be historical moments in which the patterns associated with one era are complemented by those of another. The moment between historical epochs is therefore distinguished by some degree of indeterminacy – the stamp of one epoch is fading but the other has not yet become dominant. During these periods the migration process is in a state of flux; features of the previous era are still retained even as the new process takes shape. It is argued that, beginning in the last quarter of the twentieth century, technological innovations related to the computer chip and developments in biotechnology began to shape the productive systems of industrial countries. These innovations provided the basis for the transition of these societies from industrial to post-industrial and from modern to postmodern. This has been associated with changes in social relations, patterns of travel and international economic relations, as well as with systems of organization and production within these societies (Kumar 1995; Hoogvelt 1997; Sassen 1998). In keeping with the arguments regarding the relationship between epochal change and migration, this development has been accompanied by fundamental alterations to the pattern of migration affecting the region. If this hypothesis is correct, analysis of empirical data should reveal the co-existence of return migration patterns that can be identified with specific historical epochs. In metaphorical terms, the migration process that characterizes the region during such periods would amount to a kind of image or retinal retention in which one form still lingers even though the eye has found a new object of gaze. Travel into the Caribbean by its people at the present time should therefore not be imagined to be a homogenous process. Rather, it is better understood to be a composite consisting of qualitatively different strands of movement. These are the remnants of previous eras, as well as an emerging pattern of travel that is expressive of the most recent changes in global society and of the ways in which the Caribbean is integrated into this structure.

The view that the nature of return migration is best understood in terms of the changing character of the regions' relationship with the world is based on a nuance in the Caribbean-world interface that is often overlooked (Anderson 1985; Thomas-Hope 1992).[1] Arguments that characterize the contemporary period as a continuation of the capitalist world economy that started five hundred years ago run the risk of overlooking the qualitative differences between this era and all preceding ones (Girvan 2000). In this chapter, the argument is advanced that changes to the character of technological, economic, political and social configurations in the broader world economy lead to qualitative differences in the Caribbean-world interface over time that influence the nature of the migration-return migration process in fundamental ways. This has led to changes in the nature of this process over historical time. In the contemporary period, it is suggested that the distinctive character of the techno-economic-political configuration has meant that the nature of the Caribbean's link with the broader world economy and society is historically new. It has become so complex as to produce historically new forms of movement and to raise questions about the usefulness of traditional notions of the concept, even as the return streams from the previous epoch are about to draw to a close.

In the remainder of this chapter, the analytical framework outlined above is applied to an examination of the historical migration stream that has affected the Caribbean. It is then used to examine migration as it affects the region in the contemporary period.

## Caribbean Migration and the Wider World

The close association between migration and Caribbean society is well known. What is less well documented is the association between significant movements of people into and out of the region and changes to the techno-economic-political contours of the industrial world.[2] In broad historical terms, migration as it has affected the region can be divided into two phases: one inward and the other outward, accompanied by return. The first of these consists of the movement that led the region to be populated by those not belonging to an indigenous group. This took the form of the trafficking of West Africans into a system of plantation slavery organized and managed by western Europeans from the sixteenth to the nineteenth centuries. It also took the form of indenture immigration involving, in the main, the movement of people from the Indian subcontinent into servanthood during the period 1838–1917.

The second phase emerged in the mid to late nineteenth century in the form of movement of substantial numbers of persons both within the region and outside of it. It is on the basis of this second phase of travel that return migration to the region became possible. Within the region, movement took the form of travel between the Windward Islands and the "new" colonies of Trinidad and British Guiana. The extra-regional travel took the form of movement to countries such as Panama, the Dominican Republic, Cuba and the United States. This movement subsided by the end of the second decade of the twentieth century.

After a respite of two decades, the external movement resumed in the form of movement to Britain and subsequently to the United States. The inter-Caribbean movement has also continued into the post–World War II period, shaped by variations in the levels of socio-economic development that have come to characterize the region.[3] See table 2.1 for an indication of these trends.

The second phase of travel can be broken down into a number of stages. The first lasted from the middle of the nineteenth century to the second decade of the twentieth century. The second lasted from the immediate post–World War II period to the early 1960s. The third broad phase, from the 1960s to the present, can itself be usefully subdivided into the decades of 1960 and 1970, 1980 to the end of the century, and the post–September 11, 2001, period. These phases of travel are all characterized by particular pat-

**Table 2.1**     Population Movement in the English-Speaking Caribbean 1840–1980

| Year of Census | Census Population | Annual Rate (%) | Natural Increase | Indentured Immigrants Net Total (1839–1981) | West Indian Emigrants | Migration Balance |
|---|---|---|---|---|---|---|
| 1841–44 | 863,900 | – | – | 24,500 | – | – |
| 1861 | 1,068,400 | 1.07 | 79,700 | 124,800 | – | – |
| 1871 | 1,238,300 | 1.49 | 88,300 | 81,600 | – | – |
| 1881 | 1,440,000 | 1.52 | 130,700 | 72,400 | 1,600 | 70,800 |
| 1891 | 1,607,300 | 1.11 | 122,500 | 45,200 | 500 | 44,700 |
| 1911 | 1,951,300 | 0.97 | 321,200 | 64,000 | 41,200 | 22,800 |
| 1921 | 1,999,200 | 0.24 | 146,100 | 12,500 | 110,800 | -98,300 |
| 1943–46 | 2,851,000 | 1.43 | 832,400 | – | – | – |
| 1960 | 3,766,800 | 2.00 | 873,000 | – | 245,300 | – |
| 1970 | 4,319,500 | 1.38 | 1,198,300 | – | 645,700 | – |
| 1980–82 | 4,845,147 | 0.96 | 1,092,310 | – | 566,663 | – |
| 1990–91 | 5,095,662 | 0.51 | – | – | – | – |

*Source:* Derived in part from Roberts 1981.

terns of return. They ought to be understood against the background of particular social, technological economic and political configurations that lend distinctiveness to, if not determine the character of, the period within which they operate.

The first subdivide of the later phase involved extra-regional movement from the Anglo Caribbean to the Hispanic Caribbean and Central America.[4] This was associated with the penetration of the region by American capital, a waning of the hegemony of the British and an increase in the American sphere of political influence in the region. This period was characterized by the decline of the region's sugar industry, fuelled by the emergence of technology that allowed for the economical extraction of sugar from beet. It took place against the background of changes that had already begun to take place by the middle of the century, which involved an amalgamation of the economies of the world that had not existed previously (Ashworth 1952). These economies associated and interacted on the basis of physical proximity or congruence of political order. Thus, western and central Europe formed one group, Russia and the Baltic comprised another, western Europe and North America formed one more group, and India and the Far East comprised yet another.

The increase in world trade that underlay these coalitions had its genesis in certain changes that were brought to bear on the productive process. The first of these involved its mechanization; the second entailed its division; the third had to do with the bringing of greater complexity to its organization (Ashworth 1952). The greater interaction between the previously unconnected economic groupings took the form of increased levels of migration, movement of capital, and trade in raw materials and finished products.

The state of the international market for the agricultural produce of the colonial territories was a most important factor in determining the state of society and economy within those territories. In terms of the framework presented above, this period of our study can be classified as one in which the techno-economic-political alignments, which had occurred on the globe since the advent of the first industrial revolution, were undergoing fundamental changes. Prior to 1870, innovation centred on the development of the steam engine and its application to the textile and iron industries. The post-1870 period witnessed the emergence of electricity as a major source of energy and the development of the internal combustion engine and new forms of transport. This changed the complexion of world trade by introducing into it a whole new set of goods: railway equipment, steam ships, steel, electrical products and other manufactured products (Kenwood and Lougheed 1971). These changes were transmitted to the British Caribbean via the cost of imported foodstuff and the state of the market for its agricultural produce and as a consequence the availability of employment. Beachey tells us of the distress that this state of affairs caused in the West Indies.

Grenada's production of sugar dropped from ten thousand hogsheads to four thousand hogsheads within the year and a half ending 1884. By 1886, two-thirds of the sugar cultivation in St Vincent was abandoned (Beachey 1957).

In Jamaica the reduction in the price of sugar coincided with the exodus of labourers to work on the Panama Canal and aggravated the difficulties of the sugar planters who were attempting to economize by reducing wages, which were already very low (Brown 2000).

## Travel and Return: The First Phase

It is this situation that fuelled the movement out of the territories of the
Anglo Caribbean in the closing years of the nineteenth century. The outward
movement led to the establishment of overseas Caribbean communities for
the first time in the region's history. Some, such as the community of
Jamaicans established in Blue Fields, Costa Rica, were to become permanent
and represented a loss of population. The vast majority, however, were to
return to their countries at the end of their contracts. The movement to
Panama perhaps epitomizes the character of the migration in this era.
Newton quotes a knowledgeable observer in the early years of the twentieth
century as follows:

> We believe it is correct in saying that never before in the history of this colony
> has such an event taken place; there have been in the past a few spasmodic
> attempts at emigration, but hitherto, this has been confined to the ordinary
> labourer from the country district. On this occasion, it is the youth of Kingston
> that have had to go – lads on whom we have been counting to carry on the
> duties and responsibilities of citizens. Tailors, shoemakers, carpenters, clerks,
> they have all gone, and who can blame them for going? There is absolutely
> nothing for them to do here . . . *We wish them God-speed and a safe return to
> their native land with a larger portion of this world's goods than they now possess.*
> (Netwon 1987; my emphasis)

This quotation is illustrative of the character and magnitude of the movement to Panama, the adverse local economic conditions with which it was
associated and the social composition of the emigrants. The quotation also
points to the sex-selective character of the movement. The typical emigrant
we are told was "a black male", usually an agricultural labourer, or unskilled
town dweller. He was eager to go to Panama to try to earn enough money to
build a house and purchase land on which he could make a living from farming. It also alludes to return to the country of origin (Roberts 1957). This
sometimes took the form of an ultimate return, preceded by brief visits
following the earning of some amount of monies. The wages offered to
labourers in locations such as Panama were much greater than those offered
on the local job market (Roberts 1957).[5] This encouraged another pattern of
travel involving movement from one labour-contract destination to another
in an effort to maximize lifetime job-market earnings (Roberts 1981). Travel

out of the region to the job locations was facilitated by the development of trade and shipping links between the United States and the Caribbean (Roberts 1957).[6] This made movement between the Anglo Caribbean, the rest of the region and the United States itself relatively easy and cheap.

Data relating to the magnitude of the return flow during the period 1881–1921 is sketchy. Figures provided by Newton for Barbados and Jamaica indicate that 55 per cent of those who left for Panama from 1881 to 1915 returned during that time. Prior to 1911, Panama was the main destination of emigrants from Jamaica, with smaller numbers going to the United States and other areas such as Cuba and Costa Rica. During the period 1911–21, most travel from Jamaica took place to the United States, with lesser amounts going to Cuba and other destinations within the Caribbean basin. Movement to the United States came to an end in 1924 when travel restrictions were imposed. During the respite of outward movement from 1921 to 1943, some twenty-five thousand of those who had left in the previous decades returned to Jamaica (Roberts 1981).

These then were some of the main features of the return migration movement to the Caribbean as it occurred during the nineteenth and early twentieth centuries. The world was a vastly different place then than it is now, and this was reflected in the Caribbean's position within it and hence, within the features of the travel activities as they occurred. The migration flows with which the return movement was associated took place within the context of a world in which the productive sectors and economies of the industrial countries had been transformed by fundamental techno-economic changes. These changes subsequently had adverse effects on the region's markets for primary produce, while simultaneously facilitating the growth of other kinds of trade and economic activities and the means to conduct them. These changes in effect stymied the attempts to establish anything resembling an independent peasantry in the region and led to an outward flow of young men overseas and women into the urban centres of the territories (Austin-Broos 1985). They also led to the movement of young men with working-class and artisan backgrounds from the urban areas to overseas.

The movement of those who returned was framed and defined by the terms of their labour contract. These migrants viewed the move overseas as something that was being done for a specific time period, for a specific purpose. Interestingly, this stands in marked contrast to the character of the migration process in the wider world that was initiated as a result of the techno-economic changes that have been described. It is also one of the chief markers of the difference in character of return travel to the Caribbean in the historical and contemporary periods. In the wider world, much of the nineteenth and the early twentieth century were characterized by a relaxing of the barriers to the free movement of capital, trade and people. This led to an international migration that was unlike the process taking place in the Caribbean; it was distinguished by the freedom of those migrants from any control on the part of sending or receiving countries. For these migrants, the very promise of freedom from religious and political persecution was what provided impetus for the movement.

The period between World War I and World War II was one in which the old techno-economic arrangements were being replaced by new ones. The new technologies provided the basis for productivity based on the marshalling of abundant supplies of low-cost energy in the form of petroleum and petrochemicals. The need for raw materials to feed this production – and markets in which to convert these resources into profit – fed the intense competition between the West and its European allies and the newly emerging communist empires in eastern Europe and China. One arena in which this competition was acted out was in western Europe, which was devastated by the war. A strong Europe was a necessary bulwark against communism and a pillar for the resurgence of capitalism. These considerations led to the Marshall Plan, in which US$19 billion was provided for the rebuilding of Britain, France and West Germany. The economic activity that this generated called for manpower that was not available in those countries. It also coincided with an economic downturn in the Caribbean that spawned the disturbances of the late 1930s and continued to be a source of distress to the region's people. These circumstances provided the basis for the next wave of movement out of the Anglo-Caribbean region.

## Travel and Return: The Second Phase I

The movement to Britain is well documented.[7] Suffice it to say that in its features it began to resemble the wider-world migration movement that occurred during the nineteenth and early twentieth centuries. Some 63 per cent of the total 31,347 who travelled from Jamaica in the period 1953–55 did so in order to work (Roberts and Mills 1955, 25). Despite the fact that many of these workers were recruited for jobs in Britain while still living in the Caribbean, the restrictive terms of the old labour contracts were no longer present. This wave was less sex-selective, although it resembled the previous one in terms of its socio-economic composition. Large-scale movement from the West Indies to Britain began in the early 1950s and lasted until the mid 1960s (Thompson 1990).[8] At the end of this period there were approximately 450,000 West Indians in Britain. A great deal of the movement occurred in the period 1961–62 when there was a threat of restrictions on travel in the form of the impending Commonwealth Immigration Bill. In this period some 100,000 West Indians migrated to Britain. Nearly two-thirds of these were Jamaicans.

The accounts of the process can be divided into a number of areas. One useful treatment of this literature classifies it in terms of its concerns in the early years with racial harmony and integration and in more recent times with post-colonial considerations about diaspora and identity (Chamberlain 1997). The literature on this phase of migration from the region has been critiqued on the grounds of its economic and structural focus. This it is argued provides no insight into the ways in which culture and values influence and shape the migration process (Chamberlain 1997). In terms of the argument that has been put forward in this chapter, this is an interesting proposition.

The author of this argument, Chamberlain, directs our attention to the importance of focusing on the cultural values that inform the migration process across generations of West Indian families. At first glance this argument seems to suggest continuity across generations of motives and values that have influenced and shaped the propensity to migrate within families. While this might seem to contradict the contention that the return migration process is historically specific, this is not the case since Chamberlain goes on to argue for the existence of "periodic differences" and a "structure of feeling". Both of these, she suggests, speak to the existence of a somewhat amorphous historical zeitgeist created on the one hand by the legacy of the past and on the other by the definitions of the future held by the new generation. This blend of past and future, she contends, distinguishes one historical period from another.[9] While not discounting the value of these insights, it should be pointed out that those aspects of the wider setting highlighted in this chapter provide the context within which this intergenerational dialogue takes place. They determine the ways in which these values are given practical expression and, therefore, how they affect migration and return. The values and motivations may or may not change over generations, but the ways in which they inform the *pattern* of travel that takes place will be dependent on the societal-technological context that exists. Thus, the motivation of economic betterment and upward social mobility might not have changed between the migratory streams of the late nineteenth century and the present, but the strategies used to achieve these goals have done so.

By the time of the movement to Britain, migration from the Caribbean had come to mean short-term travel abroad to work and gain resources that were needed to secure one's position at home. In addition to the integration of this conception into the general cultural milieu, many of the emigrants would have had fathers and grandfathers who had been a part of the movement to Central America and the Hispanic islands in the nineteenth century. Growing up with such a legacy would have informed their views on migration. It is therefore no surprise that many of the persons who travelled to Britain during the 1950s and 1960s believed they were leaving the Caribbean only for a brief period (Gmelch 1992).[10]

In practice it turned out quite differently. The historical colonial relationship between Britain and the West Indies meant that the immigrants were regarded as "British subjects" and Britain as something of a "homecoming".[11] By the time large numbers of black people started to arrive a few years later, the underlying prejudices and resentments of the British people came to the fore. In principle, however, apart from the pronouncements of the far Right in the person of Enoch Powell, the right of these immigrants to stay in Britain was never seriously questioned. Furthermore, black workers became an integral part of the British labour market with its chronic need for manpower (Thompson 1990). The right to stay meant that those immigrants who did not meet the success they had anticipated could keep on trying and ultimately had the option of not returning to the Caribbean if they never succeeded. Also among this category of persons were some who had fared so badly that they simply could not afford the cost of a ticket home. For those who were successful, doubts as to whether the standard of living that they enjoyed in the United Kingdom could be replicated in the West Indies deterred many a return to the society of origin. These are the societal circumstances that gave rise to the image of the return migrant as a sojourner, someone who returns home after spending many years abroad. In the contemporary period, this type of migrant forms an important part of the return stream but coexists with other types of return travel that occur within the context of the most recent techno-economic developments and the global societal changes they have spawned. It is to an examination of these that we now turn.

## Travel and Return: The Second Phase II

Beginning in the last quarter of the twentieth century, the world experienced a change in the technological basis of its productive activities. These changes form part of a process that is perhaps best characterized as a multidimensional phenomenon in which developments in the realms of information technology and telecommunications have been associated with the diminished significance of the spatial and temporal barriers to communication and production. This has been accompanied by the dissolution of the global geopolitical arrangements that emerged out of the post–World War II period and the institutionalization of economic neoliberalism as the guiding principle for the conduct of economic activities across the globe. These developments ought not to be seen merely as a continuation of the process of the expansion of the world capitalist economy that started five hundred years ago, rather they should be taken as representing a qualitatively distinct era in the history of relations between the societies of the world (UN 2002).[12] As part of this process, societies and cultures have been brought into juxtaposition as never before. Associated with this, there have been marked increases in the movement of people as tourists and labour. This has been facilitated by the transnationalization of production and the integration of national economies, the increased availability and greater capacity of air transport, and the greater permeability of national borders.

In these circumstances, the nature of international migration and by corollary the process of return has undergone fundamental changes. These changes have included the pattern of outward movement and return. The pattern of travel that we are accustomed to characterizing as "return migration", based on the migratory experiences of the 1950s–1970s, has now been altered by the presence of the pattern of travel associated with the new age. Return migration of today refers to a different phenomenon than it did in the previous era.

In illustrating this point, I draw on data from two Caribbean territories, Grenada and St Kitts and Nevis. They demonstrate the co-existence of what

I refer to as the sojourner model and the circular model. I would argue that, as time goes on, the relative importance of the two patterns of travel will change in favour of the latter.

Table 2.2 is compiled from data collected in the Poverty Assessment studies conducted in 1999, in the case of Grenada, and in 2000 in the case of St Kitts. This is a household-based survey that solicits information from a representative national sample of householders on consumption, health, education, fertility and migration patterns and experiences. With regard to return migration, the data indicate that the majority of those who have lived abroad during at least the past decade have done so only on one occasion. In the case of both countries, however, 25 per cent of respondents indicated that they intended to do so again. In the case of Grenada, more than half of those who had once lived abroad expressed their intention to do so again. While in St Kitts, one-quarter of those who had lived abroad once indicated that they intended to do so again. These data seem to indicate the existence of two main categories of return migrants. First, there is a stream made up of those who had once lived abroad and had no intention of doing so again. This amounted to some two fifths of the total migrants in Grenada at the time of the survey and, in the case of St Kitts, a little less than half. Second, a stream made up of the remainder of travellers who were engaged in a migratory process that involved residence abroad on as many as four occasions.

This latest pattern of travel has been described as a natural accompaniment to the transnationalization of the world that has been made possible by the advent of information and telecommunication technologies. According to Pessar, the contemporary period represents a new phase in global capital-

**Table 2.2**    Pattern of Return Travel During the 1990s, Grenada and St Kitts

| Country | Once | Twice | Three Times | At Least Four Times | NS | Total | N |
|---|---|---|---|---|---|---|---|
| | Population of Travellers Who Lived Abroad during the 1990s (%) | | | | | | |
| Grenada | 60 | 18 | 8 | 5 | 8 | 99 | 360 |
| St Kitts | 77 | 13 | 1 | 7 | 2 | 100 | 148 |

Source: Caribbean Development Bank Poverty Assessment Report, Grenada and St Kitts, 1999 and 2000.

ist development. It is characterized by flexible accumulation and a decrease in the significance of national borders as they affect the production and distribution of goods, ideas and people. Against this background, the value of the traditional notion of return migration becomes questionable. In the new pattern that is emerging to match the changing world, return is seen as but one episode in a continuing process of migration. Today's traveller is janus-faced, belonging to no single country, but having active linkages and connections with economic, social and political institutions both at "home" and in "host" societies.[13] The empirical data tell us that in spite of these changes to the wider global setting, the legacy of the past era is reflected in the sizable proportion of travellers in both countries who still fit the profile of the migrant who has gone abroad on one occasion and returned home for good. The transitory character of the Caribbean-world relationship is reflected, however, in the emerging pattern of the circular traveller who has lived in more than one place on a number of occasions.

The destination countries to which Caribbean people travelled in this era are also reflective of the changing character of the relationship of the Caribbean to the wider global society. See table 2.3 for an indication of these trends.

For Grenada, the data indicate that the historical pattern of movement to Trinidad has continued. In keeping with the pattern evinced by the region as a whole in the previous decade, as many as two-fifths of the return migrants from Grenada lived in countries outside of the region during the 1990s. This

**Table 2.3**   Countries to Which Grenadian Return Migrants Travelled During the 1980s and 1990s

| Destination | Return Migrants from Grenada (%) | |
|---|---|---|
| | 1980s | 1990s |
| Trinidad | 38 | 34 |
| United States | 12 | 17 |
| Canada | 7 | 12 |
| United Kingdom | 22 | 10 |
| Other | 21 | 27 |
| Total | 100 | 100 |

*Sources:* Census of the Commonwealth Caribbean, 1990–91; Country Poverty Assessment, Grenada, 1998.

**Table 2.4** Countries to Which Kittitian Return Migrants Travelled During the 1990s

| Destination | Return Migrants St Kitts (%) 1990s |
|---|---|
| Trinidad | 5 |
| United States | 14 |
| Canada | 3 |
| British Virgin Islands | 12 |
| United Kingdom | 10 |
| St Thomas | 12 |
| Guyana | 7 |
| Other Caribbean | 37 |
| Total | 100 |

*Source:* Caribbean Development Bank Poverty Assessment Survey, St Kitts, 2000.

is virtually the same amount that did so during the previous decade. In the 1990s, though, nearly one-third of the migrants travelled to North America, up from 17 per cent in the previous decade. There was a corresponding decline in the proportion travelling to the former colonial power, the United Kingdom.

The data for St Kitts are for one time period only. They are of value to our discussion of the destination countries of Caribbean return travellers insofar as they offer some indication of the extent to which the pattern evinced by Grenada applies to other Caribbean territories as well. The data reveal that North American destinations attracted the largest share of the North Atlantic travellers, as was the case for Grenada. The data also reveal a smaller percentage of total return travellers travelling outside of the geographical region to the countries of the North Atlantic. This amounted to 27 per cent of the return travellers from this country (see table 2.4). This proportion of travellers going to countries outside the region is therefore somewhat less than what obtains in Grenada's case. Although, if we consider the British Virgin Islands and St Thomas as extra-regional destinations, the picture changes somewhat.

# Conclusion

The propensity to migrate in order to increase available opportunities is an integral part of Caribbean culture and values. The strategies and patterns of travel that follow as a result of this propensity find expression, however, within the context of the techno-economic configuration that happens to dominate the world at any particular time in history. In this chapter, this proposition has provided the framework for an analysis of a return-migration process that has often been conceptualized as an abstraction, devoid of its temporal and historical dimensions. The analysis suggests the existence of a return-migration process that is historically grounded and demarcated by the particular techno-economic configuration that happens to be in ascendance at any particular time. Conceptually, the tendency to abstraction becomes particularly problematic at historical conjunctures in which the term, given meaning based on the experiences of one era, is likely to be used to describe the experiences of another. Recognizing the centrality of variations in quality and patterns of migration to the region over time is, therefore, important to the study of the phenomenon. This chapter has attempted to provide some insight into the basis for this mutability by insisting on the organic linkage between travel and its societal context.

# Notes

1. Anderson, for example, has used the core-periphery framework to argue in favour of a migratory process that is reflective of the dependent economic relationship of the Caribbean to the metropole, but does not speak to the issue of the changing character of this relationship. More recently, Thomas-Hope has used a seemingly immutable notion of globalization to make a similar sort of case.
2. Generally, there is a remarkable association between the three components of population change – mortality, fertility and migration – and techno-economic and institutional change in the industrial world. Of the three components, migration tends to be most readily responsive to these changes. In the historical epoch, sex-selective migratory movements affected fertility by creating imbalances in the sex ratios (Brown 2000; Marino 1970).
3. The pattern that obtains is one that sees the movement of persons from the poorer countries of the region to a number of relatively prosperous countries. Some of this

movement, such as the one from St Vincent and Grenada to Trinidad and Tobago, represents the continuation of a historical trend. Others, such as the movement of Jamaicans and Guyanese to Antigua, St Kitts and the Cayman Islands, are associated with developments that have taken place as a result of globalization (Brown 2004).

4. Destination countries included Panama, Cuba, the Dominican Republic and Costa Rica.
5. Roberts (1957) quotes the local rate as 1s 6d, as opposed to the foreign rate of $1.00.
6. This was in keeping with the increased economic and political dominance of the United States in the region. Roberts (1957) quotes figures that indicate that whereas in 1878 the United Kingdom took 79 per cent of Jamaica's exports and the United States 14 per cent, by 1899 a reversal had taken place with the United States taking 79 per cent of the island's trade.
7. See Peach 1986; Roberts and Mills 1955; Davison 1962; Thompson 1990; and Gmelch 1992.
8. Thompson tells us that the movement began in June 1948 with the arrival in London of 492 Jamaicans on board the SS *Empire Windrush* (Thompson 1990; Chamberlain 1997).
9. Chamberlain argues for the distinctiveness of the various migratory streams by suggesting that each of them occurred within a particular pocket of time, closely related to the past but distinguished from it (1998, 36–46).
10. Gmelch points out that less than 10 per cent of the returnees to Barbados that he surveyed believed they were leaving for good at the time of their departure (1997, 285).
11. According to one author, the first immigrants to Britain from the West Indies in 1948 were greeted with a headline in a leading British newspaper that read "Welcome Home" (Thompson 1990).
12. For a similar interpretation, see also Castells 1997–98.
13. This line of reasoning is informed by the notion that concepts are rooted in the social realities that they describe. This reality is deemed to be constantly changing and hence, so are the meanings associated with the concepts.

# References

Anderson, P. 1985. *Migration and Development in Jamaica*. Kingston: Institute of Social and Economic Research.
Ashworth, W. 1952. *A Short History of the International Economy since 1850*. London: Longman.

Austin-Broos, D. 1985. Religion, Economy and Class in Jamaica: Reinterpreting a Tradition. Mimeograph.

Beachey, R.W. 1957. *The British West India Sugar Industry in the Late Nineteenth Century.* Oxford: Oxford University Press.

Brown, D.A.V. 2000. *The Political Economy of Fertility in the British West Indies 1891–1921.* Kingston: Canoe Press.

———. 2004. Inbetweenity: Marginalisation, Migration and Poverty Among Haitians in the Turks and Caicos Islands. In *Beyond the Blood, the Beach and the Banana. New Perspectives in Caribbean Studies,* ed. S. Courtman, 135–52. Kingston: Ian Randle.

Castells, M. 1997–98. *La era de la información: economía, sociedad y cultura.* 3 vols. Madrid: Alizana Editores S.A.

Chamberlain, M. 1997. *Narratives of Exile and Return.* New York: St Martin's Press.

———. 1998. *Caribbean Migration, Globalised Identities.* London: Routledge.

Davison, R.B. 1962. *West Indian Migrants: Social and Economic Facts of Migration from the West Indies.* London: Oxford University Press.

De Souza, R.M. 1998. The Spell of the Cascadura: West Indian Return Migration. In *Globalization and Neoliberalism,* ed. T. Klak, 227–53. Lanham, MD: Rowman and Littlefield.

Girvan, N. 2000. Globalisation and Counter-Globalisation: The Caribbean in the Context of the South. In *Globalisation: A Calculus of Inequality,* ed. D. Benn and K. Hall, 65–87. Kingston: Ian Randle.

Gmelch, G. 1992. *Double Passage: The Lives of Caribbean Migrants Abroad and Back Home.* Ann Arbor: University of Michigan Press.

Hoogvelt, A. 1997. *Globalisation and the Postcolonial World: The New Political Economy of Development.* Baltimore: John Hopkins University Press.

Kenwood, A.G., and A.L. Lougheed. 1971. *The Growth of the International Political Economy, 1820–1960.* London: George Allen and Unwin.

Kondratiev, N. 1935. The Long Waves in Economic Life. *Review of Economic Statistics* 17 (6): 105–15.

Kumar, K. 1995. *From Postindustrial to Postmodern Society: New Theories of the Contemporary World.* Cambridge: Blackwell.

Marino, A. 1970. Family, Fertility and Sex Ratios in the British Caribbean. *Population Studies* 24 (2): 159–72.

Newton, V. 1987. *The Silver Men: West Indian Labour Migration to Panama 1850–1914.* Kingston: Institute of Social and Economic Research.

Peach, C. 1986. *West Indian Migration to Britain: A Social Geography.* London: Oxford University Press.

Perez, C. 1985. Microelectronics, Long Waves and World Structural Change: New Perspectives for Developing Countries. *World Development* 13 (3): 441–63.

Pessar, P., ed. 1997. *Caribbean Circuits: New Directions in the Study of Caribbean Migration.* New York: Center for Migration Studies.

Roberts, G.W. 1957. *The Population of Jamaica.* Cambridge: Cambridge University Press.

————. 1981. Currents of External Migration Affecting the West Indies: A Summary. *Revista/Review InterAmericana* 11 (3).

Roberts, G.W., and D.O. Mills. 1955. *Study of External Migration Affecting Jamaica, 1953–1955.* Kingston: Institute of Social and Economic Research.

Sassen, S. 1998. *Globalization and Its Discontents: Essays on the New Mobility of People and Money.* New York: The New Press.

Schumpeter, J.S.A. 1939. *Theoretical, Historical and Statistical Analysis of the Capitalist Process.* New York: McGraw Hill.

Thomas-Hope, E. 1992. *Caribbean Migration.* Reprint, Kingston: University of the West Indies Press, 2002.

Thompson, M.E. 1990. Forty and One Years On: An Overview of Afro-Caribbean Migration to the United Kingdom. In *In Search of a Better Life: Perspectives from the Caribbean,* ed. R.W. Palmer, 39–70. New York: Praeger.

United Nations (UN). 2002. Twenty-eighth Session. *Equity, Development and Citizenship: CEPAL.* Mexico City: United Nations.

# CHAPTER 3

# Barbadian Migrants Abroad
# and Back Home

| George Gmelch |

In 1987, Eric Hinds, twenty-two, single and without the prospect of a steady job, emigrated from his native Barbados to the United States and settled with his brother's family in a West Indian neighbourhood in Brooklyn. Over the next eleven years he held various manual jobs – deliveryman, baker, steel-band player – while attending night classes at a local university. He married Esther Hollingsworth, another Barbadian emigrant, and they started a family.

On a visit to Barbados during Christmas 1997, the couple started to talk seriously about going home. Esther did not want to raise her children in urban America and Eric missed the Caribbean climate, the sea and a more relaxed pace of life. So he began to apply for jobs advertised in the *Advocate,* a Bajan newspaper that circulated among his emigrant friends. Eventually he was offered a job with a small bakery owned by a relative. The salary was only half of what he was making in the United States; Eric and Esther agonized over the decision. They would not enjoy the same standard of living they had had in Brooklyn, but they would be home. After some months, they decided that what mattered most was the country in which they were to rear their children. Eric accepted the job and they returned home to Barbados.

The Hinds are among tens of thousands of emigrants who have returned to their native lands in recent years. During the past decade, there has been a stream of migrants returning from Britain and North America to many parts of the Caribbean, including Puerto Rico, Jamaica and Trinidad, as well as to smaller islands such as Barbados. The actual number of emigrants returning to countries like Barbados can only be estimated because as they pass through airport customs and immigration, they are often indistinguishable from those returning solely to visit. But other indicators – the transfer of foreign bank deposits, construction of new housing in rural areas and population increases beyond natural growth – provide ample evidence that return migration is rising sharply in much of the Caribbean (Gmelch 1992, 41–56).

This chapter examines the emigration and return of Barbadians from Britain and North America. While both ends of the migration cycle are described, the focus is on the experiences of Barbadians returning to the Caribbean, and on what it means to come home, for the individual and the society. In the early 1980s, I conducted a survey of Barbadian returnees.[1] The results of the survey, in which the varied lives and experiences of the migrants were reduced to statistical patterns, seemed too far removed from the reality of the migrants' lives as I knew them. More interested in giving expression to what it meant to migrate and, years later, return, I began a second study involving in-depth, tape-recorded life history interviews with a smaller sample of migrants.[2] The data in this chapter are drawn heavily from the latter research, but it is also informed by both the earlier survey work and recent fieldwork.

## Emigration from Barbados

The Barbadians in this study left their island as part of a mass migration from the English-speaking Caribbean to Britain and North America following World War II. Some went to attend university or vocational training courses, but most sought work. In the 1950s, Britain began actively recruiting workers from its former colonies in the West Indies, India and Pakistan. Labour was needed for the post-war reconstruction and to accommodate a booming economy. Tens of thousands of Barbadians, along with other West Indians, boarded ships for jobs in the United Kingdom. British companies and government agencies, including the London Transport Executive and the British Hotel and Restaurant Association, sent recruiters to Barbados. Villagers could take the bus into the capital city of Bridgetown for an interview. If they measured up, as most did, they were assigned a job, trained and transported to England. Men, particularly, went to Britain to work in post offices and on buses, trains and construction sites. Women became nurses or worked in light industry. The Barbadian government, seeing emigration as a way to alleviate population pressure at home, loaned the emigrants money for their travel.

As Britain got back on its feet, however, competition for jobs between the Britons and the newcomers created hostility and resentment towards the coloured immigrants. The British parliament responded with the Commonwealth Immigration Act of 1962, restricting further immigration. By the late 1960s the flow of emigrants from the West Indies, India and Pakistan had virtually ended.[3] However, the United States and Canada reopened their doors to immigrants, and a new stream of migration began to the north.

The post-war era was not the first time Barbadians had emigrated from their island. Since the 1830s, when slavery was abolished throughout the English-speaking Caribbean, migration had been common. On Barbados and other islands with similarly dense populations and scarce resources, emigration was a necessary safety valve. In the nineteenth century, Barbadians went to larger islands within the Caribbean. In 1905, many signed up with American recruiters and emigrated to Panama to dig the canal. By the time the canal was completed in 1914, nearly one-quarter of all Barbadians had travelled to Panama (Richardson 1985). In the 1920s, Barbadians emigrated to Curaçao, Trinidad and Venezuela to work in the newly developing oil fields. Others went to Cuba to work in the sugar industry. Even before World War II, a small number had emigrated to North America and England, which was then affectionately known as the mother country. But the flow to these "metropolitan" countries, as they are referred to in the Caribbean, was only a trickle compared with the torrent that followed after the war. In just two decades (1951–70), 14 per cent of Barbados's population of 230,000 had left the island (Richardson 1985).

## Why They Went

In my survey of 135 migrants, nearly all left Barbados with the expectation that they would find better opportunities for themselves abroad. Many also desired to see what the mother country was really like or "how the other half lives". Especially in the 1950s and 1960s, some were also influenced by the fact that other Barbadians were emigrating and that it was the "thing to do".

In the words of one Calypso artist, "the trek to England was the only craze" (Holmes 1988, 220).

The journey overseas was a momentous occasion, and the beginning of a new life. Most migrants had never travelled abroad before, much less been on a ship or an airplane. To this day, the migrants can remember the day of the week they left home and the day they arrived abroad. The migrants were "sojourners" rather than "settlers", in that they all saw their stay overseas as being temporary. Most expected to be home within five years. Nearly all, however, stayed much longer.[4] The few who came back on schedule were primarily students who had no choice because their visas had expired.

Abroad, the migrants settled in cities and neighbourhoods in which they had relatives or friends, and where work was most available. Hence, most migrants found themselves in large cities – London, Birmingham, New York and Montreal.[5] Almost immediately upon arrival, they went to work. Norman Bovell, for example, arrived in London on a Tuesday, found a job on Wednesday, and began work on Thursday. Rose Thornhill disembarked from a ship, boarded a train and arrived at the mental hospital in York at 4:30 a.m. to begin a job she had been recruited for in Barbados; she had been told to report to her nursing station for the 7:00 a.m. shift. The speed at which the migrants were employed indicates the high demand for labourers in England during much of the 1950s and early 1960s. That the migrants lost no time in finding work is not surprising given that a primary motivation for going abroad was the desire to make money. It is telling that most of the migrants can still recall their wages down to the last shilling for each job they held.

The work migrants found was predominantly manual labour. They became van drivers, bus conductors, mailmen, painters, seamstresses, nurses' aides and factory operatives. Typically the jobs available to them were the dirtiest, most boring and least compensated. Most were jobs white workers did not want. For some migrants these jobs were of lower status than the positions they had left in the Caribbean, though the wages were generally higher.

If there is a dominant theme in the migrants' stories, it is of how hard they worked; some held two jobs. Most volunteered for all the overtime available to them. Rex and Tomlinson's study of immigrants in Birmingham, England, found that twice as many West Indians worked more than forty-eight hours a week as did white British workers (1979, 113). Despite the extra hours, however, their weekly wages were not any greater.

Barbadians, like most immigrants to Britain and North America, did not wander far from the cities in which they initially settled (Rex and Tomlinson 1979, 53).[6] Remaining among fellow West Indians made it easier for the migrants to maintain relationships with other Bajans who provided moral support, as well as information about jobs and economic opportunities. Even small groups of immigrants can have some economic and political weight if they are spatially concentrated.

## *Family*

As a husband and a father, I am struck by how long many migrants were separated from their spouses and children. In many cases, five years would pass without couples seeing one another.[7] As I conducted the interviews, I wondered how well the marriages of my middle-class American friends would have endured under such circumstances. But Valenza Griffith spoke for many Barbadian women whose husbands had gone abroad when she explained that, as long as one's husband was emigrating to better the family's position, you could not cry or complain. Rather, you passed the time by "keeping busy" until they came back or until you could join them.

The separation of parents from children was also common. Children were often left in the care of grandparents or other relatives. Their children would be better off in the Caribbean, most parents believed; the village was thought to be a safer and healthier environment than the streets of Brooklyn or London. There would be more relatives to look after their welfare. Good child care was difficult to find, and many immigrants had heard stories of children who had been left with babysitters being neglected or abused. When the parents' stay overseas stretched longer than they had originally planned, their children grew up during their absence. It was ten years before Norman Bovell saw his eldest child, and when they reunited she was not sure he was her "daddy". Another elderly man painfully recalled his homecoming after more than twenty years abroad. His two sons, who were infants when he left Barbados, were in their twenties when they came to the airport to meet him. He had a photograph of them but was unable to recognize them in the crowd. When they finally did locate one another, his sons were not convinced that he was their father.

## *Racism*

Many migrants encountered racial discrimination, especially in their search for employment and housing. They told stories of signs posted in the windows of flats and on doors telling blacks they need not apply. One family recounted being turned away at an apartment just a short while after they had been told over the phone that it was available. Discrimination was also expressed in countless other ways, such as a white woman bus passenger putting her bus fare on the seat next to her to avoid having to touch the black hand of the Barbadian conductor, or a receptionist who did not ask the Bajan delivery man to sign for a delivery because she assumed he could not write. There was also the captain of the college cricket team who automatically assumed that Bajan John Wickham would be a good bowler because he was tall and black.

Even after living many years abroad, and successfully adjusting to English or North American society, the orientation of the migrants was always to the Caribbean. Most friendships were with other islanders. Many tried to visit Barbados despite costly airfares, which cut into hard-won savings. Most sent remittances home to help support parents and other relatives. Even those who have been abroad for decades with no prospect of returning home still identify strongly with the homeland. They retain what observers call an "ideology of return" (King 1978; Gmelch 1980). Their identification with the Caribbean and lack of interest in assimilating were encouraged by the white host societies, who kept the coloured immigrants at arms length. In England, the migrants were reminded in countless ways that while the country welcomed their labour – at least as long as there were plenty of jobs to go around – it was not willing to extend the privileges of full citizenship. This was a shock for migrants who believed they were going to the mother country, to a society they assumed would treat them as equals, on the basis of merit rather than colour (Foner 1976, 41). Racism diminished the respect migrants had for whites and decreased their interest in identifying with the larger society.[8] What the migrants had learned and experienced overseas was not only important to their adjustment to life in the host societies, it also influenced their decision to return and their readjustment to Barbados.

## Returning Home

Returning to Barbados from the United Kingdom, the United States or Canada is to move from a highly developed economy and nation to one that is less developed. Structurally, the move is similar to that of Mediterranean migrants returning home from northern Europe, or to Puerto Ricans and Mexicans returning from the United States. Often return migration for Barbadians also means moving from a big city such as London or New York to a small town or village at home.

For the returnees, coming home is the natural completion of the migration cycle. At the time they left Barbados, most had planned to stay away only long enough to save money to buy a house and perhaps a car, and to see something of the world. Roy Campbell's observation is typical: "On the way over to England my thinking was that I'd be away no more than five years. I had a goal of saving a certain amount of money and then coming back to Barbados and getting a little home." Yet, most overseas Barbadians never manage to return home, at least not permanently. Some cannot afford the ticket back. Others who have not bettered themselves economically are disinclined to return because they will lose face.[9] Student emigrants are expected to come back with a diploma, while working emigrants are expected to have at least enough money to buy a home of their own. The very successful may not return because it would mean giving up well-salaried positions and a standard of living that could not easily be equaled in Barbados. To return, the migrants must believe they can attain a reasonably comfortable standard of living in Barbados. Not surprisingly, the state of the home economy, employment opportunities and exchange rates all significantly influence the flow of return migrants in all countries.[10] Over the past few decades, Barbados has seen a higher rate of return than any of its neighbouring islands. This is due to the relative strength of its economy, a high per-capita income and the availability of most modern amenities.

During a holiday visit, migrants often see how much Barbados has prospered during their absence and, importantly, that black Barbadians – and not just the white elite – are benefiting from the new prosperity. They notice the increasing number of high-quality wall houses, as well as new roads, restaurants and recreational facilities – much of it associated with the growth of tourism. Those who left Barbados in the 1950s and 1960s returned to see that during their absence the country truly became independent. The people who now run the island are black, and a large number of blacks have entered the middle class. They realize that many Barbadians now have material comforts at home, while also enjoying a more fulfilling life at home in other respects.[11] Exalted by sunny blue skies, warm air, an inviting sea, the easy-going pace of life and the friendliness of their village neighbours, they seriously begin to consider returning home for good. Since it is usually Christmas or summer holidays when migrants visit, the atmosphere is festive and relatives are in good cheer; they are eager to please, driving the migrants here and there to see sights and old friends.

Not surprisingly, it is either during such a visit – while nostalgia is still fresh – or immediately upon return to Britain or North America that migrants often reach a final decision to return for good. They make plans – setting a date, buying land on which to build a house and opening a Barbadian bank account. One woman, who wanted the family to stay in England, recalled how her husband brushed aside her reservations and instead talked only about "how beautiful Barbados was, that the country was doing much better". Many migrants would later report, however, that perceptions of home acquired during these short holiday visits can be deceptive.

While migrants are drawn back primarily by what life in Barbados promises, they must also be somewhat discontented with their lives abroad. People who are entirely satisfied with their lives rarely uproot themselves. Unemployment, racial tension and personal problems push people to move. Jobs for young West Indians in England are so scarce that, in an ironic reversal of their parents' emigration, some who were born and raised in England are now leaving to seek their fortune in the Caribbean (Western 1992).

Some return migration is precipitated by personal crisis: the breakup of a marriage, the death of a spouse, trouble with children or ill health. A hotel maid in an English resort town, who returned after a divorce, said: "After my husband left, it was just me and kids in the house, and that's not good for anybody. I was lonely and bored. We needed more relatives around." A worker in the London post office returned when he injured his back and could no longer deliver the mail; a mechanic brought his family back when his mother in Barbados developed cancer. In Britain, doctors often advise West Indians with serious health problems, especially mental disorders, to re-emigrate. The change of scene and climate may be good for the patient, but it also helps to reduce the burden on the National Health Service.

Migrant parents are also disappointed in the education their children receive abroad, especially in inner-city schools. In Britain, many West Indian children drop out of school and a disproportionate number of those who remain in school perform at or near the bottom of every academic skill. Many Barbadian parents, who proudly tell you that Barbados has one of the world's highest literacy rates, believe that their children will do better in Barbadian schools.

Despite such complaints, most migrants who return home do so primarily because of their attachment to the land of their birth.[12] As one elderly man, chewing a stick of sugar cane said, "The money [in Canada] was good and the people treated me with fairness, but in the end I wanted to be home with my own people, in my own land." A woman who had graduated from Colgate University and had worked as a housing research analyst in Washington, DC, returned to Barbados to teach high school, because "Barbados is still a developing country, and I felt that any contribution that I make in my lifetime I want to make here".[13]

## Adjusting to Home

Returning is seldom as easy as a migrant expects. In my survey, 53 per cent of the respondents were so dissatisfied during their first year at home that they believed they would have been happier abroad. Friendships did not materialize as hoped. Relatives and friends from their youth often proved, at closer quarters, narrow and greedy. Neighbours who had appeared affable or chummy during return holiday visits (when presents were distributed) became distant or disinterested once the migrants returned. Commenting on the people in her village, one woman observed:

> The people say that I don't want friends, they say I don't want to share. Them that do the talking [gossiping] are the same ones that I brought goods for. I give them rice, I give them coffee, I give them dinner plates. I give all around and I try to keep friendship with them. They took my things, but then they cut me up.

Another woman said, "It makes you wonder if people really care about you, or if they just want the things that you can give them."

Sometimes old friends that the migrants had most looked forward to seeing and with whom they had hoped to recapture the lost memories of youth, were themselves gone. One man, disappointed to find that most of his former friends had emigrated, said he did not know the younger crowd of men at the rum shop or any of the children. A stranger in his own village, he wondered aloud if he had made the right decision to return to Barbados after more than twenty years away.

In their interactions with villagers and fellow workers, returnees often conclude that Barbadians who have never lived abroad are provincial and narrow-minded, an attitude which only makes it more difficult for them to establish friendships. One woman whispered to me, as though she were afraid of being overheard: "I have no good friends who have never been away. There are very few here I would want to call friends . . . their outlook on life is so small, so tiny, it's like they have blinkers on, like they're always going down a one-way street."

A man who had spent twenty-three years in England complained that the Barbadian women he met were boring and that he could not make conversation with them: "They sit there like great lumps of pudding with nothing at all to say."

Some returnees feel they no longer share the same interests as their neighbours. They say their own interests are more cosmopolitan. Returnees living in villages often complain that their neighbours are gossipy and preoccupied with the affairs of others. Having grown accustomed to the anonymity of big city life, they feel a loss of privacy as their every action – and even their new possessions – come under public scrutiny. In the words of one woman, "People go out of their way to make gossip. You can't lead your own life here. It's so small and everybody knows everybody. It's terrible." This same woman confided to me that she and her husband had made a mistake resettling in the village. "Maybe it wouldn't be so bad," she said, "if we had moved to Bridgetown."

Many sense that those who stayed behind are jealous of their prosperity, of their large houses, new cars and their children's level of education. Some villagers diminish the accomplishments of the migrants and attempt to lower their elevated status by saying that money is easy to earn abroad and that anyone who goes away can come back rich. One prosperous family I know well, rather than being credited with having worked hard, was rumoured to have received a "blessing" or to have won a lottery. Villagers rarely came to their shop, lest they add to the family's wealth. Said the disgruntled shopkeeper, who was considering re-emigrating to Canada:

> Even the people from our church don't shop here. They don't want us to have their business, except for an occasional small thing when they run out and don't want to go into town. You can't win. If you come back with money, they are jealous. If you come back with nothing, they ridicule you. . . . When I was a poor shopkeeper, before I first left Barbados, we had more friends than we have today. Then we were all at the same level.[14]

On the other hand, returnees are sometimes insensitive. They may strain relationships with friends and neighbours by making frequent comparisons of Barbados to the society from which they have returned. Some talk too much about the metropolitan society and about their experiences there; they would be better off trying to find common ground with people at home.

A common irritant to all migrants returning from the industrialized world is the slow pace of life at home. It is difficult to get things done.[15] Barbadian returnees report being frustrated at the delays in getting service-men to make repairs, getting a telephone installed, clearing an overseas parcel at the local post office and having to wait in line while sales clerks chat with other customers. Having grown accustomed to the punctuality of Britons or North Americans, they become impatient and frustrated by the absence of this quality at home. "If people agree to meet you at eight o'clock," said Roy Campbell, "they don't turn up until eight-thirty or maybe even nine o'clock, and they don't say they are sorry for being late." Esther Griffith felt there were only two speeds in Barbados: "slow and dead stop".

Retirees living on pensions often find the cost of living in Barbados higher than anticipated. Those whose savings are being eroded by the high cost of goods and energy often speak of little else – canned fruit is four times what they paid abroad, milk and eggs are twice the cost, water and electricity are three times as much, and so forth. The cost of living becomes an obsession. A retired welder, who thought the $3,600 he had saved while in England was "a fortune", was surprised to see how little it was actually worth. "The cost of things like lumber and masonry for my house [was] so high," he said, "that my money disappeared fast. I could not even hold onto my passage money to England in case I ever wanted to go back." Many returnees try to reduce their household expenses by producing some of their own food, taking advantage of kitchen gardens and fruit trees, and by raising sheep, goats and

chickens. One man who was working as a waiter earns half as much in
Barbados as he did at the same job in Toronto. He motioned to his backyard
as he said, "In Toronto I lived ten floors up in an apartment. Here I can go
out in the yard and pick a coconut, a lime or a banana, and I raise my own
animals. In Canada, I had to buy all that stuff."

For women, returning home can present special problems. Most held
wage-paying jobs while abroad; now at home they have difficulty finding
work.[16] Faced with low wages or early retirement, some become self-
employed. One sews uniforms for hotel staff, another sells soft drinks from
her house and a third keeps the books for the family bus operation. Overseas,
wage work helped these and other women gain a measure of independence.
Having money of their own, if not outright control of their paycheques,
enhanced their status and strengthened their claims for respect in relations
with their husbands.[17] Listening to women returnees describe the mind-
numbing tasks and endlessly repetitive duties of the work they did in the
sweatshops of London and New York makes it easy to underestimate the
importance of work to these women. In middle-class America these jobs are
seen as menial, even as demeaning. Typically, my field-school students in
Barbados see the alternatives for the returnee women – a life as a homemaker
in Barbados, tending a vegetable garden, having fresh air and open spaces –
as a much better way of life. But this perception is not always shared by
returnee women, who prior to their emigration had never earned a weekly
paycheque nor enjoyed the autonomy, stimulation and status that comes with
having a full-time job. For these workers, wage work – whether it is menial
or not – is an improvement over life without a paycheque.

In the villages, in particular, some returnee women find there are not
enough things to do; some especially miss shopping. While living abroad,
they had enjoyed browsing and looking for bargains in the large department
stores, and they liked the wide range of foodstuffs available in the supermar-
kets. In Barbados, most retail stores are small, the range of goods is limited
and the prices are higher.

For women who come back to Barbados without their grown children,
the most serious source of unhappiness is often the separation. Ann Bovell
was speaking for many women when she confided at the end of one interview: "To tell the truth, I feel real bad me being here and the kids being over
there [England]." Another woman's response to being cut off from her children has been to work even harder, rising before dawn to sew hotel uniforms

in order to earn enough money to travel overseas each year to visit her four offspring in Canada, England and Belgium. Parents hope that children whom they have raised overseas will someday move to Barbados, but few ever do.

Listening to returnees' woes begs the question: why do so many migrants, who are familiar with Barbados and who have visited the island on several occasions before their actual return, experience difficulty readjusting? As one local who had never been away said, "You'd think they'd know what they'd be getting into." The answer is best found in the changes that have occurred in the migrants themselves during their time abroad. Migrants often do not realize how much their attitudes have been altered by their experiences in a metropolitan society until they return. While abroad they see themselves only in opposition to mainstream Britons or North Americans. They tend to think of themselves and of fellow Barbadian emigrants as being no different from people back home. Only when they return to Barbados and try to resume relationships with old friends and relatives do they first see the differences. Returnees see themselves as having become more "broadminded". Indeed most have become less ethnocentric: they are no longer convinced that the Barbadian or West Indian way of life is the only right way. They are also less inclined to do something simply because of tradition. They have seen alternatives and some are better than the customs at home. Hence, they sometimes become impatient with time-honoured Barbadian traditions.

Many come back with a changed attitude towards work. An architect who returned from Toronto said, "I now recognize that it takes work to be successful. I didn't really understand that before." A female office worker who had lived in Brooklyn for thirty-seven years said, "I learned that money doesn't grow on trees, that even in America you have to work hard to make money. Everyone should go away and see for themselves, it would be good for Barbados." Many also come back with a clearer idea of what they want in life. As one middle-aged man explained, he saw a change in himself: "I'm not interested in hanging around the way I did before I left. I want to go forward, to make something of myself. A lot of people here don't want a lot. As long as they have a roof over their head, own their own home, they're happy."

Meanwhile, Barbados is not the same place today as it was a decade or two before the migrants left. Although most welcome the new prosperity, the increased volume of cars (which has tripled since 1970) has snarled traffic; crime and drug use have increased; and the development of hotels to accommodate tourists has driven up land prices on the coast, limiting opportunities to buy a house near the sea. As well, young Barbadians are less courteous than they were a generation ago. These changes do not fit the nostalgic image of Barbados that many migrants retain from their youth, images that brief vacations at home do not correct. In short, the cause of dissatisfaction among many migrants is the lack of fit between what they expected to find at home and what they experience. The most disgruntled are those who were most unrealistic about what Barbados could provide them. Their discontent is caused less by the actual social, economic and environmental conditions at home than by their own expectations.

With the passage of time, however, the dreams and fantasies of most returnees fade and they learn to cope with the inefficiency and petty annoyances of life at home. Gradually, expectations about what can be accomplished in a day's work are lowered, and the slow pace of Barbadian life is no longer an irritant. Many also cope by occasionally leaving the island, whether on business, to visit relatives or just for a holiday on a cheap charter package to Miami. Whatever the occasion, a trip to an American or British city can satisfy the appetite for the things that returnees miss in Barbados, including good movies, particular forms of cuisine and discount merchandise. Being abroad once more also serves to remind them of the drawbacks of life in a metropolitan society – the impersonal nature of the place, the inability to feel safe on the streets at night, racial prejudice and the "rat race". This helps to make them appreciate Barbados again and enables them to accept island life more easily.

While many returnees experience some difficulty readjusting, most do adapt. After a year or two, most are satisfied to be home. The figure cited earlier, which identified 53 per cent of returnees as being dissatisfied during their first year back, drops to 17 per cent after the end of three years.

## Local Perceptions of Returnees

Let us briefly turn to what Barbadians who have never lived abroad think of returnees. Do they look up to them? Do they see them as role models? Most Bajans readily agree that returnees have been changed by their overseas experiences. They say that returnees are more "broadminded" than those who have never left the island. The term broadminded is such a common response that it seems almost a cliché. When pressed to explain exactly what they mean, people usually say something about the returnees having had more experience or having a greater knowledge of people and of the world. Another widespread perception is that returnees are harder-working and more goal-oriented. "When they come back here they know what they want from life and they go forward," one man remarked. "In that score you have to give them full credit, because they apply themselves diligently." When asked directly, most Barbadians also concede that returnees are less tolerant of racism and sexism and more willing to support unpopular causes, such as putting environmental protection above business interests.

Barbadians are also critical of some returnees, particularly those who do not make enough of an effort to assimilate back into society and those who think they are superior to their non-migrant countrymen because they have lived abroad. One of my neighbours in the village of Josey Hill said, "They feel that because they've been overseas in a big country and you ain't been nowhere that they are better than you." Another man said, "They think because you were here in Barbados all the time that you didn't learn any-thing, while they being abroad learned all about life. Some of them, because they've been in a big country [they] come back down here to this small coun-try and they think they is the world."

Several villagers related incidents in which a returnee tried to appear worldly by pretending to have forgotten or never to have known some local custom: "Sometimes they try to play the stranger. Like if you have a bread-fruit in your hand, they might ask you, 'Is that a breadfruit?' Now, you know they haven't forgotten what a breadfruit is."

Speech and dress are also mentioned as ways in which returnees stand out. Many have an English or a North American accent when they return. And as one villager explained, "They try to put their words in the proper places, they try to raise their language up." If the returnee's accent is pronounced, locals may suspect it is intentionally put on. "You find that lots of them pick up a foreign accent," one person commented, "whether it's genuine or not. It's something they put on to let you know that they've been somewhere."

Locals say that migrants who have been away for a short period, say three to four years, often have stronger accents than those who have been away much longer. The explanation given is that locals are more likely to forget that a person who was away for only a short period had in fact lived abroad, whereas no one forgets the experience of the man or woman who was away many years. Commenting on the latter, one woman said, "They don't need to remind people by talking like they've just left England. You know they have been away."

Some returnees also stand out because of their clothes. "You can tell them by the way they dress. They wear stockings and sweaters and clothes like they were still living in a cold country. I always wonder how they manage underneath all them clothes, it must be so hot," said one villager. Older Barbadians recall that in the past the attire of returnees stood out even more than it does today. When Barbados was poorer and the island had less contact with the outside world, those migrants who came home were often a spectacle and the object of much attention. Speaking of the 1950s, one man recalled:

> Them back from England would wear these three-piece suits and stockings, and they'd all come back with a watch. Even if it was a really cheap watch they'd want you to see it. If you hadn't noticed it, they'd pick up their wrist and look at the watch and say, "Gee, it's already two-thirty!" That was just to draw your attention to it, because having that watch was a great achievement.

Today most Barbadians deny being impressed by the speech or dress of returnees, although their large houses and cars are a different matter.

Locals also believe that Barbadians who have been away are less religious when they come back. They are also said to have become less strict with their children. "They no longer flogs their children to put them right," said one man. "They think that talking to the child, more than whipping it, is the better way. But I don't see their kids turning out any the better."

Nothing annoys Barbadians as much as hearing returnees complain about their country. This is often done in the context of comparing Barbados with the country the migrant has returned from. Barbados invariably comes out short in such comparisons. Locals say they do not want to hear how expensive the vegetables are in Barbados, that the cashiers are slow and discourteous or that medical service is not what it is in Britain or Canada. They have heard it all before and do not want to hear it again. One woman told me about two migrants who had returned from England that she had overheard on the local bus. "They were laughing at our buses," she said, "making fun of our buses, about how much better the buses were in England and that the roads there don't have no holes in it. It's not fair to stack up Barbados against a big country like England."

## Some Impacts of Return Migration

One question governments and anthropologists alike are now asking is whether migrants have any impact on economic development when they return home.[18] Do they bring back new ideas and attitudes that might rub off on local people? Do they bring back work skills or invest their overseas savings in ways that contribute to their society's development? Or in returning home do they merely add to the island's overcrowding and create pressure on its scarce resources?

Early on, many social scientists took the latter view, that returnees played a minimal role in introducing modern ideas (Dahya 1973; Rhoades 1978; Griffiths 1983; Rubenstein 1983). They found that returnees rarely invested their repatriated earnings in new enterprises that created jobs or benefited the region. Writing about the Mediterranean, Russell King concludes: "The notion that returnees help in the development of their home country is falsely utopian" (King 1978, 17). For the English-speaking Caribbean, Hymie Rubenstein suggests that return migration and remittances actually added to the "deterioration of already trouble-ridden economies" (Rubenstein 1983, 298). In a review of the literature, Michael Kearney (1986, 246) concludes that, "few migrants learn any new skills, or if they do, rarely put them to use in the home community". However, these conclusions are largely drawn from research conducted among migrants who returned to rural areas, where agrarian economies provided little opportunity for them to make use of the skills and training they had acquired in urban-industrial settings abroad.

The Barbadian experience paints a different picture. About half of the migrants I surveyed believed they had initiated at least one constructive change in their workplaces based on knowledge they had acquired overseas. Those who were college-educated or had received technical training abroad were twice as likely as the non-trained workers to believe they had been innovators.

In some fields, new innovations were directly attributed to the influence of return migrants. An American-trained accountant, for example, introduced the electronic processing of financial accounts to a Bridgetown firm. A minister of health who had spent many years in New York, introduced halfway houses for those who were mentally incapacitated but able to care for themselves. A movement to de-institutionalize childcare in Barbados came from returnees working in the Ministry of Social Services who had become familiar with new approaches while working in Canada. Important innovations in computers, medicine and engineering have also been attributed to the influence of returnees.[19]

Opportunities for migrants to apply their foreign experience are greater in private-sector jobs than in the public sector (Gmelch 1987). Foreign work experience, in fact, is considered important by many in the Bridgetown business community. An owner of a retail sales firm said he preferred to hire returnees because of their wider experience. Perhaps with some exaggeration, one businessman claimed, "There is nobody in business in Barbados who is moving up who has not been away."

There is less room for innovation in government. Barbados's civil service, established by the British and modelled after their own system, is hierarchical and rigid. Its bureaucrats, say many Bajans, are primarily interested in defending their own positions. Unlike the business community, where the pressure of competition forces people to be at least minimally open to new ideas, there is no such need in the civil service. One civil servant who had returned from England talked about his superiors who had not been away: "Because you've been away and maybe know more about something, they feel threatened. They don't want to admit that maybe you have the answer, especially when you've only been on the job half as long."

The resistance to the foreign ideas of returnees is by no means restricted to government bureaucrats. Barbados is a conservative society where people are slow to accept change, especially foreign ideas brought back by their own countrymen. "When proposing some change to my parishioners", said an Anglican rector, "I have to be very careful not to let them think I learned it in England." Another man said of returnees: "They have the same ideas as North Americans who live here. The difference is that people will listen to what the foreigner has to say, but not to their own kind. They'll say, "Who the hell is he to tell us what to do. He's only a Barbadian like us."

Sometimes innovations are resisted because they require extra work, something many Barbadians admit they are not prepared to do. Said one woman who returned from England with a PhD in education, "Most Bajans are happy with the status quo, they take the path of least resistance. Don't ask them to change if it's going to mean more effort." In fact, she gave up trying to convince her teaching colleagues to hold "parent-teacher nights", modelled after those she'd seen in Canadian and British schools. "The teachers were somewhat open to the idea until they realized it was going to mean more work."

In occupations in which there are many return migrants, they may collectively have an impact. This was the case with nurses at one hospital, who by strength in number, modernized some procedures and upgraded their positions. In the words of one, "If you try to change things, there is opposition. But there are certain standards in the hospital and one is that they have meetings, and nurses are allowed to give their opinions. Since a lot of us have worked or were trained overseas, some things we say are heard."

Because of jealousy and resistance to new ideas, the influence of returnees at the local level is much less than it could be. Some of Valenza Griffith's ideas were rejected by her fellow nurses:

> The standard of nursing in England is completely different. . . . Up there you are exposed to more equipment and teaching than here, and you have more different kinds of cases there. But you can't apply what you learned up there without being criticized. They'd [fellow nurses] soon tell you should've stayed up there.

A teacher recalled the way her colleagues would "push up their faces" at her suggestions. Outside the workplace, the influence of migrants as purveyors of new ideas is especially difficult to measure. For example, there is no evidence of returnees having influenced the attitudes of locals towards racism. Yet, I am certain that it occurs. While some migrants may not say much about their encounters with racism overseas, others freely recount their experiences to neighbours and friends. Specifically, they relate the stereotyped remarks they have overheard white Britons and Americans make about black people being dirty, ignorant, loud and lazy, as well as how they live off the backs of taxpayers and eat smelly food. Anthropologists Connie Sutton and Susan Makiesky (1975) believe that in the two Barbadian villages they studied, return migrants had a significant influence in awakening the racial and political consciousness of villagers who had not been away. It was largely from migrants that villagers learned how black people were regarded in predominantly white Britain and North America. It is not that Barbadians had never known racism, for there is ample white bias in Barbados. Rather, they assumed that the prejudice of their own whites was a perversion of the true metropolitan culture and that whites in England or North America were somehow different. Living abroad had taught the migrants a different reality, which they communicated in various ways to Barbadians at home. Sutton and Makiesky (124) consider the influence of the returnees in raising racial consciousness to be greater than that of the Barbadian middle-class or student radicals. They also note that while the media keep Barbadians abreast of happenings in the outside world, it is often the returnee who interprets the news from overseas for the villager and, in the course of doing so, shapes public opinion.

Technology is probably the easiest place to look for evidence of the influence of returnees, as items of material culture are more easily transferred from one culture to another than are ideas. In an earlier period, Bon Richardson (1985) notes that Barbadians returning from work on the Panama Canal introduced window screens which keep out disease-bearing mosquitoes. Today's returnees have introduced little more than the peculiar use of wallpaper, wall-to-wall carpeting and drapes, none of which are suited to a tropical climate. On the positive side, returnees who have become accustomed to new products and technology abroad are quicker to adopt new ideas and goods when they appear in Barbados.

The problem with assessing the influence of returnees in the larger community is trying to disentangle their role as agents of cultural change from other external influences on Barbadian society. Barbadians today have much contact with the outside world through movies, foreign television programming, contact with tourists and travel. In the realm of material culture, there is little that migrants can introduce that locals have not already seen, either on television or while visiting relatives abroad.

But returnees have a clear impact in another way. After years of hard work, most emigrants arrive home with a sizable amount of capital from savings and from the sale of overseas assets: house, car and furniture. Most use their savings to purchase housing or to improve the home or property they already own.[20] Returnee housing is invariably of high quality; most buy or build substantial and high-status wall houses, rather than the more common wood houses many had grown up in. In the villages, large, solidly constructed and brightly painted returnee housing often sets the standard to which others aspire.

Most returnees also buy a car. Successful migrants are expected to buy a car in Barbados or bring one home when they return. Car ownership is an important status symbol among middle-class Barbadians, who shun public transportation. But buying an automobile does not benefit the island's economy, since all are manufactured outside Barbados. Worse yet, car ownership adds to air and noise pollution, creating severe congestion in Barbados's urban areas.

Anthropologists in other settings have argued that it would be far better if return migrants invested their savings in business enterprises that create new jobs and capital rather than in housing and automobiles.[21] It is largely the returnees' failure to do so that leads some scholars to conclude that returnees have little or no impact on their homelands. Only one in seven Barbadian migrants participating in the survey had invested their savings in a business.

Barbadian returnees admittedly spend their repatriated savings primarily on consumption. Improved housing, furnishings and automobiles raise their living standard and their social status, which was their reason for emigrating in the first place. It seems unfair to expect them to invest their savings in a business before providing for their own shelter. Often the problem is not the returnees' investment priorities, but simply not having enough capital. Many more returnees would start businesses if they had enough money remaining after taking care of their housing needs. And some who are financially successful at home will later start up businesses of their own. It was nearly twenty years after Richard Goddard returned from Canada that he finally had enough capital to buy a sugar estate. He then diversified into different crops and livestock. His estate is now a small but important part of the national effort to find alternatives to growing sugar.

## Conclusions

Since the bulk of post–World War II English-speaking Caribbean migrants emigrated to North America and Britain, the skills and cultural knowledge they returned with are Western in character. Hence, in the Caribbean context, "development" means becoming Western. At the national level, progress or development becomes a measure of the country's proximity to the institutions and values of British and North American society (Thomas-

Hope 1985). The ethnocentrism inherent in this position is unfortunate, but in assessing the impact of migrants returning from Western metropoles, it is difficult to avoid. The problem (suppressing an indigenous culture at the hands of Westernization) is mitigated, however, by the fact that Barbados is not a traditional non-Western society. The aboriginal Arawak and Carib inhabitants of Barbados were gone by the time of British settlement in the 1600s, and from that time until 1966, the island was a colony of Britain.

Furthermore, both black and white Barbadians have always been orientated towards Britain and more recently North America. They still look to these nations for their social and economic goals. In short, in the minds of most Barbadians, the transfer of culture and capital from the metropolitan countries to their island nation does represent development.

With regard to labour and capital, the return of migrants to their homelands is also beneficial to the host countries. It is in the interests of the United Kingdom, the United States and Canada to have migrant labourers go home as they age and become less productive, and as their children begin to occupy spaces in the schools and universities. When migrants return home, Barbados bears the cost of their retirement. As capitalist economies mature and their populations age, temporary labour migration becomes preferred over permanent immigration (Kearney 1986, 344). It is not surprising that most industrial countries in the post–World War II era preferred guest worker programmes to permanent immigration.

Finally, it is also legitimate to ask what would have happened to Barbados had these migrants, and the many more who permanently remain abroad, not left their island? Young, healthy and ambitious at the time of their emigration, we do not know how they would have changed their society had they stayed behind. Nor can we be sure how Barbados would have responded to and been changed by the increased unemployment and elevated pressures on scarce resources that would have likely resulted.

# Notes

1. Results of the survey research, which involved 135 Barbadian returnees, can be found in "Work, Innovation, and Investment: The Impact of Return Migrants in Barbados" (Gmelch 1987).

2. Twenty migrants participated in this study. Some of the life histories were published in Gmelch 1992.

3. For more discussion see Holmes 1988, 257–60.

4. Of 135 migrants surveyed, those who went abroad to work were away an average of 15.3 years, and those who went to study were away an average of 9.7 years before resettling in Barbados.

5. Most took up residence in inner-city areas. West Indians in both Britain and the United States tend be clustered in the inner city. The reason for this, as Peach (1968, 85) notes of British cities, is that the older, more dilapidated and therefore less costly housing is found near the centre. Not surprisingly, as British towns evolve, the newer and more desirable housing is built further from the centre.

6. See also Holmes 1988 and Western 1992.

7. See Chamberlain 1997 for a good discussion of migrant family life.

8. The situation was somewhat different for Barbadians and other West Indians in the United States, where there was already a large American black population. Hence, the West Indian immigrants settled in neighbourhoods that were predominantly black. White Americans, knowing perhaps even less about the Caribbean origins of the migrants than white Britons, merely lumped them in with American blacks. Their status as immigrants was invisible. As a result of their treatment as black Americans, argues Sutton, West Indians have been discouraged from assimilating: the immigrants see that the group they are identified with "possess[es] the lowest incomes and the highest school drop-out and unemployment rates" (1987, 21).

9. I have heard Barbadians tell stories about migrants who returned home only to discover that their wives or families had frittered away the sent remittances. These frustrated and unhappy migrants, often with nothing to show for the years of effort and saving, often re-emigrated.

10. For more detailed discussions of the influence of macro-economic conditions on return flows in other settings, see Paine 1974; Rhoades 1978; and Piore 1979.

11. Similarly, many of the returnees interviewed for earlier studies on Ireland and Newfoundland also said that favourable experiences during a holiday visit home were the impetus for them to return permanently (Gmelch 1983, 52).

12. The desire to return is usually stronger among men than women. In fact, a

number of the women I interviewed admitted that they had initially resisted their husbands' desires to come home.

13. For a detailed discussion of gender and the reasons for return migration, see Gmelch and Gmelch 1995.

14. This quotation was taken from an interview for a documentary video and, therefore, the wording is slightly different than the version that appears in the oral history in Gmelch 1992.

15. For examples from other cultures, see Gmelch 1980, 143–44.

16. The official unemployment rate in Barbados, which seldom drops below 25 per cent, is two to three times the level of unemployment in the host societies.

17. Michael Whiteford's observations among Columbian migrant women that migration is a "liberating process which results in a modicum of sexual equality" (1978, 86), applies equally well to these Barbadians.

18. For an excellent review, see Kearney 1986.

19. For details see Gmelch 1987.

20. For details see Gmelch 1987.

21. The preference to use one's savings to buy and improve housing has been widely described among returnees elsewhere. For a detailed discussion, see Rhoades 1978; for a review of similar cases, see Gmelch 1980, 148.

# References

Chamberlain, M. 1997. *Narratives of Exile and Return.* New York: St Martin's.

Dahya, B. 1973. Pakistanis in Britain: Transients or Settlers. *Race* 14 (3): 241–77.

Foner, N. 1976. Male and Female: Jamaican Migrants in London. *Anthropological Quarterly* 49 (1): 28–35.

Gmelch, G. 1980. Return Migration. *Annual Review of Anthropology* 9: 135–59.

———. 1983. Who Returns and Why: Return Migration Behavior in Two Atlantic Societies. *Human Organization* 48 (1): 46–54.

———. 1987. Work, Innovation, and Investment: The Impact of Return Migrants in Barbados. *Human Organization* 46 (2): 131–40.

———. 1992. *Double Passage: The Lives of Caribbean Migrants Abroad and Back Home.* Ann Arbor: University of Michigan Press.

Gmelch, G., and S.B. Gmelch. 1995. Gender and Migration: The Readjustment of Women Migrants in Barbados, Ireland, and Newfoundland. *Human Organization* 54 (4): 470–73.

Griffith, D.C. 1983. The Promise of a Country: The Impact of Seasonal US Migration on the Jamaican Peasantry. PhD diss., University of Florida.

Holmes, C. 1988. *John Bull's Island: Immigration and British Society, 1871–1971*. London: Macmillan.

Kearney, M. 1986. From the Invisible Hand to the Visible Feet. *Annual Review of Anthropology* 13: 331–61.

King, R.L. 1978. Return Migration: Review of Some Cases from Southern Europe. *Mediterranean Studies* 1 (2): 3–30.

Paine, S. 1974. *Exporting Workers: The Turkish Case*. London: Cambridge University Press.

Peach, C. 1968. *West Indian Migration to Britain: A Social Geography*. London: Oxford University Press.

Piore, M. 1979. *Birds of Passage: Migrant Labor in Industrial Societies*. Cambridge: Cambridge University Press.

Rex, J., and S. Tomlinson. 1979. *Colonial Immigrants in a British City*. London: Routledge and Kegan Paul.

Rhoades, R. 1978. Intra-European Return Migration and Rural Development: Lessons from the Spanish Case. *Human Organization* 37 (2): 136–47.

Richardson, B.C. 1985. *Panama Money in Barbados, 1900–1920*. Knoxville: University of Tennessee Press.

Rubenstein, H. 1983. Remittances and Rural Underdevelopment in the English-Speaking Caribbean. *Human Organization* 42 (4): 295–306.

Sutton, C. 1987. The Caribbeanization of New York City. In *Caribbean Life in New York City,* ed. C. Sutton and E.M. Cahney, 3–30. New York: Center for Migration Studies.

Sutton, C., and S. Makiesky. 1975. Migration and West Indian Racial and Political Consciousness. In *Migration and Development: Implications for Ethnic Identity and Political Conflict,* ed. H.I. Safa and B. DuToit, 113–44. The Hague: Mouton.

Thomas-Hope, E. 1985. Return Migration and Its Implications for Caribbean Development. In *Migration and Development in the Caribbean*, ed. R.A. Pastor, 157–77. Boulder: Westview Press.

Western, J. 1992. *A Passage to England: Barbadian Londoners Speak of Home*. Minneapolis: University of Minnesota Press.

Whiteford, M. 1978. Women, Migration and Social Change: A Colombian Case Study. *International Migration Review* 12 (2): 236–47.

# Trini to the Bone

## Return, Reintegration and Resolution Among Trinidadian Migrants

| Roger-Mark De Souza |

All these years ah spent abroad
In the cold longing to be home
Trini to the bone, Trini to the bone
Lord I pray that some sweet day I will no longer have to roam
Trini to the bone, Trini to the bone
The problems we have are plain to see
... There's no place like home, some people say
Though some had to leave to make their way
In their hearts they know their destiny
To come home and big up they country.
— *Calypsonian David Rudder, "Trini to the Bone"*

West Indian mobility patterns reflect a growing complexity of interwoven transnational relationships, socio-cultural associations and survival strategies among a people accustomed, and historically predisposed, to migration. For Trinidad and Tobago, like many other islands in the region, emigration has long served as a way of overcoming the limitations of life on small islands. While many Trinidadians emigrate, official statistics suggest that the majority return for visits or long-term resettlement. Many of those who resettle come back because of homeland attachments. These attachments are rooted in a sense of home and of belonging – of being "Trini to the bone".

The most obvious of these attachments are socio-cultural connections, kinship bonds and interpersonal relations. This chapter examines the life stories of one hundred Trinidadian long-term returnees to examine the saliency of socio-cultural factors that influence return movement, particularly this sense of belonging. It will illustrate that while social attachments are the main reason for return, it is the area where returnees experience the most problems. Government policy can help address these problems by facilitating re-entry into the country. However, it is ultimately the combination of official policy with individual and community strategies that will minimize these problems and enable returnees to use their skills and knowledge acquired abroad "to come home and big up they country".

## The Context of Return Migration: Investigating Return

Return migration is an enduring feature of West Indian societies. As long as there has been emigration from the region, there have been countervailing streams of return. This movement, however, is poorly recorded by immigration statistics. Official estimates point to a return flow of 85 to 98 per cent. These figures capture anyone returning, including return visits and long-term return. Investigating return is all the more difficult in this context.

One of the first challenges is how to define return. For the purposes of this analysis, return is characterized as the re-entry of a citizen who left with the intention of spending at least a year abroad and upon returning intended to spend at least a year in the homeland. This is consistent with the United Nations' identification of one year as a significant time frame for defining a migrant and coincides with research suggesting that those who stay beyond the time allocated on their visas (that is, "overstayers") do indeed leave the host country within one year (Conway 1994).

In order to further examine return, information was garnered from the Central Statistical Office, contemporary newspaper reports as well as a survey and interviews with one hundred return migrants. Informants were contacted through a non-probability snowball sampling technique based on friendship networks. A preliminary profile of the returnees interviewed suggests a reasonable mixture of respondents. At the time of return, 61 per cent of the sample were not married; 54 per cent were thirty years old or younger. The two largest ethnic groups were represented: 49 per cent were Afro-

Trinidadian and 18 per cent Indo-Trinidadian. In addition, 60 per cent were female and 5 per cent were blue-collar workers. The host countries from which migrants returned were primarily Canada, the United States and the United Kingdom. Other countries where migrants had lived or returned from were France, Holland, Spain, Guatemala, Mexico, Venezuela, St Martin, Jamaica and Barbados. Most migrants in the sample returned to Trinidad and Tobago during three decades – from the 1970s to the 1990s.

## Motives for Return

Why did these people return? Return was primarily an individual and household strategy. Emigration was not an expression of a desire to reside abroad, but rather a strategy for accumulating sufficient savings or upgrading skills so that individuals might ultimately reside comfortably in the homeland. Select household members emigrated to diversify household income or to increase the household resource portfolio. For some, planned return was accelerated by the need to remedy an urgent situation back home or the desire to flee unfavourable conditions abroad. Many others returned hoping to take advantage of opportunities back home afforded by newly acquired skills or to gain from socio-political developments in the island homeland. For all, however, the decision to return home was driven by homeland attachments.

These attachments are location-specific assets that cannot be replicated in the host country or elsewhere in the world (De Souza 1998). The most important of these attachments is a sense of belonging. This sense of belonging suggests easy reinsertion into the homeland and fits into a larger repertoire of historical, anecdotal and cultural images of return. All returnees interviewed, regardless of the reason for return, benefited from the positive associations connected with this image of return and enjoyed the prestige and increased status that return confers.

## A Positive Image of Return

Important drivers in the decision to return are popular perceptions of return migration, and those perceptions have influence in the individual consciousness. In Trinidad and Tobago, the collective attitude towards return migration is that it is beneficial, status-conferring and a valid path to upward mobility.

Historically, upward mobility for the Trinidadian middle classes could only be accessed through foreign education. This trend is clearly evidenced in the sample. Fifty-five per cent mentioned education as one of the main reasons for emigration. The fact that an overwhelming majority, 75 per cent, had attained education beyond the secondary level while abroad confirms that returnees have the potential to be a highly trained group. Many of those returning with advanced degrees are able to secure employment. Fifty-four per cent of the returnees were professionals at the time of the interview, clearly supporting the belief that returnees enjoy occupational success and prestige in Trinidad and Tobago.

This potential for upward mobility is closely tied to the image of success that is buttressed by consistent return streams and positive descriptions of returnees in the local press, folklore and literature. Once they leave, many Trinidadian emigrants do not forget their commitments in the homeland and often fulfil these obligations by running announcements in local newspapers. These announcements hold up to society the image of a "son or daughter of the soil" who has succeeded abroad against all odds and invariably include a photo, the individual's migration history, a synopsis of achievements (usually educational or professional) and the individual's local connections. The latter may include a host of relations who may have in some way contributed to the individual's upbringing or who may derive prestige from being mentioned. These are usually parents, but may extend to siblings and members of the extended family such as aunts and uncles, grandparents, and even dead relatives.[1] In some cases, this is an opportunity for those abroad to partially fulfil their obligation to those who helped them; for others, it is a way to herald their return and to prepare for reinsertion into the homeland.

If these announcements reinforce the prestige attached to a foreign education by emphasizing the accomplishments of recent graduates of British and North American universities, articles dealing with the success of Trinidadians abroad reinforce the idea of a return and stress an obligation to Trinidad and Tobago. One such article ends:

> So will she use her education to live comfortably up in the Great White North? No way, she declared: "I want to come back home . . . (She) sees

Trinidad's present economy as an exciting opportunity for people who have been educated abroad. . . . Far from giving up on her homeland, she wants to return and make it into the financial heart of the Caribbean. (*Sunday Guardian,* 13 June 1993, 19)

The image of returnees and foreign education in the local press is significant because it illustrates the pervasiveness of emigration from and return to Trinidadian society, and serves as an indicator of return expectations.

## Expectations of Return

Key messages about return and reinsertion into the homeland shape expectations about return. While some of the earliest emigration may have been due to economic opportunities abroad, since the turn of the century, Trinidad and Tobago's economy has enjoyed relative prosperity due to oil production. This prosperity facilitated major changes in Trinidadian society. The government implemented ambitious development plans and revitalized the country's infrastructure and social services. This not only encouraged locals living abroad to return, but it meant that upward mobility was now within reach for a larger percentage of the population who could go abroad, upgrade their skills and return to enjoy a better life.

Return to Trinidad and Tobago held out the promise of opportunity, prestige and recognition in the homeland. Comma (1980, 22) suggests that given the limited training offered in Trinidad and Tobago, an increased number of students also emigrated with the intention of returning to benefit from the new opportunities. These developments made return attractive to expatriates.

The migrants who returned during these boom years had no problems finding employment. It was a period when jobs for the foreign-educated were abundant, and virtually all those in the sample who returned at that time had little difficulty in securing work. Richard Chen Wing[2] was one such case: "I came back during the boom years. I went for an interview and one week later I had a job. There were many openings then and the salaries were good. The idea of coming back was greater, more attractive." These opportunities facilitated the decision to return and provided an opportunity for initial professional re-entry.

Long-term reintegration, however, centres not only on initial re-entry, but also on the general manner in which returnees are received over time – this is based on expectations of returnee behaviour. These expectations date back to as early as the eighteenth century, when the French and British creoles had children in Trinidad and Tobago, were sent abroad for a foreign education, and returned to assume leadership positions in the society. Two centuries later, expectations of returnee behaviour came to be conditioned more and more by North American influences.

During World War II, under an agreement with the United Kingdom, huge American military bases were built in Trinidad. During this time, Trinidadians took advantage of the economic benefits to be derived from the American presence in Trinidad, and many were quick to mimic the mannerisms of the foreigners, particularly their speech patterns and "languid drawl" (Anthony 1983, 47). "Fresh-water Yankee", a popular derogatory term that originated in this period, referred to a Trinidadian who had acquired an American accent simply by visiting the US Embassy or one of the US Naval Bases (Mendes 1986, 58). Today, it commonly refers to returnees who have spent time in North America and come back with a heavy American accent. It is also used to denote returnees who exemplify general North American values and mannerisms. This kind of behaviour is reminiscent of the pervasive images of North American lifestyle as portrayed by the cable television that is available on the island. The returnee, even when not overtly displaying these kinds of mannerisms, is expected to have taken part in this kind of lifestyle.

These observations point to four important conclusions with regard to the reintegration of return migrants. First, return is a historically viable means of upward mobility. Second, socio-cultural forces and a historical legacy have resulted in returnees generally being held in high esteem and being accorded a certain degree of prestige. Third, returnees value homeland attachments and come back home anticipating that they will be warmly received. Fourth, returnees are expected to demonstrate foreign values and mannerisms, which often reinforce the perception that they enjoyed a luxurious life abroad. These social forces – history, culture, homeland attachments and returnee behaviour – all culminate in a positive image of return that, in turn, determines how the returnees will experience reintegration.

## Reintegration: The Returnees' Dilemma

### The Re-entry Crisis

Once migrants come back, their reintegration is determined by the accuracy of the information they have gathered about return. Successful short-term reintegration occurs when anticipated benefits in the perceived environment are fulfilled, or when the returnee develops mechanisms to cope with the unanticipated difficulties of return. The more inaccurate the perception, however, the more likely the returnee will experience difficulties.

Several researchers refer to re-entry difficulties of this nature as the "W-curve phenomenon". The W curve refers to the double accommodation process that the returnee undergoes. The first U-curve component traces the migrant's adaptation to the host society from an initial feeling of elation, to diminution of adjustment to the new culture and finally to an improved stage marked by easier adjustment. As a result of these stages, the migrant experiences a change of attitudes, habits and perspective. A second U-curve adjustment, creating the complete W curve, occurs when the migrant returns and encompasses the returnee's adjustment to the receiving country and readjustment to the home culture (Comma 1980, 31). This second phase of the W curve is referred to as "the re-entry crisis".

### Readjustment Problems

The re-entry crisis is paramount and may be complicated by three factors: first, having to readjust to the original society may come as a surprise to returnees; second, the original society itself may have gone through changes; and third, individuals may not appreciate the effects of the U curve on their expectations, values and feelings of alienation. The impacts of these factors reveal themselves in three areas of readjustment difficulties for returnees: self-perception, interpersonal relations and connection to the homeland.

### The Self-Perception of Returnees

The period shortly after return can be one of the most decisive and most difficult, when the experience abroad is still fresh in the mind of the returnee and, in almost immediate juxtaposition, he or she has to readapt. It is almost as if a double persona has to be adopted. Davindra Ramlalsingh explains:

> When I returned [in 1969] I went through a process of reverse culture shock. I looked at the airport and said to myself, "Look at dem [their] airport! Look at the prices in dis [this] country." I would look at the society very harshly. Soon I had to resolve it in my mind, intellectually, and I said to myself, "This is my country." . . . I had heard stories about that, about returnees being cautioned about losing their nexus.

Many other returnees saw this as a key phase in their readaptation. Natasha Hunte said that when she came back, she saw Trinidad and Tobago "through visitors' eyes". Alvin Mark claims that he experienced a culture shock: "The mentality of Trinidadians is something else. They don't give a damn, Monday could fall on a Tuesday." Similarly, Marcia Warner proclaims that "you have to deal with Trinidadians never answering questions that you ask them, the inefficiencies in the government system, the mentality of the people who serve you who always give you the impression that they are doing you a favour". It is important to note that these returnees distinguish themselves from those who have not gone abroad. The fact that the latter are *Trinidadians* is emphasized. On the one hand, this reflects a common habit among the local population of criticizing the actions of countrymen by stressing that these actions are typically Trinidadian. This situates the criticized action from which the speaker wants to distance him or herself in a Trinidadian context. On the other hand, several returnees use this labelling to refer to the non-migrating population to emphasize that they exhibit characteristics which are typically Trinidadian and have been strengthened by the fact that they have remained in Trinidad and Tobago.

For many of the respondents, this time was one of re-apprenticeship. It was a time when experiences that they had undergone in adapting to life abroad had to be relived. In fact, they had to rediscover their homeland. Brian and Elizabeth LeBlanc describe their experience: "When we came back I couldn't even find Frederick Street [a major street in Port of Spain]. Friends had changed. We had so much to learn. I never drove in Trinidad. I started driving in the States." Typically, returnees experience initial difficulty. It is the time when they experience the greatest isolation. This is normally resolved as years pass and the individual reassesses perceptions and develops strategies to facilitate reintegration.

Dealing with personal changes and a changing perception of self may be difficult if returnees are not fully aware of how they have changed while abroad. The reactions of others make them aware of these changes, which, in turn, help them define ways of coping with reintegration. For the local population, changes in a returnee can be easily detected. At the most obvious level, these would be in differences in language (accent and vocabulary) and mannerisms. These may be interpreted as putting on airs, and remind others of fresh-water Yankees and a time when Trinidadians imitated American servicemen. Mathilda Slinger tells us:

> People always tell me that I have an accent and that I like to play white woman. For example, when I buy "fags" [cigarettes] or call everyone "love". I have lots of problems with that. It's not that I mean it, but it's a way of calling [addressing] people . . . People here . . . always tell me that I always talk about England and why I don't go back where I come from.

The reactions to Mathilda confirm that certain of her mannerisms are more British than Trinidadian, and this provokes a denial of her Trinidadian origins.

For other returnees, expectations of a changed appearance or comportment are such an ingrained aspect of the returnee stereotype that if the returnee does not fulfil them, some locals may doubt whether time was actually spent abroad. Kamla Boodram explains: "People ask me why I came back. They are very impressed that I studied in England. They still have that mother-country attitude. But because I don't have an accent some people don't believe that I went to England." While Mathilda's difference in speech attests to her time abroad, Kamla's lack of obvious signs of having lived abroad leads others to question her returnee status. In both instances, the women experience a degree of isolation. These feelings of isolation were shared by most returnees, but were particularly acute among those whose success abroad was apparent.

### Interpersonal Relations

The isolation that returnees experience is also reflected in their social relationships, gender relations and professional situations. Even though it is rarely a problem with family, the success of a returnee may cause friends who remained in Trinidad and Tobago to feel inferior and act distant. When

Horace Andrews returned from Canada he brought back all his household possessions, bought a new house and car, and opened a business. "I wasn't really treated differently by family when I returned," he describes, "a few friends were ignoring me. Probably they thought that I was better off than they were." In Horace's case some of this distance is undoubtedly created by the possessions that he brought back which created an image of a successful life abroad.

The desirability of emigration is effectively perpetuated by this image of success resulting from a repertoire of references to extravagant return as well as the returnees themselves who strive to uphold the image. Carolyn Sahadeo worked illegally in the United States, but felt that it was important that no one in Trinidad knew this. She explains: "I didn't want to be traced [by Trinidadians] . . . I went brave and never looked back. People in Trinidad don't know what I did in the States. They all think I went to study and that I lived with my uncle." It is important to note that she was careful not to reveal to others the true motivations of her emigration, nor the actual conditions of her time abroad. On her return, she presented the image of success. She needed to save face, especially as others knew that she had been remitting money to her sons in Trinidad.

The majority of the returnees had little difficulty, however, in readjusting to family life, but instead experienced value conflict with regard to social and interpersonal relationships. "When I got back, it was difficult to get accustomed to the attitude of people," John Aguiton explained. "It was difficult to adjust to things such as people not being on time, the pushing in queues, the lawlessness." Similarly, Harry Rampersaud, an opera singer, and his wife experienced extreme difficulties in reintegrating:

> When we returned I was sixty-five years old. I hoped to teach in Trinidad, perhaps return to [the town where I grew up]. But it has been difficult . . . Trinidadians are not really interested in opera. I want to sing opera. But Trinidadians say, "What happen to that Indian man singing in Spanish and thing?" They want me to sing Indian songs.

In one case, a returnee had changed so much that she had many problems interacting with Trinidadians on the whole. Sally Walcott had been back almost four years, yet claimed that "[after Canada], I don't know how to make friends with Trinidadians . . . I feel separate and hold myself apart from people."

Part of this isolation is brought about by attitudinal changes. In discussing how their time abroad has changed them, returnees feel that they are more determined, independent and ambitious than when they left. Their experiences and qualifications abroad help them to seek out new opportunities and be more creative. Irma Spicer, a light-skinned Trinidadian of African descent, describes her experience as such:

> Now that I am back some people may look upon me as a fresh-water Yankee, but it's just that I now have a wider range of experience. A friend tells me that I would always get where I want to because of my colour. When my boyfriend tells people about my job, they tell him that I couldn't be black. But I disagree, I am simply a hardworking, striving young black woman.

The fact that Irma is sometimes considered a fresh-water Yankee is a reference to the perception of a different value system and to the noticeable changes which are attributed to the time she spent abroad. These changes centre largely around her work ethic, and this is no accident, for part of the image that the local population of the 1940s held of the "Yankee" servicemen was that of an industrious hardworking group.[3] Nicola Ragoonath also demonstrates a similar attitude of industry, independence and resourcefulness:

> I came back highly qualified and very independent. When I returned in 1984, I knew that there were jobs out there and I was determined to find one. When I came back I had to work in a bar to make money – that was something that I would never have done before.

For female returnees, these attitudes and changes sometimes present special readjustment challenges with regard to gender expectations.

Accomplishments abroad allowed women to grow personally and enter new domains that had been previously reserved for men. They have emerged more assertive and less willing to accept boundaries imposed on them by their home society. This success, however, compounds the difficulties of readapting to the homeland. Nicola Ragoonath explains:

> If someone tells me I am female and that I can't go somewhere, if I want to go, I go . . . [At work] I am the only female in a male department. That causes problems. I work long hours and report directly to the general manager. I have had to put in longer hours because of the added stress of being the lone female in the office.

Sally Walcott finds that the independence that she enjoyed in Canada is curtailed in Trinidad and Tobago. She elaborates:

> Here life is difficult for a woman, up there you're really independent, you could move on your own and be your own person. You feel safe up there, you don't need to be with someone. Here you don't feel safe. . . . Here women look at themselves in a particular way. They only expect so much for themselves, and if they get less than that, they are unhappy . . . they are caught up in appearances.

These changes have also affected women's relationships with men. Kandis Mohammed, for example, also perceives herself as different from non-migrating women and describes how this perception has changed her expectations of men:

> A Trinidadian man who has been abroad is different. . . . Here men are pampered by their mothers. They expect everything to be done for them. They have the same expectations of a mate. A lot of Trini women focus on getting married. It gives them a sense of achievement, a husband and children. Looking for a husband becomes their goal in life. When I go out on a lime [outing] with friends I never go out with the direct purpose of looking for men, it does not mean that I won't check out the potential, but it is not a priority.

Similarly, Cynthia Tiwari found that on her return, Trinidadian men were unable to deal with her independence. Nicola Ragoonath shares this perspective: "I don't bother to pamper Trinidadian men. They have this 'I am the man' attitude. . . . They don't set out to impress and I am not competing with all the other girls – that intimidates them."

While abroad, these women were able to extend themselves beyond the gender limitations usually imposed on them by Trinidadian society. Now, as returnees, they experience difficulty in adjusting to these limitations. These women all refuse to conform to the gender expectations imposed by their homeland and experience difficulties in their social and professional interactions as a result.

Return also represents a special challenge to married couples. Their relationships have evolved in a different setting and being back once again may give rise to problems. Donna Solomon complains that returning has adversely affected her marriage:

> My husband is the typical Trinidadian male. In Canada, we were isolated, we weren't totally integrated. He belonged to a West Indian club, but it wasn't the same. He clung to us. We had more family life. Since we have returned, he is out more often, friends come to pick him up to go out. . . . Here he feels safe

Kenneth Chin Fatt had a similar experience with his wife: "I didn't want to return, we came back because my wife at the time insisted that we return. We got divorced three years later. Once in Trinidad, she changed. She was spending less time at home, and she was always out with friends."

Among returnees overall, overseas experience can lead to new habits and attitudes that may give rise to misunderstanding and the deterioration – or even break up – of social relationships. Abroad, migrants often discover new-found independence and drive, allowing the emergence of self-reliance, open-mindedness, respectfulness, thrift and self-discipline. Return may complicate previously held relationships. Returnees realize how they have changed and how the homeland may have changed. Reintegration is a constant process of readjustment – personal and interpersonal. This adjustment process is also evident in their professional lives.

One of the first readjustment problems for returnees is not finding employment. Since the mid-eighties, when economic problems affected the job market and the unemployment rate went up, returnees have experienced difficulties securing meaningful employment. Nicole Mendes tried to get a job based on her qualifications:

> I came back qualified as a nurse and expected to get a job. I applied to Mount Hope [Medical Centre] the year before I came back and got good feedback. Then I got a letter from them stating that they were not hiring and that I would be better off staying in London.

Not only was she told not to return, but she also met resentment because of her foreign exposure:

> When I finally did have an interview with the ministry, they kept harping on the fact that I was foreign-trained and that I am white. One of the interviewers told me, "I don't know if you know how it works *here* – you need to learn *our* system." I've talked to English nurses who have married Trinidadians, and they are pulling their hair out. They feel that they are knocking their head against a wall. You have the impression that [in Trinidad] you need to pull strings.

Similarly, sixty-five-year-old Indira Rampersaud is convinced she has been unable to secure a job because of her years spent in Britain. She claims, "When I came back I went for several interviews. Once they recognize you're from England, they don't want to know more. They are not interested in giving you work."

Hostile feelings towards returnees perhaps date back to the boom years, but have become arguably more acute in recent times because of the economic downfall. Rhonda Williams, a twenty-seven-year-old who returned in 1992, suggests that modern developments necessitate a re-evaluation of the image of return. She suggests that going abroad is no longer a major event, and returnees are no longer held in such high esteem: "I don't flaunt that I have been abroad. I have no expectations, my attitude is not 'I've come for the job.' People are wary of those who come back. [Returnees] can't try it anymore. Bachelor degrees are no longer foreign, everyone has one."

Recent returnees must contend with the economic and social difficulties of the country and an attitude of "returnee fatigue" – a backlash from the era when those who returned were favoured for top positions over those who remained. With this precedent, it is not surprising to discover that there are feelings of hostility. Rhonda even questions the motivations among some returnees:

> When people say that they come back to make a contribution to Trinidad and Tobago, that is kind of selfish. It's a way for self-aggrandizement. These people know that they can make good money in here. They have a good competitive advantage and they are here for their own personal goals.

This hostility is not the only difficulty that returnee job seekers face. Their search is complicated by networking channels that are closed to them. Many returnees are unprepared for the significance of home-based networks in the search for employment. Dawn Thomas expresses frustration at being unable to secure a position in her field and feels that her experience abroad should help her find a job:

> When I returned with experience from Canada, the United States, Barbados and St Martin, I expected to find a job. But I recognized that you needed a strategy based on who you knew. I was stupid. I was still in the Canadian mode of thinking and expected to be hired on merit.

Giselle Chin Cheong notes that "the importance of 'contact' and 'who you

know' versus ability and performance and the high proportion of self-
employed, especially among professionals" came as a surprise to her. This
was a frequently mentioned value conflict. Nicola Ragoonath agrees: "Now
that I am back, I am a stronger person and more independent. I will never
pull strings to get a job. I will achieve things by working for it. I have also
learnt that I am never too old for education."

While these locally based non-migrant networks may be unavailable to
returnees, as they move up the corporate ladder and find themselves in a
position to make hiring decisions, an informal network, based on the shared
experience of being a returnee, develops. Vidia Chen Wing, who came back
in 1985, believes that returnees should profit from their comparative advantage. Just as important as the level of education abroad, she argues, is the
issue of experience and exposure. She elaborates: "When I am part of an
interview panel I tend to look more toward applicants who have had an
experience abroad. It's not just the fact that they went abroad, but the struggles that they had to face and what that experience would have taught them."

Vidia is able to recognize the added maturity and independence that life
abroad brings. She is quick to add that this did not systematically mean that
a returnee would be offered a position over a locally educated or experienced
candidate; it just means that it is an advantage that returnees enjoy. Her husband agrees: "I get more respect because I went abroad. People look up to me
more. It is an edge. Just being on your own and having had other experiences, having had more exposure." Nicola Ragoonath staunchly supports this
view and found that local experts in her field were behind the times:

> A foreign degree is better than a local degree. I taught for a while [in Trinidad
> and Tobago] and I was doing freelance training with an agency. I was teach-
> ing people who had been in the field for at least three or four years. They had
> been doing a lot of second guessing, especially when compared to graduates
> from the United States.

There is a general sense that this feeling prevails and is revealed in the admiration that returnees receive from their co-workers.

Some of the more common work-related problems that returnees face are
as follows: no ready market for newly acquired knowledge, lack of stimulation, inadequate facilities, shortage of materials, the necessity of further
accreditation and difficulty in keeping abreast of the latest developments in
their respective fields. The area, however, that has provided the most prob-

lems is interaction with others at work. The workplace, in particular, is a potential hornets' nest of difficulties for interpersonal relations as the qualifications and experience that returnees bring to the job are invariably recognized by employers and co-workers.

The aura of success, be it real or imagined, surrounding returnees may lead to resentment and power conflicts in the workplace. Traditionally, there has been some respect and awe for those who have left the shores of Trinidad and Tobago and returned educated. As a result, expectations placed on returnees may be higher. Donna Solomon reiterates that "at work they expect you to do things better because you were away". Michelle de Gannes says that "people look up to you because you studied abroad. At work people say, 'Ask her, she studied abroad, she'll know.' "

Such a reverence can be easily reduced to derision. Margaret Clarke recounts: "At work they make jokes. For example, if someone can't figure something out, other people in the office always say ask me. It's almost as if they are mocking my [foreign] education." Giselle Chin Cheong, Nicola Ragoonath and Marcia Warner all agree that reactions from co-workers are ambivalent. Nicola Ragoonath raises an important point:

> People look up to me, but there is also a certain amount of jealousy, especially from people at work who have been there for a number of years. They feel that I have just walked in and got the job. . . . People see that you're educated abroad and they feel intimidated. They have their heads in the sky, they figure that I have a lot of money.

She illustrates how easily the local population associates return and success with grandeur, and how easily that leads to speculations of financial well-being. The returnees believe that the local population negates their hard work and effort by perceiving their material and professional achievements to be automatic. If the gap between the migrant's position at departure and that at return is great, especially if the non-returnee has not advanced as much, this may be an understandable perception.

The disparity between returnees and non-migrants may often lead to power conflicts and personal attacks. In Marcia Warner's case, feelings of jealously culminated in a published attack in the local press against her.

> There is much jealousy about my position at work. There were people who expected to have this position based on connections. They feel a certain degree of resentment that I went abroad and got qualified and based on those quali-

fications I was able to get the job. They, on the other hand, remained here and cultivated connections with the hope that would advance their career. There was a very nasty article in one of the weekly newspapers based on inaccurate and unreliable information about me and my job. It gave me a pseudonym, but described my position so clearly that it was obvious that it was me. . . . It hurt, but at least you know who your enemies are and you deal with them only in a business sense.

Marcia's story reveals a perception by non-migrants that returnees are treated better. This can actually lead to a refusal to allow the returnee to employ skills learned abroad. Laurence Bain, an electrician, laments:

My supervisor refused to acknowledge the qualifications and training that I had got in England. . . . No one would show respect for the knowledge [I gained abroad], it wasn't that they owed me it, I would have earned it, but there was no motivation to move forward and go higher. . . . It is a pity. The company was robbed of what contribution I had to make.

The problems that Laurence encountered were similar to those blue-collar Barbadian returnees faced in Gmelch's sample (1985, 44). Gmelch suggests that white collar returnees are better positioned to institute change. White-collar returnees, however, are also confronted with criticism from locally trained co-workers. Larry Joseph recalls:

I recently met someone in Diamond Vale[4] who asked me to which university I went, and when I told him Howard, he ridiculed it, calling it Diamond Vale University. . . . Everyone I know went to Howard. [University of the West Indies] graduates feel that those who can't get into UWI go to Howard, they thus look down on them. UWI graduates feel that a UWI degree is worth more.

Hostility is therefore expressed at all levels. Edward Daniel (1983), an expatriate professional, goes so far as to state that the training and skill of the returnee may be viewed as a threat to members of the elite who want to preserve the status quo.

Even in the workplace, the re-entry crisis is, therefore, marked by stressful interpersonal relations. These difficulties often lead to feelings of isolation. Reintegration difficulties also force returnees to reassess their feelings about their homeland. In some cases this isolation may lead to feelings of hostility towards the homeland; for others, life abroad has reaffirmed their attachment to the homeland and given them a greater appreciation of what it has to offer.

### Trini to the Bone?

Reverse culture shock is most pronounced in those who expect everything at home to be the same as it was when they left it. The standard of living, the political climate and even family relationships may have changed during their time abroad. Petrodollar investment created opportunities for returnees and fuelled expectations of a successful professional reinsertion into Trinidadian society, but it has also become a source of instability. Since 1982, the combined effect of an international recession, the fall in oil prices, a diminished demand for heavy oil, competition from major US refineries and a downturn in production rates brought about a 26 per cent decrease in oil revenues for 1983 (Instituto del Tercer Mundo 1990). The government responded to this crisis by implementing austerity policies such as the elimination of subsidies, a decrease in public investment and the containment of public salaries. These measures, however, contributed to social unrest among the general population.

Teachers, nurses and other health workers led rallies in the urban centres to decry these measures. At the same time, unemployment increased significantly, doubling from the early 1980s to the 1990s (Thomas 1988, 293). Large building projects, such as the Mount Hope Medical Complex and the Jean Pierre Sports Complex, physically transformed the landscape, but did not actually provide many of the basic services needed by the population nor offered opportunities for employment.[5] Around this time the crime rate rose dramatically. Trinidad and Tobago's Central Statistical Office reports that serious crimes reported to the police increased by almost 83 per cent from 1982 to 1993 (Central Statistical Office 1993, 56).[6] By the end of 2001, the country reported a record murder rate of 151, an increase of about 7 per cent from a previous high in 1994.[7] A report by a cabinet-appointed committee to examine criminality among Trinidadian youth (Cabinet at the Office of the Prime Minister 1994) attributed this spate of violent crimes to high unemployment levels and unequal income distribution.

Conditions of social unrest, uneven economic distribution and inadequate services have made readjustment difficult. Donna Solomon explains:

> Trinidad had changed in the period I was away [from 1967 to 1980]. The oil boom had come and had almost gone. The people had become materialistic and more "mimic men"[8] than ever, perhaps a reaction to the "colonial days of massa"[9] being over, or the advent of Americanized television. Whatever Trinidad meant to me, as far as people were concerned, has gone forever.

Donna's husband, Robert, finds it difficult to accept the negative aspects of change:

> Trinidad, during the time of my stay abroad, had changed in its habits, way of life, social amenities etc. While you are away you somehow accept change that is taking place where you live. It is, however, difficult to come to terms with change that has taken place in one's country in one's absence, especially if it is negative change.

This negative change has an adverse effect on the returnee because reality does not meet the expectations of return. Francis Duke notes, "What I liked about Trinidad is no longer there. The level of crime is terrible. People give credence to mediocrity. I am one of those silent rebels who don't compromise." Socio-economic change has therefore had an important impact on reintegration. On the one hand, it has facilitated the return of expatriates by providing avenues of re-entry; on the other hand, it has made adaptation difficult by adversely modifying other elements that lured migrants back.

Many returnees' reactions to their homeland are conditioned by how they are received once back. Often the reaction of others towards returnees is a reflection of the attitudes of the time. Sylvia Donawa gives us an idea of how others reacted to her in the boom years: "When I returned I was surprised at people's expectation of what my behaviour or attitude should have been, having studied and lived abroad for some time. They expected me, at that time, to be 'snotty' and they were disappointed when I was not." It was felt that returnees brought with them an attitude of superiority and intolerance for things local. Whether this is fully substantiated or merely a jealous reaction by those who remained is unclear. It is perhaps a combination of both. What is significant, however, is that many believe this to be pervasive among returnees.

Like Sylvia, Mathilda Slinger experiences a certain degree of criticism and isolation because of her adopted British mannerisms and values. This makes her extremely frustrated and critical of Trinidad and Tobago. Here is what she has to say about being back: "Where I live in Laventille, there is no water. There was a man who used to beat his wife if she wouldn't give him money for fags [cigarettes], and she used to run out into the street naked, screaming for help. White people don't do that."

She constantly consciously and subconsciously compares her situation on return to her life abroad, a comparison that ultimately leads to extreme discontent with the island homeland:

> T&T is not my home. [If I leave again] I will never come back here. I don't want to be buried here. I don't like how Trinis carry on. I wish that someone would just pass in a plane and bomb the whole place and just start over. . . . From Neil who stole all my money to that man I chop up with a cutlass who was selling coke in front of my house to children, everything a Trini do I get to hate Trinis [makes me hate Trinidadians] a little more. There is this English girl where I work. I talk to her more than I talk to Trinis. I tell her, "Girl, go back to England." Imagine she went around the Savannah and they charge her TT$5 for boil corn.[10] Trinis again. In England, it's the same price for everybody. You see why I cannot like my own country.

Mathilda was also cheated out of her chance for upward mobility. On her return she opened an import-export business, but all the money invested in it was squandered by one of her associates (Neil), and the business fell through. She keeps old business cards and a photo of the associate who betrayed her in her purse as her nemesis and a reminder of her difficulties in Trinidad and Tobago.

Homeland attachments – a sense of belonging, of being home, of being "Trini to the bone" – are often the deciding factors in the decision to return home. Yet, it is often these areas that present the greatest reintegration difficulties. The following section explores strategies, government as well as personal and community based, to address these difficulties.

## Resolution

> With respect to migration [Trinidad and Tobago], has, in the past, focused attention on emigration, particularly the "brain drain" effect. However, the new phenomenon of return migration, with its positive and negative consequences, and the processes involved in reintegration into mainstream society is now receiving government's attention. (Ramsaran 1999)

Throughout the Caribbean, there is a belief that returnees can be driving forces behind progress. Some West Indian governments, notably Jamaica, Guyana, Barbados, and Trinidad and Tobago, have implemented policies to utilize the vast stock of Caribbean human capital that is abroad on a temporary as well as on a permanent basis with the hope that such policies may facilitate the reintegration of expatriate professionals. Several types of government policies are likely to ease some returnee reintegration difficulties. Strategies outside of government control also facilitate reintegration. This section explores some of these options while making a distinction between the potential role of government policy and community mobilization, and drawing on examples from two island states where migration is significant – Jamaica and the Philippines.

## Government Policy

Government policies that are likely to ease return usually fall into two categories. A first set of approaches deal with procedures related to re-entry such as customs and immigration policies. Other schemes endeavour to address the difficulties of reintegration, such as the inability of returnees to use the skills they developed while abroad or inadequate health care for returning retirees. Often, the first step in developing a comprehensive reintegration scheme for returnees is to pass legislation that provides a framework for these different measures.

The Ministry of Foreign Affairs of Jamaica has established such legislation. In 1993, the Jamaican government established a Charter for Long-Term Returning Residents. Specifically, the Charter seeks to address the re-entry problems that returnees face by coordinating with the appropriate ministries to identify potential problem areas for the re-entry of residents abroad, reducing red tape and working on solutions to common bureaucratic obstacles that returnees may face. The implementation arm of the Charter is the Returnee Residents Facilitation Unit. While not all West Indian countries have implemented such policies, Barbados has implemented a similar policy based on the Jamaican model.[11]

A legal mandate and even financial resources to assist those contemplating return, however, do not guarantee the successful implementation of such policies. Policy implementation is particularly difficult when government agencies do not have the orientation or the proper structures that can lead and operate a coherent national reintegration programme. Recent studies have shown, for instance, that many Filipino migrants are unaware of the multiple reintegration services offered by various government agencies in the Philippines (Economic Resource Centre 2000).

One of the key premises of government policy, therefore, must be information provision. In the case of Jamaica, its Returnee Facilitation Unit coordinates the efforts of designated officers in Jamaican embassies along with high commissions and consulates in the United States, Canada and the United Kingdom, and provides an information pack on procedures and regulations for returning residents. The unit works with returning residents to ensure that they understand government concessions that may facilitate their relocation. These concessions cover the duty-free import of personal and household effects, motor vehicles, machinery and equipment. In various countries, such concessions are sometimes as part of a proactive re-entry assistance programme.

The Jamaican Unit collaborated on such a programme in 1993 with the Commission of the European Communities and the International Organization for Migration. The programme, called "Migration for Development", sought to facilitate the return and reintegration of forty professional Jamaican nationals. Over two and a half years, the programme targeted Jamaicans living in industrialized countries, offering financial incentives and "important vacant development positions" such as managers, engineers and policy analysts (IOM 1996). These programmes are, however, not without problems.

The programmes tend to be short term. In addition, evidence shows that financial incentives such as those offered in these programmes are not the only factor that intervene in the migrant's decision to return or not. These return programmes can be expensive and difficult to implement, and many have not been particularly successful in encouraging large-scale or sustained return. They also lead to tension with non-migrants, particularly if financial incentives are offered and are not available to the non-migrating population (Ouaked 2002).

In other cases, government can introduce policies that are ultimately beneficial to both the migrating and non-migrating population. One such policy is that of dual citizenship. In 1998, the government of Trinidad and Tobago introduced an amendment to the Citizenship of the Republic of Trinidad and Tobago Act that indicates that "a citizen of [Trinidad and Tobago] by birth or by descent, who acquires citizenship of another country shall not lose his citizenship by reason only of such acquisition" (1988, 153). This development gave legal sanction to dual citizenship, thus permitting migrants to secure citizenship from their host country and return to Trinidad and Tobago without fear of losing citizen privileges in either country. Non-migrants may also benefit by emigrating and returning. Overall, such policies allow for greater circulation.

In a recent round table on high-skilled migration and sending country issues, participants noted the need for new policies that support circulation of the highly skilled between developing and developed countries (Ouaked 2002). Participants suggested that programmes such as the US cultural exchange visa, known as the "J visa", could be applicable in other countries. Not only do they allow for short durations of stay, but they also require migrants to return home after completion of their programmes. Such programmes may increase the effectiveness of return policies by helping source countries develop and raise their scientific and economic standards.

In addition to measures that facilitate circulation, other policies have been adopted that target retirees and overseas workers. In the Philippines, for example, a government agency called the Philippines Retirement Authority is implementing a national scheme offering incentives to Filipinos who choose the Philippines for their retirement (Rodriguez and Horton 1995). Another government effort in the Philippines is the Overseas Workers Welfare Administration (OWWA). The OWWA supports an inter-government agency referral system called the Replacement and Monitoring Centre. The centre falls under the jurisdiction of the Department of Labour and Employment and offers returnees job placement services, skills training, livelihood programmes, job opportunity assessments and a database of skilled migrant workers for employers. The OWWA also offers limited social counselling for the families of overseas workers that are left behind (Uda 1999).

Programmes of this nature are not without difficulties. The director of the Philippine OWWA notes, for example, that whenever the agency changes its top officials, policies and programmes get disrupted. In addition, the need to produce immediate and tangible results may curtail social or psychological assistance programmes as these services are unable to produce such benefits in the short term (Philippines Center 1999).

One tangible result that is often pursued is the promotion of returnee spending or investment in the homeland, often through partnerships with the government and the private sector. In Guyana, for example, the Guyana Office for Investment was established in September 1994 to attract and facilitate increased investment in order the fuel the country's economic growth by providing efficient and effective investor services. Along with targeting foreign investors, it was particularly interested in targeting expatriate Guyanese. In the Philippines, the private sector supports a government returnee programme called the "Balikbayan" (returnee) programme. The programme offers returning Filipinos (including former Filipino citizens) tax-free shopping up to US$1,500, visa-free entry for a year, travel tax exemptions and special areas in the ports of entry to expedite the processing of documents. The private sector supports the programme by issuing a Balikbayan Plus card that gives discounts in stores, banks, hotels, transport fares and overseas phone calls. In addition, the government offers short-term seminars and financing for the establishment of short-term businesses.

Anecdotal stories point to the short-term nature of some programmes. They note that returnees were given loans after setting up a business plan, establishing credit and following a seminar, but that in some cases the businesses failed, and the migrants founds themselves in even greater debt (Inq7 Commentary 2002). Remittances also often go to consumer spending, payment of debts, long-term investments such as education, building and improvement of houses, and do not create widespread employment. Some analysts suggest that the private sector could help establish a bank to manage and re-channel the earnings of overseas workers. These banks would ensure that earnings are invested in projects that will create a greater demand for local goods and services as well as employment and livelihood opportunities. These projects, they note, should be geared to the needs of migrants and their families, particularly those returning and reintegrating into their communities.

While possible government policies include providing information, implementing re-entry assistance programmes, introducing new policies that facilitate reintegration, and promoting micro-enterprise through government–private sector cooperation, non-governmental efforts also support returnee reintegration. These non-governmental approaches include individual strategies, diaspora policies and homeland community mobilization.

## *Non-Governmental Approaches*

Many responses to deal with reintegration difficulties naturally depend on the resilience and tenacity of individual migrants. Returnees use the same skills to readapt to the homeland as they did in preparing to emigrate. One mechanism that allows returnees to better deal with reintegration difficulties is to prepare for the stresses of return. Some migrants prepare by keeping abreast of political, economic and social developments at home. This may include using Internet resources for updated information, maintaining contact with friends and family, and travelling home on a regular basis. These visits may also be a way of transmitting hand-to-hand remittances and maintaining homeland assets, such as a house, that will ultimately facilitate reinsertion into the homeland. In some cases, migrants contact local chambers of commerce or similar bodies in the host country for listings of companies that may be interested in candidates with a foreign education and/or experience.

Others prepare for interpersonal difficulties by forming bonds with others who have been through similar experiences. This association with other returnees may mean building a network for return. Once in the homeland, some returnees also maintain links with contacts in the receiving country who continue to provide information on the latest developments in their professional fields.

The shared experience of life abroad sometimes reminds returnees of the benefits of life in the homeland. There were also many respondents who found that their time abroad opened their eyes to the reality of life in Trinidad and Tobago. It helped to demystify life abroad and "things foreign". With this awareness sometimes came a greater appreciation for the homeland. Desiree Simpson explains her feelings: "Once I got back I was surprised at how *green* green could be and how people griped and complained and did not appreciate what they had. Many think that it's greener on the other side." The experience abroad can very clearly reaffirm an attachment to Trinidad and Tobago. After a bad experience as a nanny in Canada, Rookmin Singh proclaims that "people say that in Trinidad we have devils, I say that we have angels here". Lisa des Vignes on the other hand, even though more appreciative of Trinidad and Tobago, still finds it difficult to deal with the negative aspects: "I appreciate more the uniqueness of Trinidad and Tobago, the warmth and the caring of the people and the extended family unit. I am disappointed with the level of corruption and the poor level of delivery of almost all services." Such sentiments were characteristic of most returnees. The vast majority were happy to be back, but were more critical of the society and as such had problems readapting. Others just learned to live with these difficulties. Peter Maynard notes:

> Now that I am back I am more impatient when certain things take much longer than expected, since everything worked like clockwork in Canada. When you go away and experience a different lifestyle, you begin to realize and appreciate all of the positive aspects of home. You also learn negative things and you can adjust yourself to them and make the necessary changes.

Others prepare for reintegration by developing strategies to deal with cultural differences of which they are aware. For example, Steven Moore, a company executive, anticipated that a return could potentially be detrimental to his marriage, so he and his wife developed a strategy to deal with such an impact: "My wife and I have this unwritten rule that we always socialize together. . . . Here there is a lot of pressure to socialize. People always tell me, 'You're the boss, why not lime [hang out]? You shouldn't have to tell your wife where you going.' " It is significant that integration in England was difficult for them, but that they were able to work it out together. Once they had dealt with adaptation abroad as a couple, they were able to deal with reintegration together.

There are other ways of maintaining contact with the host country to facilitate return. These strategies rely on the diaspora to establish networks and offer new openings. The diaspora could form a strong lobby in the destination country, be the source of remittances and favour technology transfer. One common example of this is what some scholars refer to as transnational philanthropy. This refers to how migrants in the receiving countries bond and allot their earning for the development of their communities in the homeland (Inq7 Commentary 2001). These kinds of diaspora approaches are facilitated by transnational lifestyles and circulation. Often the existence of a large diaspora forms part of the impetus behind government policies, and very often can work to support these policies.

More often than not, though, mobilization efforts among returned communities in the homeland work towards making reintegration easier. In Jamaica, for example, there are at least ten local returnee associations.[12] These associations, run by returnees themselves, fulfil a multiplicity of roles including providing advice and assistance to those contemplating return or to those who have returned and are engaging in philanthropic work in the communities where they live.

These associations also support government efforts at providing information to prospective returnees. Many of them provide information, guidelines and procedures about issues relevant to return and reintegration. These usually include issues related to health, social welfare and pensions; customs, investments and legal affairs; housing, real estate and construction as well as education. As the brochure for one association notes,

> Those who have returned have experienced great difficulties with Government and other agencies. Some are exploited, treated like strangers, and feel isolated. Returning residents have contributed, are contributing and will continue to contribute to the development of Jamaica. Returning Residents must be afforded the courtesy, rights, duties and responsibilities as true citizens of Jamaica. It is against this background that the International Returning Residents Association was formed – with the primary aim of supporting returnees in the re-adaptation process. (Personal communication, Returning Residents Association, St Thomas Eastern)

Other local associations form support networks and perform philanthropic acts. One association president observed the following:

> To date we have mostly been engaged in socialization activities, e.g. trips around the island, community involvement, e.g. the local citizen association, fundraising activities for the local hospital, where we buy small, but necessary items for them. Other things like curtains and chairs. We work closely with other returning residents groups in the island. . . . To date we have thirty members and the group grows slowly, although there are many returned people in the area, most of them are reluctant to participate. . . . We do not in any way try to attract expatriates to Jamaica. What we do is to try and engage people returned to become part of the Association. (Leaflet, International Returning Residents Association, Jamaica)

There are other ways that civil society can play a role in facilitating reintegration. Through migrant savings and alternative investment programmes, non-governmental organizations in the Philippines have enabled migrants to establish small-business ventures. Similarly, local churches have launched micro-enterprise activities, and one organization even provides services of videoconferencing to establish contact between the family left behind and the migrants. Other groups provide welfare and protection for families left behind. These efforts reveal how important it is for social development workers, policymakers and implementers, as well as the migrants and their families themselves, to work together to ease reintegration (Gilig Payot 2002).

## Conclusion

The evidence in this chapter supports Pessar's (1988) findings that the principal problems encountered by the repatriate population are not economic. Even though those who go abroad to study are disappointed when they are unable to secure meaningful employment on their return, difficulties with interpersonal contact and value conflict weigh more heavily on their minds. Those who return after living and working abroad for some time usually anticipate downward occupational mobility. All returnees derive some prestige from having lived abroad, but this also provokes jealousy. Most returnees go through a period of isolation and readaptation, during which they redefine their relationship to Trinidad and Tobago and to those around them, in both their personal and professional spheres. This experience is found throughout the Caribbean where long-distance migration has become part of the lifestyle.

While most migrants return to re-establish ties with Trinidad, for many this means interpersonal relationships, a sense of being "Trini to the bone". This chapter has shown that it is here, however, that reintegration is the most difficult. Several types of government policy are likely to ease some returnee reintegration difficulties. Possibilities include providing information on procedures for re-entry, implementing re-entry assistance programmes, introducing new policies that facilitate return and promoting micro-enterprise and investment opportunities through government–private sector cooperation. Systems outside of government control also facilitate reintegration. These usually involve individual migrant strategies, efforts that engage the expatriate population in development concerns in the homeland (so-called diaspora policies) and community-based returnee efforts in the homeland.

# Notes

1.  One case containing all of these was found in the *Daily Express,* 30 May 1993, 50.
2.  Pseudonyms have been used for all respondents.
3.  Anthony notes that the Americans were so demanding that one of the contractors, W & D company (Wash and Driscoll), was known among the locals as the Work and Dead company (1983, 46). In fact, to motivate the local labourers to work hard, the Americans adopted a huge, constantly turning signboard on which were printed the words "Keep Moving" (55).
4.  A middle-class residential area in Diego Martin, in the suburbs of Port of Spain.
5.  The Mount Hope Medical Complex, also known as the Eric Williams Medical Sciences Complex, is one of the most modern health and medical training institutions in the region. It stands at the foot of Trinidad's Northern Range, on 142 acres of landscaped grounds east of the capital Port of Spain. It serves as a training centre for doctors, dentists and veterinary surgeons, and boasts a number of clinical facilities such as a 334-bed adult hospital, a 210-bed children's hospital, a woman's hospital, a dental clinic and an animal hospital (*FT Caribbean,* No. 21, 1990/91).
6.  Serious crimes are those that carry a penalty of five or more years in prison, for which prosecutions have been instituted in the high court.
7.  See the SpiceIslander TalkShop Editorial. http://www.spiceisle.com/talkshop/messages/115888.htm (accessed 12 December 2002).
8.  This is a reference to V.S. Naipaul's book *The Mimic Men* where he portrays Trinidadians imitating foreign values and mannerisms.
9.  Here Donna makes reference to the saying "Massa day done". This means slavery days are over (Ottley 1980, 100).
10. This is almost twice the regular price.
11. In personal communication, the head of the Returning Residents Facilitation Unit of the Ministry of Foreign Affairs and Foreign Trade in Jamaica indicated that after consultations with the Jamaica unit, the Ministry of Foreign Affairs in Barbados had put in place a programme and unit very similar to the Jamaican model.
12. Information from personal communication.

# References

Anthony, M. 1983. *Port-of-Spain in a World at War: 1939–1945.* Vol. 2 of *The Making of Port-of-Spain.* Port of Spain: Columbus Publishers and the Ministry of Sport, Culture and Youth Affairs.

Cabinet at the Office of the Prime Minister. 1994. *Report of the Cabinet Appointed Committee to Examine The Juvenile Delinquency and Youth Crime Situation in Trinidad and Tobago.* Central Bank Tower, Independence Square, Trinidad, January.

Central Statistical Office of the Republic of Trinidad and Tobago and the Central Bank of Trinidad and Tobago. 1993. *Annual Statistical Digest 1991.* No. 38. Port of Spain: Central Statistical Office.

Citizenship of the Republic of Trinidad and Tobago (Amendment) Act: Legal Supplement Part A. 1988. *Trinidad and Tobago Gazette* 27 (202): 5 August. Port of Spain: Government Printery.

Comma, J.L. 1980. Trinidadian Adjustment/Readjustment to Trinidad After Acquiring Post-Secondary Education in the United States of America. MEd thesis, George Washington University.

Conway, D. 1994. The Complexity of Caribbean Migration. *Caribbean Affairs* 7 (4): 96–119.

Daniel, E. 1983. Perspectives on the Total Utilization of Manpower and the Caribbean Expatriate: Barriers to Returning. In *Caribbean Immigration to the United States,* ed. R.S. Bryce-Laporte and D.M. Mortimer, 158–68. RIIES Occasional Papers, no. 1. Washington, DC: RIIES.

De Souza, R.M. 1998. The Spell of the Cascadura: West Indian Return Migration. In *Globalization and Neoliberalism The Caribbean Context,* ed. T. Klak, 227–53. Lanham, MD: Rowman and Littlefield.

Economic Resource Center for Overseas Filipinos. 2000. The Development Potential of Migration. http://www.philsol.nl/org/ercof/DevPotential-mar00.htm (Accessed 28 November 20002.)

Gilig Payot, J. Wanted: A Reintegration Program for Returning OFWs. *Cyber Dyaryo,* 4 February 2002. http://www.cyberdyaryo.com/opinion/op2002_0204_01.htm (Accessed 28 November 20002.)

Gmelch, G. 1985. Barbados Odyssey. *Natural History* 10: 38–44.

Inq7 Commentary. 2001. Is It Despair Or Hope Waiting for OFWs Returning Home? Posted 15 November. http://www.inq7.net/opi/2001/nov/16/text/opi_commentary1-1-p.htm (Accessed 28 November 2002.)

———. 2002. Turning Migration's "Weakest Links" Into Assets. Posted 6 April. http://www.inq7.net/opi/2002/apr/07/text/opi_commentary1-1-p.htm (Accessed 20 November 2002.)

Instituto del Tercer Mundo. 1990. Section on Trinidad and Tobago. *Third World Guide 91/92,* 537–39. Uruguay: Instituto del Tercer Mundo.

International Organization for Migration (IOM). 1996. *Second Annual Report: Return and Reintegration Programme of Qualified Jamaican Nationals for Development.* Washington, DC: IOM.

Mendes, J. 1986. *Cote ci, Cote la: Trinidad and Tobago Dictionary.* Arima, Trinidad: J. Mendes.

Ottley, C.R. 1980. *Creole Talk of Trinidad and Tobago.* Port of Spain: Crusoe Publications.

Ouaked, S. 2002. Transatlantic Roundtable on High-Skilled Migration and Sending Countries Issues. *International Migration* 40 (4): 153–66.

Pessar, P.R., ed. 1988. *When Borders Don't Divide: Labor Migration and Refugee Movements in the Americas.* New York: Center for Migration Studies.

Philippines Center for Investigative Journalism. 1999. Many OFWs Face Bleak Life after Migration. http://www.pcij.org/stories/1999/ofws2.html (Accessed 28 November 2002.)

Ramsaran, Manohar. Permanent Mission of Trinidad and Tobago to the United Nations, New York. 1999. Statement to the twenty-first session of the General Assembly on the Five-Year Review and Appraisal of the Implementation of the Programme of Action of the International Conference on Population and Development (ICPD+5). 1 July, New York.

Rodriguez, E., and S. Horton. 1995. International Return Migration and Remittances in the Philippines. Working Paper UT-ECIPA-Horton-95-01, Department of Economics and Institute for Policy Analysis, University of Toronto.

Thomas, C.Y. 1988. *The Poor and Powerless: Economic Policy and Change in the Caribbean.* London: Latin American Bureau.

Uda, E. 1999. For Many Overseas Filipino Workers, Home Is Where the Hurt Is. *Philippines Center for Investigative Journalism.* http://www/pcij.org/stories/1999/ofws.html (Accessed 28 November 2002.)

# Inter-Generational "Return Migration" to St Lucia

## A Comparative Analysis

| Francis K. Abenaty |

## Introduction

It seems almost inevitable that to some of the British-born Caribbean population, given their cultural heritage, combined with the growing number of
West Indians who are returning, or planning to return to their respective
homelands, the allure of the Caribbean islands would prove irresistible. This
chapter seeks to compare, in the light of their relocation, the experiences and
responses of a group of British-born or British-reared returnee respondents
to those of some St Lucian returnees who had migrated to Britain in the
1950s and 1960s.

The data for this chapter are based on oral history interviews related to a
wider study of St Lucians in Britain and in St Lucia, undertaken in 1996.[1]
The respondents comprised twenty-eight returnees (fifteen women and thirteen men), who had spent an average of twenty-seven years in Britain and
had returned to St Lucia between 1972 and 1995 and ten British-born or
British-reared Caribbeans who relocated to the island between 1976 and
1995. Among them were seven who had been born in England, while the
other three had migrated with, or joined, their parents between the ages of
five and eight. They had spent their formative years in Britain and are therefore subsumed under the British-born umbrella. Their average age on arrival
in St Lucia was twenty-five years.

## Migration and Return

For the people of the Caribbean generally, migrating in order to improve their lot and return has long been a cherished ambition (Conway 1988; Richardson 1980, 1985; Rubenstein 1979; Thomas-Hope 1978, 1992) and in that respect, the mass migration to Britain, which began in the mid-1950s and peaked in 1961 (Peach 1968, 1991) in response to the forthcoming Commonwealth Immigrants Act, was no exception. This Act effectively ended primary immigration from new Commonwealth countries.

While West Indians were returning to the Caribbean from Britain in noticeable numbers from the mid-1960s (Davison 1968), that stream has gathered momentum in more recent times. Indeed, the movement from Britain has represented the largest voluntary return of migrants from a single destination that the Caribbean has ever witnessed. Peach, extrapolating from demographic trends, estimates that the Caribbean-born population in Britain declined from 330,000 in 1966 to a 1991 figure of 264,591 (1996, 26), a discrepancy largely attributable to a significant re-migration of West Indians from the United Kingdom to their country of origin. Not surprisingly, Jamaicans and Barbadians, who constitute the bulk of the West Indian migrants in Britain, have also returned to the Caribbean in greater numbers. Consequently, the government of Jamaica was encouraged to establish the Returning Residents Facilitation Unit within the Ministry of Foreign Affairs in 1993 (*Weekly Gleaner,* 26 October 1993) to monitor the number of returning nationals. This example was followed by the Barbadians, who set up the Facilitation Unit for Returning Nationals in 1996 (Goulbourne 1999).

No such facility has been extended to returning St Lucians and indeed, it is only since February 2002 that a database was established by the Customs and Excise Department to monitor, specifically, returnees from Britain (interview with Joan Lawrence, Customs Officer, 27 November 2002). Therefore, the number of those who returned in the preceding years can only be estimated. It has been tentatively suggested that some 2,800 had done so between 1966 and 1988 (Peach 1991, 13), but it is reasonable to assume that this figure has now been far surpassed. Whatever their numerical size, the evidence suggests that for an increasing minority of former migrants, the dream of returning home has been realized, borne out by their highly visible presence and the contentions that have arisen from their interactions within St Lucian society.

A commonality between the West Indians who migrated to Britain in the 1950s and 1960s is that the overwhelming majority of the twenty-eight returnees regarded their migration as a temporary affair, with a period of five years being perceived as the favoured amount of time in which to accomplish their goals (Abenaty 2000). While the process had taken far longer than anticipated, the vast majority had prepared themselves as best they could for their return to St Lucia. They had visited the island, kept in touch with family and friends, and laid the material foundations for life in the old country.

## The British-Born Caribbeans

As the pace of Caribbean migrants returning to their country of origin has gathered momentum, an increasing number of their offspring have either accompanied their parents or relocated to the Caribbean on their own initiative. The actual numbers involved are difficult to pinpoint and in the case of St Lucia, as noted above, records of returning nationals have been hitherto non-existent. Crucially, however, for relocation purposes, the authorities in St Lucia, as in Jamaica and Barbados, do not differentiate between Caribbean-born nationals and their foreign-born spouses and offspring. All are classified as returning nationals and entitled to a range of concessions on their belongings, provided that certain criteria are fulfilled. For example, under the Saint Lucian constitution, a foreign-born spouse is defined as a returning national if he or she is the "spouse of a citizen by birth or descent, coming to St Lucia to settle after a minimum of ten years residence abroad" (St Hill 1978, 99–101). The minimum ten-year resident overseas qualification applies to all returning nationals but, additionally, citizens by birth or descent must have attained the age of eighteen in order to qualify. While this makes it convenient to refer to these British-born Caribbeans as "returnees" (see, for example, Nutter 1986; Plaza 1999), it is felt that this label empties the term of the dynamics inherent in a process which reconnects a former migrant to a place from which he or she originated and of which memories have been retained. In essence, therefore, they are migrants, albeit migrants with strong family connections in the Caribbean.

The British-born Caribbeans who have relocated to the Caribbean thus far would appear to consist predominantly of young women (Plaza 1999) who are, in the main, professionally qualified or who possess a range of trans-

ferable skills. It could be that the phenomenon is reflective of the higher educational attainment of female students within the British educational establishments as Goulbourne (1999) suggests. This is an important consideration,
but the ratio of British-born women to men in the relocation process appears
to be so overwhelming that other explanations beyond the bare matter of
qualifications may need to be proffered. Although arguably a related point,
Plaza (1999) identifies a lack of confidence on the part of British-born males
that has led to an aversion to risk-taking because of the opprobrium, which
might ensue from their peers, should they not succeed in their venture.

## The Employment Market

The twenty-eight returnees considered it an essential prerequisite that they
should be either employed or financially independent, or a combination of
the two, and all conformed to that aspiration to varying degrees. Given that
sixteen of them had returned before retirement, the employment sector
formed an important part in their settlement plans. Similarly, for the
relatively young British-born respondents, who were at the height of their
productive life cycles, finding worthwhile employment was a major preoccupation. See table 5.1 for clarification of this trend.

**Table 5.1** Occupational Profile of Employed Returnees

| Occupation in Britain | Occupation in St Lucia |
| --- | --- |
| Sewing machinist | Clothing shop proprietor* |
| Electrician | Clothes shop proprietor* |
| Sewing machinist | Sewing machinist* |
| Sewing machinist | Sewing machinist* |
| Factory operative | Farmer* |
| Factory operative | Farmer* |
| Lithograph printer | Bakery proprietor* |
| Electrician | Electrician* |
| Factory operative | Taxi driver * |
| Staff nurse | Staff nurse |
| Local authority officer | Executive accountant |
| Secretary | Secretary |
| Clerk | Tourism officer |

*Source:* Respondents' interviews, 1996.
* = self-employed

Most of the returnees who were below the age of retirement were self-employed, a phenomenon which would seem to be the preferred option of many returnees throughout the Caribbean and elsewhere (see, for example, Cerase 1974; Gmelch 1992; Byron 1994, 1999). It is worthy of note, however, that the occupations of the four non-self-employed returnees were not qualitatively different from those of the British-born sample. Also, respondents from both groups had managed to obtain employment with relative ease, as reflected in the data clarified by table 5.2 as well as the personal account of Leslie Johns who, although born in St Lucia, had left at the age of five and visited just once before she returned to settle in 1978: "I had loads of job offers. Once you said you were from away . . . you'd be working and somebody would call you and try to take you from your employer. You had no difficulty in getting work."

Their rapid absorption into the workforce underscored, to some extent, the shortage of skilled and trained personnel that prevailed in certain key sections of the labour market. Roy Rodriquez[2] observed: "One of the aspects that has been identified by the World Bank, which is in short supply, is middle management. And if somebody is coming with a skill or work experience at that level it is likely that they will find readily available jobs at their level."

**Table 5.2** Occupation of British-Born Respondents in St Lucia

| Year of Migration | Occupation |
| --- | --- |
| 1976 | Electrical engineer |
| 1976 | Civil engineer |
| 1978 | College lecturer |
| 1983 | Catholic priest and educationalist |
| 1988 | Advertising manager |
| 1989 | Secretary |
| 1990 | Accountant |
| 1991 | Accounts officer |
| 1994 | Accounts officer |
| 1995 | Marketing executive |

*Source:* Respondents' interviews, 1996.

It meant that returnees and British-born Caribbeans alike tended to be employed in relatively responsible positions and this was not always well received by many within the local workforce. This reaction was related both to the fact that they came from overseas and that they brought with them attitudes which were perceived to be different from those prevailing among the local working population. Indeed, the similarities in their testimonies in that regard were striking. Ruth Myers returned to St Lucia in 1989 having spent twenty-seven years in Britain. As far as she was concerned,

> The attitude of the employees is very much different from what I'm accustomed to. They are not committed to their jobs at all. The two institutions that I worked for in England were of such high standards that I came here with the approach that I had disciplined myself into. And when I find that people are slapdash in their work, I find that difficult to cope with.

Similarly, Pauline Redburn, secretary to a firm of lawyers despite having returned since 1979, had not been able to come to terms with what she saw to be the poor attitude to work, which prevailed in St Lucia: "My point of view where work is concerned is completely different. You'd be on time, because having lived in England as far as I'm concerned I have come to work and at the right time I leave and go home. St Lucians don't really work that way."

Stacy Richards, an advertising manager, assessed the reasons for the prominence of British-born employees in positions of authority thus:

> In my opinion, that is because of the work ethic that you have been exposed to and that you've adopted and your level of education and exposure is different. A lot of assistant managers, still at that level, they must wait to be told rather than to use their initiative and take a chance. I think people from England are not so much like that. We do go the extra step because we're used to it.

This attitude was seemingly endorsed by a number of employers who deemed arrivals from Britain to be far more flexible, possessing the ability to view developments through a wider lens than the local workforce. The perception that employers favoured returnees and British-born Caribbeans has, not surprisingly, given rise to resentment and petty jealousies on the part of local employees, leading to non-cooperation in some cases. This was particularly so if new ideas were being proposed and formulated, as Mary Nugent, a staff nurse and returnee in 1991, recalled, "If there's something which they've always done and you try to do it differently because you think it's a better way, they criticise and tell you that's not how we do it in St Lucia. It's like a one-man band because they're not really interested in implementing changes here."

## Expectations and Social Interactions

The returnees considered themselves to be returning "home" to either deploy the work skills they had acquired in the metropolis, retire or simply luxuriate in the Caribbean sunshine. They had achieved what they thought to have been the expectations of the society. During their stay in Britain, they had kept in touch with family and friends, visited St Lucia when they could and many on the island had benefited directly, through remittances, from this migration. More importantly, the majority had achieved a measure of economic or professional success, which was the *raison d'être* for migrating in the first place.

The challenge to their identity, therefore, has proved to be a profoundly vexatious experience for many of these returnees, since, far from being embraced by the community at large as they expected, their "St Lucian-ness" was being repeatedly scrutinized. Rita Floyd, who suffered some hostility, particularly in the workplace, explained, "I think it was initially that there was this girl from England. Because when you've lived and worked in England for a while and you come down, your very friends don't even see you as a St Lucian but as an outsider."

Similarly, Mary Nugent was aggrieved at the treatment meted out to her by the bureaucracy: "I went to get an ID card and the girl said to me that I don't look like a St Lucian and she had my birth certificate and everything in front of her. And I had to spend so many hours waiting to try and get this sorted out."

Their desire to be accepted as part of the society was being thwarted, partly because they were prepared to question certain practices, especially in relation to the provision of goods and services. Carl Simmonds, a returnee from Canada, although not a respondent, was of the opinion that "When one returns to St Lucia it's as though people, and the administration in particular, expect you to be humble. It's as though you don't know anything about anything and must therefore take whatever comes and keep quiet. Well, I'm afraid I'm not prepared to do that."

It was also because many of these returnees dressed differently, projected different body languages and had what local St Lucians call "an accent", which immediately marked them out. Significantly, a most enduring, but less tangible, aspect of their stay in Britain – considered by most of these returnees to be one of the main positive outcomes of the sojourn – relates to the wider view of the world with which they perceived themselves to have been imbued. This perception, juxtaposed with what many have interpreted as the narrow, insular attitudes of non-migrants, has been one of the principal areas of conflict between the returnees and other St Lucians. This broadening aspect was emphasized on numerous occasions, and Joyce Green expressed it well when she contended,

> The knowledge I gained there I would not have gained in St Lucia. It's been an education in itself. I've got a wider knowledge because when I was in St Lucia, I lived in a community, all sheltered and we have all these prejudices about class and I went to England and I thought it was something completely different, so my mind is widened now and this sort of thing irritates me.

In other words, these returnees were not the entities they were in the pre-migration period. They had been Anglicized to a very large extent in habit, thought and outlook, as Angus Proctor, a resident of the United Kingdom for twenty-two years before his eventual return in 1979, surmised, "There are certain things that you're exposed to when you're away and so it's difficult to fit in. All the disciplines, the things you learned, you either have to shelve them or be isolated."

The returnees had all experienced difficulties in coming to terms with St Lucian society to some degree, and this was acknowledged by Peter Bates:

> I still have problems but they're not great ones because I used to come back regularly and tried and adjust myself between that time. But up to now you always find problems because when you think of the short time I've been here compared to the time I've lived in England there's a lot to get used to. When you get used to certain things and you come here and it's not the same, naturally you're disappointed.

However, while most of the male returnees seemed to have found a *modus vivendi,* with just one wishing to re-migrate to England, the strong attachment to Britain among the women persisted over time. Indeed, eight (53 per cent) expressed grave reservations about different aspects of their return.

They struggled to embrace their new life, partly because they missed their children, as Tina Charles so vividly articulated:

> It was very hard uprooting everything I had in England because when I left here I had nothing and after a couple of years in England I sent for my children and living in England for twenty-six years where you're settled and have a family. It was very, very hard to uproot all that and leave your children behind, which was a tragic thing. And when I got over here, all I could think about is my children, my children, my children [*sic*].

Boredom too, after having led a relatively active life in Britain, would seem to have been a particular concern for some of the female returnees and a number of contributory factors were identified. First, they considered there to be a lack in the variety of public entertainment that they felt able to attend on their own. There was not, for example, a purpose-built, public cinema anywhere in Castries, the capital of St Lucia. Second, the means of getting to what little entertainment was available were not always accessible. While public transport was improving, it remained at a fairly basic level. Third, only three of these women were driving at the time of the interviews and this inability, or disinclination, imposed severe restrictions on their freedom of movement. Rita Floyd, approaching retirement and actively considering the prospect of dividing her time between England and St Lucia, considered this issue:

> Life here is very different from England. There's a lot more to do in England as far as the arts are concerned. We've got just one theatre here, the Cultural Centre. We do hear of concerts in other parts of the island but because of the mad driving one is scared to leave Castries to go to perhaps Vieux Fort, if ever there was one. In London, you can hop on a bus or get on a train in safety. There aren't many places that one could go to during the day and relax. One has to think very carefully I would say, before coming here and deciding to be a full-time housewife because it can be very boring.

These frustrations combined to create a level of dissatisfaction whereby slightly over 50 per cent of the female respondents were either so dissatisfied with life in St Lucia, even after an average of four years residence there, that most would gladly return to Britain were it not considered imprudent to do so.

Of the respondents, these female returnees did not, nevertheless, represent the majority but comprised 53 per cent of the women interviewed and 29 per cent of all the St Lucian returnees. While having some reservations, the majority of the returnees were pleased to have returned and had come to accept St Lucia as "home" for the foreseeable future. Peter Bates considered that life was qualitatively better for him in St Lucia than it would have been in England:

> Yes, I'm quite happy and as I say, it all depends on what you make of it. Because going back to England on the past three or four times, looking at it in the area where I last lived and some of my old friends there in my age bracket, I see they all stand by the street corner and telling me boy, things ain't so nice at all. It was just like back in the 1960s when we first came. So I'm quite happy.

Similarly, Pauline Redburn, who seemed to have had little difficulty in adjusting to St Lucian ways, concurred, "St Lucia is not a paradise. There are many problems here but I'm a lot more relaxed here. I'm happier here because this is my home."

## Differential Aspects of Settlement

While the circumstances which propelled each of the British-born respondents to St Lucia were different, one common factor was crucial in sustaining them. Of the ten, eight had been preceded by their parents, one had returned with her St Lucian husband and one had grandparents on the island. This family connection helped to mitigate the impact of some of the difficulties they were likely to encounter and made for smoother adjustment than might have otherwise been the case. Visits to the island were facilitated which, in turn, enabled these respondents to become accustomed to the ways of the society, establish contacts and decide whether to relocate on the basis of their own observations. Marion Paul's experience was not unusual among this group:

> I've been coming back every six months over the last three and a half years. In that way, I managed to build up my own group of friends and kept in touch with them. My parents came back twenty-two years ago, so I've been coming back to visit my parents regularly and for the last four visits, I've been looking at St Lucia very critically in terms of settling.

It meant also, that unlike their parents' generation, who, on their migration to Britain, had to seek rented accommodation as a matter of urgency and in some cases had great difficulty in so doing (Burney 1967; Jones 1961; Rex and Moore 1967), most of these respondents were able to live in relative comfort in St Lucia, in some cases rent-free, until they were in a position to rent or buy their own homes. Equally important was the sense of security and moral support that stemmed from these relationships.

Nevertheless, it seemed reasonable to assume that the identity of the British-born respondents would be scrutinized far more closely than that of St Lucians, who were returning with some knowledge of the culture and the society, and that the adjustment problems of the British-born returnees would be correspondingly more acute. Interestingly, they did not express the sense of displacement which coloured the lives of some of the female returnees. There were frustrations and disappointments, to be sure, since they shared certain values with the returnees that were reflective of their common experiences within the British social system. For example, concern was expressed about what they thought to be the favouritism and unfair manner in which goods and services were acquired within the economic and social system, and comparisons with the way in which such transactions were conducted in the British context were drawn. May Walters, whose parents had returned a few years earlier, was critical:

> If you want something done in England, you go to A, B, C and you pay your money to get it done; but here, it's like C, B, A. And it's like if you know this particular person, you can get this done and it's a bit of a hustle sort of thing. That part, I think, is really unfair, because if somebody, for example, who lives out in the countryside and they don't know some body in a particular position, it would be really hard on them to try to get something or do something. Whereas in England, you pay your money and it doesn't matter who you are.

Also, a recurring theme in their reflections related to what they perceived to be the incivility which permeated some sections of St Lucian society. This sentiment was expressed by Father Ray Jacobs, who had lived in Britain since the age of eight, was ordained as a Roman Catholic priest and moved to St Lucia in 1983, at the age of thirty-two. Like many of the other respondents, he was disturbed by what he considered the lack of respect and sensitivity which inflected social interactions and particularly the manner in which some in positions of authority responded to their subordinates:

People treat others very rudely. "Who do you think you are?" kind of thing. I've heard nurses speak to patients like that in hospital. You see it with teachers and students; the student is down there and shouldn't answer back. In England, we would never dream of speaking to a student like that or to a patient.

While there was some correspondence between the responses of returnees and the British-born contingent, the latter had not brought with them memories and perceptions of St Lucia as it existed twenty or thirty years ago; consequently, they were unable to make then-and-now comparisons. So, unlike former St Lucian migrants, who had returned with expectations based upon their pre-migration experiences, these respondents were more likely to accept the society at face value. It could be, too, that they were less confident than the returnees both in articulating their concerns and in challenging bureaucratic procedures directly. This more measured response seemed to have helped to lessen the intensity of the challenges to their identity, which might have been the case otherwise.

There were occasional references to their "Englishness", expressed in such terms as "the English woman" or "the English gal" (May Walters, interview, 2 May 1996), but few, serious challenges were recounted by these respondents. Indeed, in certain situations, they considered this "Englishness" to be a boon. Teresa McDonald presented her opinion cryptically: "A lot of people who have companies are foreigners and work-wise sometimes it's an advantage. When you answer the telephone the comment is always you're not St Lucian are you? They always ask me this question. I haven't seen any disadvantages."

In various other ways they demonstrated that they had adapted to the rigours of the society. For example, in marked contrast to the female St Lucian returnees, eight of the British-born women owned and drove a car. And while most of them missed the variety of British life in terms of shopping, the cinema and the theatre, the boredom experienced by some women returnees was not evident in the testimonies of this group. Most felt that they had relatively active lives. Rachel Barratt, for example, had much to occupy her time: "Apart from work, which is very demanding, I'm also on the executive of professional engineers, I exercise a lot, I go horseback riding all day on Saturdays, I socialize in the evening with my friends and there's always a beach party or something like that." Leslie Jones, the oldest of the respondents at forty-seven, was similarly fully occupied: "When you finish work you can go out, you can go to the beach. I've joined the Lions Club and I'm a Lion, so I do a lot of community work and we meet socially. So I have a very full life."

## Prospects for Returning to Britain

The links which the British-born respondents maintained with (and their attitudes towards) Britain were variable. Some considered Britain to be "home", although not in the same way that their parents, while in Britain, had regarded St Lucia as "home". This was because the impetus to return was largely absent from their future plans. Nevertheless, they acknowledged the influences that both traditions had brought to bear upon them and seemed to have little difficulty in reconciling the two. This realization was reflected in the words of Marian Paul:

> I think I've always seen myself as a West Indian child growing up in England and culturally I've always looked towards the West Indies. But in actual fact there are bits from both cultures that I've adopted. I'd like to think that I've chosen the best from both worlds and adapted the two.

And May Walters, although married to a St Lucian, was a regular visitor to Britain: "I go back every year for a holiday and to see friends, go and eat popcorn and hot dogs, to see what's happening and work-wise, to see whether there're any ideas I could pick up to bring back."

For some, however, visiting England only served to strengthen their decision not to return on a permanent basis. Leslie Johns had visited on a number of occasions but emphasized the following: "I go to England on holiday and I just want to be there on holiday and I want to come back. The London I knew has no pull. It's nice to go up to see mummy and my brother and after about four weeks I've had it."

As migrants, their parents' generation had considered returning to St Lucia as the culmination of a dream. However, whatever difficulties they may have encountered during their residence in St Lucia, none of these British-born migrants thought them grave enough to make returning to England a serious proposition. Indeed, they compared life in England unfavourably to that in St Lucia. Stacy Richards expressed the view that, in employment terms, the success which she had achieved in St Lucia may not have been forthcoming had she remained in England: "My son will return to finish off his education; he's expressed a desire to do that. For myself, no, because the way my career is now . . . I've had pretty good opportunities here, that I think I would not have got back in England."

Not only did they consider that they had progressed professionally, but the affordability of goods and services reflected in a better standard of living for themselves and their children. This factor also featured as an important justification for not returning to Britain. This meant that in terms of housing, for example, they were able to purchase much more spacious homes than would have been the case in England. They also perceived that the combination of the tropical atmosphere and the sense of space created a less pressured and constrained environment. This afforded their children the opportunity to pursue a wide range of outdoor activities in relative safety. These respondents concluded that their lives, and those of their children in St Lucia, were different but more fulfilling than would have been the case in England. Penny Gray, who in career terms had been a success by any yardstick, was ebullient about life in St Lucia.

> In the six years I've been here . . . I've got to the top of my ranking for my profession. The other aspects are my children. My eldest daughter is now nine, she enjoys going to school, she goes to the beach a lot, she has tennis lessons, she has ballet lessons. She has exposure to a lot more things here I feel I can afford than if I was in England. So I feel my quality of life is much better than in England. Even though when I first came to St Lucia I had to take a tremendous pay cut, I was still able to drive a new car, which I couldn't do in London.

Teresa McDonald, too, evaluated her stay in positive terms.

> Nice for the children, almost free of crime at one point. It's a safer place to live in, it's a much cleaner place to live, the schooling is very good. My children have the advantage of both because they can go to England if they want to study. The only thing I miss, I guess, are the shops. I miss being able to go to the High Street and just pick up whatever I need and the parks for the children.

Father Ray Jacobs, for different reasons, was pleased with his decision to settle in St Lucia.

> For me it's certainly been a positive experience. I do not think I'd readily go back to England; I certainly like the climate here. Despite all the difficulties

with the clergy here, I would still prefer to work in the Caribbean as a priest, although in England, as a priest, I would have far less difficulty. In a certain sense I'm a counterbalance for the clergy here and in education I still think I have a lot to offer.

The returnees and the British-born respondents were at different stages of their respective life cycles and would have travelled, to some extent, with different priorities and preoccupations. Most of the latter were in the company of their parents and children and this was juxtaposed to the returnees, many of whom had left some, if not all, of their own children behind in Britain. For them, Britain was a place where families had been reared, friends made and countless experiences gained. It is therefore not surprising that these returning St Lucians, in common with returnees from other parts of the region, would wish to maintain these transatlantic attachments (see, for example, Western 1992; Byron 1994; Goulbourne 1999; Chamberlain 1997, 1999) even though returning to Britain was not a practical proposition for the overwhelming majority.

Arguably, pursuing a career was a more pressing matter for the British-born respondents, who perceived St Lucia to be a more favourable environment in which to foster their professional development, as well as to bring up their children. Consequently, while they too maintained links with Britain, it did not exert the economic or potential developmental "pull" that had enticed many of those very returnees away from St Lucia in the first instance.

## Conclusion

The majority of the returnees had prepared themselves in material terms for their return, but even so, resettlement proved to be a far more complex process than had been anticipated. This stemmed largely from values and expectations which they harboured on return, but also those inherent within St Lucian society. The attachment to Britain proved stronger among female returnee respondents and correspondingly, the transition had been more painful for them. The majority were, however, content with their lives in St Lucia.

The return of their parents to St Lucia was instrumental in motivating most of the British-born respondents to relocate themselves. This provided them with a base from which to explore the opportunities available, establish contacts and generally familiarize themselves with the functioning of the society. Like some of the returnees, they found that the skills and profession-alism which they were thought to possess were in demand. They therefore readily obtained worthwhile employment. While they were ill at ease with some of the practices of the society and missed aspects of life in Britain, they seemed to have adjusted well to St Lucian ways and had no plans to return to Britain on a permanent basis, although they continued to maintain links with that country.

## Notes

1.  The interviewees were as follows: Rachel Barrett, 12 May 1996; Peter Bates, 22 April 1996; Rita Floyd, 4 April 1996; Joyce Green, 15 April 1996; Penny Gray, 19 May 1996; Father Ray Jacobs, 11 April 1996; Leslie Johns, 18 April 1996; Teresa McDonald, 29 April 1996; Ruth Myers, 2 April 1996; Mary Nugent, 19 April 1996; Marian Paul, 5 May 1996; Angus Proctor, 21 April 1996; Pauline Redburn, 28 April 1996; Stacy Richards, 2 May 1996; Roy Rodriquez, 13 March 1996; Carl Simmonds, 12 May 1996; May Walters, 2 May 1996; Joan Lawerence, 27 November 2002.
2.  Roy Rodriquez is from Dominica but lived and worked in St Lucia over an extended period. He is currently chief economist at the Commonwealth Secretariat in London.

## References

Abenaty, F.K. 2000. St Lucians and Migration: Migrant Returnees, Their Families and St Lucian Society. PhD diss., South Bank University.

Burney, E. 1967. *Housing on Trial: A Study of Immigrants and Local Government.* London: Oxford University Press for the Institute of Race Relations.

Byron, M. 1994. *Post-War Caribbean Migration to Britain: The Unfinished Cycle.* Aldershot, UK: Avebury.

————. 1999. The Caribbean-Born Population in 1990s Britain: Who Will Return? *Journal of Ethnic and Migration Studies* 25 (2): 285–301.

Cerase, F.P. 1974. Expectations and Reality: A Case Study of Return Migration from the United States to Southern Italy. *International Migration Review* 8 (2): 245–63.

Chamberlain, M. 1997. *Narratives of Exile and Return.* London: Macmillan.

———. 1999. The Family as Model and Metaphor in Caribbean Migration to Britain. *Journal of Ethnic and Migration Studies* 25 (2): 251–66.

Conway, D. 1988. Conceptualising Contemporary Patterns of Caribbean International Mobility. *Caribbean Geography* 2 (3): 145–63.

Davison, R.B. 1968. No Place Back Home: A Study of Jamaicans returning to Kingston, Jamaica. *Race* 9 (4): 501–10.

Gmelch, G. 1992. *Double Passage: The Lives of Caribbean Migrants Abroad and Back Home.* Ann Arbor: University of Michigan Press.

Goulbourne, H. 1999. Exodus? Some Social and Policy Implications of Return Migration from the UK to the Commonwealth Caribbean in the 1990s. *Policy Studies* 20 (3): 157–72.

Jones, P.N. 1961. *The Segregation of Immigrant Communities in the City of Birmingham, 1961.* Occasional Papers in Geography, no. 7, Hull, UK: University of Hull Publications.

Nutter, R. 1986. Implications of Return Migration from the United Kingdom for Urban Employment in Kingston, Jamaica. In *Return Migration and Regional Economic Problems,* ed. R. King, 80–102. London: Croom Helm.

Peach, C. 1968. *West Indian Migration to Britain: A Social Geography.* London: Oxford University Press.

———. 1991. *The Caribbean in Europe: Contrasting Patterns of Migration and Settlement in Britain, France and the Netherlands.* Research Paper in Ethnic Relations, no. 15. Coventry: Centre for Research in Ethnic Relations, Warwick University.

———. 1996. Black Caribbeans: Class, Gender and Geography. In *The Ethnic Minority Populations of Great Britain: Ethnicity in the 1991 Census,* vol. 2, ed. C. Peach, 32–48. London: Office for National Statistics, HMSO.

Plaza, Dwaine. 1999. Desires and Actions for "Return" Migration among Second Generation Caribbeans in Britain. Paper presented at the Society for Caribbean Conference, South Bank University, London, 5–7 July.

Rex, J. and Moore, R. 1967. *Race, Community and Conflict.* London: Oxford University Press.

Richardson, B.C. 1980. Freedom and Migration in the Leeward Caribbean, 1838–48. *Journal of Historical Geography* 6 (4): 391–408.

———. 1985. *Panama Money in Barbados 1900–1920.* Knoxville: University of Tennessee Press.

Rodriquez, R. 1995. Returning to St Lucia. Paper presented at the Eastern Caribbean Commission, London, 2 December.

Rubenstein, H. 1979. The Return Ideology in West Indian Migration. *Papers in Anthropology* 20 (1): 21–38.

———. 1982. Return Migration to the Caribbean. In *Return Migration and Remittances:*

*Developing a Caribbean Perspective,* ed. W.F. Stinner, K. de Albuquerque and R.S.
    Bryce-Laporte, 280–306. Washington, DC: Smithsonian Institution.
St Hill, L. 1978. *A Constitution for St Lucia.* Castries: CM Pamphlet St Lucia.
Thomas-Hope, E. 1978. The Establishment of A Migration Tradition: British West
    Indian Movements to the Hispanic Caribbean in the Century after Emancipation. In
    *Caribbean Social Relations,* ed. C.G. Clarke, 15–29. Liverpool: Centre for Latin
    American Studies, University of Liverpool.
———. 1992. *Explanation in Caribbean Migration, Perception and Image: Jamaica,
    Barbados, St Vincent.* London: Macmillan.
Western, J. 1992. *A Passage to England: Barbadian Londoners Speak of Home.*
    Minneapolis: University of Minnesota Press.

# Building Home

## Being and Becoming a Returned Resident

| Heather A. Horst |

> We are not continuous returning residents. Yes, when we are thinking about
> returning to Jamaica and when we do return, yes we are returning residents
> then. But after we have settled down here in society and we have made it our
> home – we bought our homes here, we've brought all our worldly possessions,
> we are Jamaican!
> – Female caller, *Exploring Connections,* 1 November 2000

*Exploring Connections,*[1] a weekly radio programme hosted by the president of
the International Returning Residents Association, John Small, highlighted
issues of interest to Jamaicans who lived abroad and returned to their island
home to permanently resettle. The programme's guests ranged from
returnees to tax accountants to politicians to local academics who could talk
about the experience of migration and return. During the second half-hour
of the programme, the public routinely phoned the radio station to ask questions of the host or his guests, and callers often commented upon a recent
event or the general treatment of returnees across the island. Such was the
case when a woman who identified herself as a returnee phoned the programme complaining about nomenclature: "Should we refer to return
migrants as returning or returned residents and when are returnees considered Jamaican?" As the caller and other returnees noted, this was not simply
an issue of semantics. Rather, it had everything to do with a feeling of acceptance and belonging in Jamaica. Ultimately what to call this group of individuals was a commentary on their ability to adjust or adapt to life in their

homeland, despite changes in the social, cultural and political landscape over the past thirty to forty years. More importantly perhaps was the woman's insistence that the symbol of this process and one's commitment to becoming a "returned resident" was intricately tied to the purchase, construction and furnishing of a home.

This chapter, which is based upon twelve months of ethnographic research with Jamaicans who moved from the United Kingdom to Mandeville, Jamaica, in the 1990s, examines the relationship between building a home and becoming a returned migrant in Jamaica. In particular, it questions how the movement from "returning" to "returned" resident, a signal of the establishment of belonging in returnees' new setting in Jamaica, is mediated through the house. I begin with an overview of the conditions of Jamaican homes with attention to the historical significance of homeownership in Jamaica and the United Kingdom. I then introduce one case study of a returnee with particular attention to the interaction between the biography of the individual's return and the biography of the house. The case study demonstrates how returnees' construction and organization of the home, and in turn the household, expresses a tension between completion and incompletion, a tension fundamentally linked to being and becoming a returned resident.

## The Jamaican House: A Brief Description

Homes in Jamaica range from small one to two-room dwellings built of corrugated tin, wood and/or cinderblock to large ten-room mansions constructed of steel and concrete with modern appliances and amenities. Over half of the homes in Jamaica are constructed of concrete block and steel while just over one-quarter of homes still use wood as their primary material (Statistical Institute of Jamaica 1997). The remainder use concrete nog,[2] a material associated with Spanish walling (Hudson 1997). Jamaica's use of concrete and steel continues to increase due to the perception that these materials are the best defence against hurricane damage as well as their association with status (Statistical Institute of Jamaica 1997).

Sixty per cent of Jamaicans are homeowners and 72 per cent of homeowners live in rural areas (Statistical Institute of Jamaica 1997).[3] While 14 per cent of individuals live rent free, almost one-quarter of Jamaicans rent, and the highest proportion of renters live in the Kingston Metropolitan Area. In addition, a number of Jamaicans live as squatters on "captured" land or unused land owned by the government or other individuals and corporations. Captured land ranges from pieces of habitable property to toxic waste dumps where individuals and families construct dwellings out of materials they can obtain, such as corrugated tin. While the Jamaican government has, in practice, negotiated with more established squatter settlements for better access to water or electricity, often on the condition that the individuals and families purchase the captured land, in general few squatters have access to utilities or water closets.[4] Although the exact number of individuals living on captured land varies significantly due to survey methods, the *Jamaica Survey of Living Conditions* reports only 3 per cent of Jamaicans are squatters (Statistical Institute of Jamaica 1997). However, Eyre's (1997) analysis reveals that approximately 66 per cent of Montego Bay's population live in self-help housing, defined as dwellings constructed by the poor outside of legal or state-sponsored frameworks in response to an inadequate supply of shelter. Eyre also contends that almost "half of Spanish Town's population, at least 49,000 out of 99,000, inhabit the 36 present or former shantytowns within the urban perimeter and occupy homes which were first built by self-help on either capture or rent land" (1997, 77). He also suggests that slightly less than half of Kingston's population lives in self-help housing.

Over three-quarters of Jamaicans live in detached dwellings, whereas another 14 per cent live in "part of a house", meaning that they occupy or rent a room or larger division of a single home (Statistical Institute of Jamaica 1997). A small number of Jamaicans reside in semi-detached dwellings, apartments, townhouses or other commercial buildings, primarily in the Kingston Metropolitan Area. While the homeownership rates are generally high, one should be cautious of inferring that homeownership alone provides an accurate assessment of quality of life. For example, although an overwhelming number of the poorest Jamaicans (91 per cent) live in detached houses (over three-quarters of which are owned), 82 per cent of Jamaica's poor[5] use a pit latrine. While the prevalence of electricity continues to increase, 41 per cent of Jamaica's poor continue to use kerosene as their primary source of light. In terms of water, one-third of Jamaica's poor access water through public standpipes, about the same number which use untreated water from rivers, ponds and streams. The conditions for the poorest Jamaicans contrast with the general figures whereby two-thirds of the general population has indoor taps and only 15 per cent rely upon untreated water as their primary source of water.

The situation becomes even more marked when one examines the conditions of Jamaica's elderly, who comprise 9 per cent of the general population (Statistical Institute of Jamaica 1997). Over half of Jamaica's elderly still use pit latrines and cook outside using stoves or coal pots. Access to refrigeration among Jamaica's elderly also remains relatively low as does access to piped water, which is less than 40 per cent among the elderly population (Eldemire 1997, 82–83). In addition, only one-third of the elderly receive a government pension, while the remaining two-thirds rely upon their family for money or food stamps. Less than 4 per cent of the elderly possess health insurance (Eldermire 1997). As will become evident in the following section, the material conditions of Jamaica's elderly (for whom retirement remains unattainable and is often experienced only as a consequence of ageing or debilitating illness) contrasts rather dramatically with the material worlds of Jamaica's returnees.

## Concrete Castles:
## Returnee Homes in Mandeville

On virtually every route in and out of Mandeville, taxi drivers and locals readily identify the number of houses built by returnees, especially returnees from England (Horst 2005). In contrast to retirement homes in Europe and North America[6] where the space available for domestic life and the attendant processes of divestment and appropriation is often reduced in the name of necessity or desire to ease one's domestic responsibilities, returnee homes are large concrete structures, usually one or two stories, with grilled verandas and visible burglar bars attached inside or outside of the windows (Marcoux 2001; Percival 2002). A fence encloses each house and separates one yard from another. The front area of the yard consists of green grass and a flower garden alongside a driveway painted in non-slip paint leading up to the house, and a red or grey concrete border surrounds the house. Around the sides and back of the structure sits a kitchen garden filled with yams, bananas, oranges, scallions and other local produce. Each house is typically located on a quarter-acre plot.

Unlike in some of the smaller towns and communities in Jamaica, returnee homes in Mandeville are neither the largest nor most elaborate in the town.[7] A green, manicured lawn sets the front of returnee yards apart from other housing which features decorative flowers, hedges and trees which are pruned and shaped with a machete when they appear too big, long or unruly (Austin 1984; Hudson 1997). In addition to their lawns, returnee homes often include doorbells, electric gate openers and security systems[8] as well as modern kitchens with refrigerators, stoves, ovens, microwaves, freezers and other amenities; flush toilets, piped and treated water (hot and cold); and electricity. Washing machines, spa-like bathing tubs, showers, televisions and stereos are common throughout returnee homes as are auxiliary water tanks to supplement the unreliable water service in town. Most homes contain an average of eight rooms, including three bedrooms, two bathrooms, a kitchen, living room and dining room, with many homes possessing additional spaces for laundry and sewing facilities, a bar, multiple verandas, garage or car port, storage and walk-in closets.

Quite aware that their material wealth and possessions mark them, returnees often admit that their sense of self is wrapped up in the house. In fact, the importance of building the dream house, as one returnee couple noted, is the root of some returnees' struggle with health care and the expense of living in Jamaica. As one couple explained: "We've heard a lot of terrible stories about people who have trouble when they return . . . some people build [their houses] so big that they cannot manage them."[9]

As this discussion suggests, the house is more than shelter or a functional place to live. With money and materials from "foreign", the dream house single-handedly represents and validates years of hard work. Many returnees began saving money to purchase and build a home after their arrival in the United Kingdom. Their household items were, in some instances, stored in a separate room abroad, awaiting the moment they would be shipped in a container to Jamaica. Other returnees purchased their household goods over a period of years before moving back to Jamaica, slowly collecting possessions to add to the homes. However, because all of the returnee homes I studied in Mandeville were built to near completion within five years of return, they diverge from a common West Indian pattern of building gradually, beginning with two to three basic rooms, adding rooms as money and resources become available (see Williams 1991).

## Land, Property and Respectability in Jamaica

> A house is of prime importance to Jamaicans. . . . A house displays to the community a family's character. Jamaicans say they are houseproud and their homes and gardens reflect this. This is especially true of the Jamaican upper middle class, whose homes are well cared for, solid concrete structures, built with wide verandas, louvered windows for cross-ventilation, and surrounded by lush greenery. (Douglass 1992, 70)

The ethos of owning land and constructing a big, dream house has an historical foundation in Jamaica's colonial plantation culture. In the plantation economy, African-Caribbean slaves received plots of land to tend. While these small plots removed a degree of responsibility for feeding by the plantation owners, Caribbean slaves employed these small plots located in mountainous and "wasted" land to cultivate food for personal consumption or sale in the market on Sundays (Henke 1996; Higman 1984; Mintz 1974, 1985). In the movement from plantation to peasant economy, land – that is owning land and property – became a way in which Caribbean peoples acquired freedom and "hoped to escape from the stigma of slavery and from the drudgery of plantation wage labour on the land of others" (Mintz 1985, 139). Moreover, property was often a prerequisite to vote and/or hold office in the colonial and post-colonial Caribbean (Lazarus-Black 1994; Maurer 1997a, 1997b). As a result, land and property became the way through which Afro-Jamaicans could achieve personhood.

While the value placed upon land ownership resulted in the emergence of a rural proletariat, Mintz suggests that very few of the peasantry were ever able to subsist entirely off the fruits of their land or property. Thus, many former slaves were forced into continued interaction with the plantation system. Often the plots were too small or infertile to effectively provide income for the family. Nevertheless, owning a parcel of land symbolically signalled membership and provided status within Jamaican society. Moreover, land ownership enabled the creation of a more permanent or transcendent sense of being, as exemplified through the institution of family land, which Besson (1984) and others have argued is widespread throughout the anglophone Caribbean (Olwig 1995, 1997). Arguing against interpretations of family land which conclude that there must be a "limiting mechanism" (such as migration and non-residence) to restrict the number of claimants (Clarke 1966;

Davenport 1961; Solien 1959), Besson contends that Caribbean peoples possess a paradoxical view of land (Besson 1995, 2000, 2002). Specifically, Besson and others have demonstrated that family land is perceived as a scarce resource, with voluntary non-use and lack of development being a common practice in the region. In addition, access to and control over the land represents one of the more cogent examples of Wilson's exposition of "crab antics" and family law disputes (Lazarus-Black 1994; Maurer 1997a, 1997b; Wilson 1973). However, land also comes to be understood as unlimited, such that Jamaicans consider the ownership of even a small plot of land to represent an insurance policy in difficult times, a place where they have the right to pick the fruits of the land or build a little house (Chevannes 2001). Moreover, in constituting the land as "family land", the plot becomes available to future generations.

In addition to land- and homeownership, the ability to control space plays a central role in enacting and asserting a lifestyle of respectability (Abrahams 1983). In Jamaica, respectability continues to be tied to proper manners, education, church membership as well as the institution of marriage.[10] These values, coupled with an English-influenced respectability, emerged in the transition from the plantation system to emancipation as the church sought to create a group of individuals and families who could carry out law and order (and a moral system more generally), creating an emergent creole class. The new creole class attended church; lived quiet, non-public lives; sent their children to private schools; trained children in piano and other arts; and restricted their access to the potential tainting of lower-status Jamaican children. For instance, in an analysis of tenement yards in West Kingston, Brodber (1975) discusses the stigma associated with urban residential units. In government tenement yards, the house in the yard is quite small and may be used almost exclusively for sleeping. All other activities take place within the purview of people outside the yard.

In contrast, a respectable home conceals these activities and places them under the control of the wife. Kitchen and bathroom facilities are also located at the back of the house, often outdoors, to ensure that no matter what the reality of the family's economic situation, the outward or front facing status is upheld (see Austin 1984; Foner 1971; Sobo 1993).[11] Homes, therefore, should include communal indoor space, such as a living room, a proper table at which to dine as well as distinctive spaces for sleeping, bathing and eating. In addition, women overseeing respectable homes hire helpers to mop floors, hand-wash laundry and do other activities associated with cleanliness (see Austin 1984; Douglass 1992; Sobo 1993).[12] The house becomes an important element of respectability, granting legitimacy to a husband and wife's relationship. As Edith Clarke notes, "It is not considered correct for a man to propose marriage unless he owns a house and, preferably, a bit of land" (1996, 51). One could say that marriage waits for the house, often occurring after a couple participates in visiting relationships for many years. This house-based practice of marriage persists despite the continued efforts of the church, over multiple generations, to encourage formal marriage prior to childbirth and the creation of nuclear families (see Olwig 1993). Moreover, the house provides a space to enact a respectable lifestyle. Thus, the respectable home must be structured to ensure the morality and privacy of the family.

## Migration and Property

Thomas-Hope (1995) argues that, in the post-plantation era, migration[13] became a way through which the value of home and ownership were attained. Described as a symbol of freedom from both slavery and the social (class) system in Jamaica, migration provides access to money as well as formal and informal education, the latter gained by experiencing the world through travel. This is particularly the case for men who, as Chamberlain suggests in the case of Bajans, narrate their migration as a heroic adventure during which they "succeeded against the odds" (1997, 98). There is also evidence that the very idea of family land as a cultural institution continues to adapt to sustained migration patterns in the Caribbean. Explicating her notion of the home/family land as a cultural site, or "cultural institutions which have developed in the interrelationship between global and local ties" (1997, 17), Olwig finds that the land and homes built on the land in Nevis serve as an "emotional, cultural and social" site of identification (28). Rather than a location for daily living, the family land and family house keep the family members connected to their island home. Although they may only spend a week or two at the house or site each year, sending money or goods for the house materially and emotionally links them to the place they call home. Olwig concludes that this practice reflects the same interest in family and continuity but stresses the house rather than land due to the increased value of land on Nevis associated with tourism. As with family land, it is not the capital gained through the house that is of consequence, but rather the very notion that one owns a home on Nevis. Thus, ownership confers a sense of belonging as well as status and prestige.

While migration often affirms or reinforces the value of property ownership, returnees' conceptions of homeownership are influenced by the experience of living and seeking housing in England. When West Indians first arrived in the United Kingdom, they were excluded from housing on the basis of colour and prejudice. In 1965, for example, the Milner Holland Committee reported that 27 per cent of the housing owners in Britain "overtly barred applicants, and only 6 per cent of the housing owners indicated that coloured people would be welcome" (Byron 1994, 129). In addition, West Indians were virtually absent from council housing due to residence restrictions as well as lack of information concerning the possibilities of attaining such accommodation. While this practice was later restricted by the state in the 1968 Race Relations Act, Byron (1994) argues that by this late date, black tenants had already devised strategies to avoid facing discrimination. With the difficulty of paying high rents as well as finding spaces in which they could cook, socialize and raise children (see Chamberlain 1997; Olwig 1993), West Indian immigrants resorted to purchasing homes in the inner-city areas. Through a combination of partner schemes, rental arrangements (such as renting out part of their home), savings and bank loans (which offered higher mortgages), by 1975 half of the West Indian households in Britain lived in owner-occupied accommodation. Another 26 per cent of West Indian immigrants became council housing tenants in the 1970s (a rate that has continued to increase) with a number of these tenants opting for the ability to purchase their council flats in the 1980s (Byron 1994). Foner observes that, for Jamaicans living in England, "changes in the availability of these two amenities [that is, homes and cars] in England seem to have enhanced their importance as status-defining criteria among Jamaican migrants" (1978, 139), adding that "home ownership is a more highly valued goal . . . Home ownership not only symbolizes self-sufficiency and success, but it is an economic asset" (140). Agnew (1982) also notes a general increase in homeownership among West Indians in the United Kingdom between 1966 and 1970–71; this increase coincided with the increasing strength of a conservative ideology, fostered by Margaret Thatcher, that tried to denigrate those who lived in council housing (Goulbourne 1998). The government's promotion of private homeownership is also likely to have reinforced the initial preferences as they were taught during returnees' socialization as children in Jamaica.

In the following section, I present a case study of a returnee living in greater Mandeville to illustrate the economic and gender dynamics of house construction and the attendant desire to become a "returned" migrant. By examining the dilemmas of return experienced by one returnee, I highlight the values that are negotiated through the creation of home.

## The Empty Fortress

Mr Reid, a single man in his mid-seventies, moved from London to Mandeville in 1997 after forty years living in the United Kingdom. After a brief sojourn in North America as a contract farm worker in the 1950s, Mr Reid returned to Jamaica only to discover that all his friends had left for England. Shortly afterwards, he decided to join his friends in London. During his time in the United Kingdom, Mr Reid worked as a builder with a construction company as well as in the transport industry driving vehicles throughout greater London. He returned to Jamaica only twice the entire time he lived abroad.

Mr Reid's return was alone and, as he termed, "blind". Rather than restarting his life in England after a divorce, Mr Reid decided to return to Jamaica. He planned his return rather abruptly, moving back without a house or any permanent place to stay. He eventually built a house on a plot of land because he liked the size and "look" of the property, and he met with a contractor to plan the home. His sketch of the house closely resembled his friend's house next door, with whom he arranged to stay while the building was being completed. However, when Mr Reid asked his neighbours to reimburse him for the customs duties paid on the extra kitchen appliance that he shipped on their behalf in his container, the relationship soured and he had to ask the contractor to speed up the work on his house. Mr Reid moved into his new house within the month.

Mr Reid's home is a source of pride as illustrated by the meticulous care given to his yard and hedges and the two white lion statues proudly protecting his front gate. The hedge on the right side of the house separates the lawn and garden and the hedge on the left side of the house is carefully manicured to block his view of his neighbours so he can "put them out of his mind". Mr

Reid also spends a good deal of time on his back veranda where people cannot see him, some days pulling his car around to the back so people think he is not home. He also installed a six-foot corrugated tin fence and invested in a security system because he felt he was at risk of "being attacked". While he now feels safe, Mr Reid admits that he is also uneasy with the idea that he is locked in the house.

Mr Reid's days are often lonely because his children live in England,[14] and he does not enjoy visiting his extended family living nearby because he feels that they always "want something from you". In response to his loneliness, Mr Reid joined one of Mandeville's returning resident associations. While he welcomes the company of other returnees with similar experiences and knowledge of the world, he admits that part of his motivation in joining the association was to find a female companion. Mr Reid claims that he is not looking for a person that he "could get" at the rum bar over an evening of drinks and dominoes, as some of the other returnee men do with young Jamaican women. His feeling is that all these young "girls" could be after is his money, and he does not want to worry about leaving someone in his house when he goes out or (as rumour has it) being murdered in his sleep – his claim is that "young women like to kill them [returnee men] off!" He wants to find someone more his own age who is attractive, travelled, has her own money and is not too religious (which effectively rules out most single female returnees). Despite his stringent criteria, he does have two more serious candidates he is "working on", both of whom lived in England.

While Mr Reid was involved in selecting the windows, tiles and other basics of his house, he remains hesitant to complete the home because he is constantly preoccupied with his missing companion. He purposefully left one entire room empty because he envisions the room to be the new master bedroom when he "gets a woman". The other rooms also have very few decorations; almost all of the pictures and photographs hang in the living room. The living room also contains two leather settees, a leather chair, a table with a small artificial flower arrangement, a television and a stereo purchased locally in Jamaica. This room is partially finished because he wants the main room to look presentable; it might possibly encourage a potential girlfriend to further enter the house (and his life). Although the home is neat and clean, he often apologizes for its sparse décor, noting that he needs a woman to come in and "dress it" because "women are better at these things". Like Mr Reid's presentable formal room, the house also contains a large open area in back for dancing and enjoyment. The backyard also has a barbecue as well as stereo outlets for his speakers, making it possible to host small gatherings and parties. Since returning three and a half years ago, however, he held a party only once when a "lady friend from England" came to visit. Mr Reid lives with the hope that he will one day be able to finish his house.

## Completion and Incompletion: Being and Becoming a Returned Resident

In his analysis of "the birth of the house" in South Sulawesi, Indonesia, Gibson (1995) describes the laying of steel, the setting and raising of posts, and the offering of food to the house spirits in the construction of a home. The building's construction culminates in a protective ritual wherein the children of the house dress as bride and groom. Critical to the ritual, and thus the house, is that the couple produce a daughter and a son to perform the role of the bride and the groom. Ideally, they will also bear a third child to stand as the ritual product of their union. As Gibson summarizes, "the successful rearing of three children thus serves both to reproduce the household with an increment and definitively transform marriage/affinity into sibling-ship/kinship" (1995, 145). But what happens when a returnee *cannot* complete their house? Is the house so intricately tied to the process of returning that one cannot achieve return and thus become a "returned resident" without it?

Return migration coincides with retirement. The home, specifically the meticulously painted tall white concrete walls, extensive grilles and burglar bars, announces one's arrival and re-entry into Jamaican society. The house further expresses a returnee's success and ability to adjust to life abroad. However, and as Mr Reid illustrates, while building and owning the dream home remains a key tenet of return, it does not guarantee general member-ship in Jamaican society. To properly return to Jamaica, a returnee's house must be completed before they can enter into relationships with other returnees and the wider society. The structure of the house must be estab-lished, the windows must be in place, the grilles affixed to the windows and doors, the tiles situated and all of the fixtures in the kitchen and bathroom installed. The interior and exterior walls must be painted and all of the wiring and cabling must be ready for hooking up water, electricity and telephone service. In other words, the house must be finished before they can participate in the *work* of returning, the transition from returning to returned. In fact, many returnees wait a few years until the "bits and pieces" of the house are complete to join a returning resident association or church.

Although the returnee's house must be complete, it should not be entirely finished. Most returnees leave projects around the home to be added to, altered, improved or changed to prevent boredom during retirement. Gardens and yards must be built, grown and tended to, small cabinets should be constructed to fill "empty" spaces, and chairs must be constructed or repainted, depending upon one's particular talents. Beyond occupying one's time, tasks around the house also provide returnees with opportunities to go to the town to interact with others while purchasing tools, paint and other supplies. The house and its upkeep also present a ready set of topics to discuss among other returnees and homeowners. At least in the early years following the move from abroad, the house becomes a social world that arouses a returning resident's sociality.

The tension between completion and incompletion is compounded by the gendered constitution of the ideal Jamaican household, particularly in relation to the division of labour. Ideally, husbands accept responsibility for the hard, heavy labour of the home, repairing and building appliances and furniture as well as maintaining the yard's clean, neat appearance. But largely due to physical ailments, such as high blood pressure, diabetes or heart conditions, older men cannot lift heavy objects or overexert themselves. These physical constraints frustrate some men to the point that they will try to do a little work, often behind the backs of their wives. However, when discovered, their wives report feeling worried and even angry that they would dare to risk their health, fearing being left in Jamaica to fend on their own. To mitigate this tension, some men resort to obsessing about the quality of workmanship by the hired help.

Although in this particular case study I focused on a single, male returnee, women's lives are also structured by the tension between completion and incompletion. In an ideal world, wives accept responsibility for the presentation of the household interior, adding the finishing touches through decoration, cleaning and general aspects of beautification. As the woman of the house,[15] they clean and polish the floor tiles, maintain the carpeting through sweeping and vacuuming, wash and iron the laundry, dust the shelves, and keep the house interior neat and clean. They also might hire and oversee a female helper who assists them with these tasks. In addition to keeping the house "clean and bright", returnee women also spend their time in the kitchen cooking (although some of the younger returnee men assume this task on a regular basis). Cooking and related housework creates a sense of warmth, cleanliness and comfort which allow women to feel house-proud.

As a life project associated with marriage[16] and upward mobility, the returnee house ideally expresses and achieves respectability. Once a couple is married, both members of the couple work towards familial respectability. The construction and care of the dream house announces the return to Jamaica; it becomes the medium through which the couple works towards respectability. Women create a sense of home by cooking and cleaning the house interior. Men concern themselves with the external features of the house and yard. However, it appears that for those who are not married when they return to Jamaica, attaining respectability through the material culture of the house proves to be a dilemma, real or imagined. Mr Reid is perfectly capable of decorating a home, purchasing furniture, hanging photographs and pictures, and attending to other aesthetic features of the home. But despite its neat appearance, Mr Reid feels his home lacks "a woman's touch" and thus the house remains incomplete. For this reason, he refrained from hosting a house-warming party until a "lady friend" visited. Although it is debatable how much choice Mr Reid has regarding a companion, at his age, fitness level and economic status, he could easily enter into a visiting relationship with a woman, but he is keen that his future companion join both his life and his household.

Confirming the incompletion of return perceived and felt by single returnees, women who managed to elude the stigma of spinsterhood were those who maintained active social networks and/or were heavily involved in the church and returning resident associations. More often than not, the successful female single returnee possessed a car and a reasonably large disposable income utilized, in part, for travel and cultural events. They also become involved in charitable activities and church functions. Moreover, most of these successful women were widows[17] who therefore already enjoyed the sanction of marriage and associated respectability.

An incomplete house suggests lack of preparation for return and a perpetual state of transition, as we see with Mr Reid. Although he has no intention of returning to England, it is because he believes that a woman "makes" a respectable home[18] that Mr Reid does not feel he has fully achieved return.

As a result, he works very hard at finding a woman who meets his high standards. He wants to make his relationship with a woman, and thus his return, successful.

## Conclusion

Among the Zafimaniry of Madagascar, the mutual development of the household and the material structure of the home are realized upon the discussion of marriage (Bloch 1996). Before the wedding ceremony, the groom builds a simple frame house in close proximity to his parent's home. The house consists of three stones for the hearth placed near the central post as well as two other posts to support the remaining house frame. The spaces between the posts are filled with bamboo and reed mats, which are often quite permeable and allow other members of the village to see and hear members of the household. In addition, before the house can be inhabited, the Zafimaniry ritually rub taro on the central post (the hearth) of the house. As each child is born, the husband and wife strengthen and embellish their home with hard wooden planks which replace flimsy bamboo. Patterns are also carved into the central post. The Zafimaniry describe this process of hardening the house as "growing bones" which signifies the strength of the marriage as well as the creation of descendents. At this time the house is transformed into a holy house, and the responsibility for the upkeep and continued hardening of the house shifts to the descendents of the original couple, entrenching the family line within the village. Yet, when a Zafimaniry village was burned by the French in 1947, Bloch reports a reluctance to return to the ancestral village to rebuild it, a predicament which he later attributes to the fear of retribution by the ancestors for permitting the destruction of the solid houses and temples that provide connection to ancestral lineage.

The Zafimaniry quandary mirrors the dilemma that many returning residents possess in constructing their lives in Jamaica. Unlike many incarnations of the house which are initiated through the typical rites of passage – birth, marriage and death – returnee homes are built at the onset of retirement after the sale of a first or second home in England. Very few returnees move back to the island with children and they rarely relocate to land shared between family members. Moreover, the homes are built without certainty of what will occur after their deaths, such as the passing and use of the home to successive generations to inhabit, due to the fact that their offspring continue to live in England. In other words, like the Zafimaniry who reconnect to their roots by recreating the marriage and the foundation of the house, thereby performing a ritual "resurrection", returning residents attempt to reconstitute themselves through the acquisition of a respectable life exhibited through their dwelling. How the house is built, its state of completion or incompletion (actual or perceived) and its subsequent use as a vehicle of sociality becomes part and parcel of the project of achieving respectability – a key value of becoming a Jamaican returned resident.

Yet the house may also thwart the process of becoming a returned resident. Unlike many of the homes that are built at the onset of marriage, these homes are erected in retirement. One does not have a lifetime to add to or "harden" the house, but rather the house is a symbol of previous strength and achievement. To achieve the dream house, one must have economic assets and the ability to maintain and "beautify" the home. The division of labour in these large, white homes, complete with yards and gardens, conceptually necessitates that two individuals complete and maintain it, a man to deal with the outside and a woman to dress the interior. Without each person, aspects of the house may remain incomplete, thereby restricting one's ability to participate in life within and outside the home.

But even if a returnee successfully attains the home and, by extension, achieves their dream of return, the house presents other dilemmas. Many Jamaicans are sceptical of returnees' claims that they truly want to return to Jamaica because the returnees tend to live close to each other, in the same areas and neighbourhoods. While this conglomeration of homes reflects the purchase of land and division of these areas into quarter-acre plots at a particular point in time (rather than an explicit desire to set themselves apart and remain secluded from the wider Jamaican population), returnee neighbourhoods effectively take the form of exclusive gated communities, what some refer to as a "little England" (Horst 2005). The sheer size of the homes, installation of burglar bars and use of security systems creates the same effect and many local residents wonder why returnees' homes are so large, given that they are only inhabited by one or two individuals. While the homes may seem excessive to outsiders ("the homes could hold two families!"), for returnees the size of the homes are not only appropriate for their age and status but also provide enough rooms and space to host their children and grandchildren when they come to visit. This factor is critical for many men and women who miss their children and grandchildren. In addition, many returnees have safeguarded themselves from the potential problems of ageing and have installed a full bathroom and bedroom on the first floor in the event they might one day be unable to traverse the stairs of their home.

A series of misunderstandings and miscommunication may also reflect the decision to return to the semi-urban town of Mandeville (population 50,000) as well as the length of the time this particular group of returnees lived in the United Kingdom (Horst 2004). The average returnee in my study lived in the United Kingdom for thirty-eight years and visited Jamaica less than five times during their sojourn abroad, less often than their counterparts who migrated to North America. In other words, many returnees in Mandeville appear out of context. This means that non-returnees fail to appreciate the work and sacrifice that went into the construction of the house and "how far they've come", as many returnees phrase it (see Byron 1999). In particular, younger Jamaicans struggling with lack of opportunity perceive the lifestyle enjoyed by returnees as simply "lucky" and feel that if only they had the opportunity to travel abroad they could also achieve the same status. This attitude tends to antagonize returnees who dislike the notion that they do not deserve or have not *earned* their retirement. Many returnees subsequently feel compelled to communicate their life of struggle to the local youth. Despite their best intentions and their desire to "give back" to Jamaica through charity, employment and experience, the interactions are often interpreted as another example of returnees (or "the English") being "miserable" or "better than we". The many recipients of this wisdom opt to ignore the message of work and struggle associated with the long-term migration journey. In its place, they fixate upon the house and the material rewards. For this reason, returning home through the building of houses may ironically undermine the welcome reception many returnees anticipate upon their arrival in Jamaica and unintentionally perpetuate the dream of return.

## Acknowledgements

This chapter is based upon research carried out for the completion of my PhD thesis (Horst 2004) at University College London. I thank Dwaine Plaza and Frances Henry for the opportunity to publish this work.

# Notes

1.  The programme aired on KLAS FM 89 on Wednesday evenings between 5:30 and 6:30 until the summer of 2001 when the station was reorganized.
2.  Following Ann Hodges, Hudson (1997) states that concrete nog builds upon traditional forms of Spanish walling wherein the builders use a mixture (in this case stone, sand and cement) to fill in the sides of the house surrounded by wood boards.
3.  All figures have been rounded to the nearest whole number.
4.  See Eyre 1997 for a discussion of five different forms of squatter settlements in Jamaica, as well as Klak 1997 for an analysis of the Jamaican government's attempts to construct housing to meet the needs of the poor.
5.  According to the Survey of Living Conditions (Statistical Institute of Jamaica 1997), which estimates income in terms of consumption and non-consumption expenditure, the poorest Jamaicans earned less than J$14,966 annually. With the exchange rate in May 1996, this amounts to US$417 annually.
6.  Research focusing upon the housing of the elderly or older populations in retirement emphasizes the sale or de-construction of the home due to the general acknowledgement that the "elderly are less likely to move than other age groups" and most often do so "to adjust their housing expenditure to their means or for companionship and care following widowhood or increasing frailty" (Williams 1990, 116–17). Elderly housing studies tend to focus upon what people bring to the apartments, how the rooms are arranged as well as how the elderly manage visits with family members, meals and mobility concerns (Percival 2002). While some studies of retirement communities have revealed positive aspects of new moves, the vast majority stress movement and the associated divestment and reconstitution of a smaller domestic living space as troublesome and difficult particularly due to the psychological effects of slowing down and leaving a phase of one's life. The emerging field of international retirement migration provides a different picture of the relationship between movement, retirement and domestic space that is strongly influenced by the more stable economic conditions of retired international migrants as well as previous experiences of migration (King, Warnes and Williams 2000; Williams 1990).
7.  For instance, few returnee homes install swimming pools. In addition, few have elaborate security systems with private security guards, acres of land or full-time helpers or nannies employed as do many Jamaicans living in the wealthiest homes and neighbourhoods of Mandeville.
8.  Approximately one-third of the people I interviewed have been burgled and/or robbed either by strangers, acquaintances (often individuals hired to do day work

in the house or yard) or extended family. In everyday conversation, however, *discussions* regarding crime, murder and burglary sometimes reach mythical proportions (Horst 2004).

9.  Most returned migrants from England build or purchase their homes within five years of their official return.

10. In nineteenth-century Nevis, Olwig reveals that "it became common to consecrate a new house, or a house which had been enlarged or rebuilt by holding a social gathering" by the Methodist church rather than through the common practice of celebrating a new house with a secular (African) celebration (1997, 83).

11. The clustering of kitchen and bathroom in modern homes corresponds with the desire to reduce the cost of laying pipes for the water supply.

12. As with family land practices, the value accorded to marriage is closely related to British colonial policy. For example, M.G. Smith, in his introduction to Clarke's 1966 edition of *My Mother Who Fathered Me,* discusses Lady Huggins's (the wife of the governor of Jamaica) attempt to end concubinage with the Mass Marriage Movement in 1944–45. The movement failed and therefore ended by 1955 (Clarke 1966, xxiii). R.T. Smith (1988) also discusses the link between marriage, status and colonial policy in his work concerning the dual marriage system.

13. The migration tradition and value of owning a home has been consistent over the last two centuries, but each migration destination has tended to have particular items of material culture associated with the migration and return. Many of the individuals I interviewed in Jamaica had parents and grandparents who migrated to Panama to build the canal. Their return was symbolized primarily by a gold timepiece or watch rather than the home.

14. Eldemire (1997) and the *Survey of Living Conditions* (Statistical Office of Jamaica 1997) note that in Jamaica older men live alone more often than older women.

15. This is similar to what Chamberlain (1997) finds among female migrants in England who said they were more concerned with their living conditions (such as a decent kitchen) than a house at home in the Caribbean. Many struggled to convince their husbands that they should concentrate on life in England rather than saving every last penny for a home in Barbados. One strategy some of the women utilized was to push for the purchase of a house in England, justifying that it was an investment for their Barbados home. See also Byron (1998) for a discussion of women's status in England.

16. During my fieldwork, there were a number of scandals surrounding returnee men who had affairs and/or decided to divorce their wife of decades for a younger Jamaican woman. While there were some who implicitly approved (or envied) these men, most returnees' sympathies rested with the woman being left "on her own" in Jamaica.

17. A proportion of female widows often desire to return to England to join their children.

18. Foner states that "West Indians in England have clearly been influenced by certain norms of English family life which differ from practices of lower-class Jamaicans, one example being the tendency to establish legal marriage at an earlier age" (1978, 77). In addition, men's roles increased with the division of the labour in the household.

# References

Abrahams, R.D. 1983. *The Man-O-Words in the West Indies: Performance and the Emergence of Creole Culture.* Baltimore: Johns Hopkins University Press.

Agnew, J. 1982. Home Ownership and Identity in Capitalist Society. In *Housing and Identity,* ed. J.S. Duncan, 60–97. New York: Holmes and Meier.

Austin, D.J. 1984. *Urban Life in Kingston, Jamaica: The Culture and Class Ideology of Two Neighbourhoods.* London: Gordon and Breach.

Besson, J. 1984. Land Tenure in the Free Villages of Trelawny, Jamaica: A Case Study in the Caribbean Peasant Response to Emancipation. *Slavery and Abolition* 5 (1): 3–23.

———. 1995. Land, Kinship and Community in the Post-Emancipation Caribbean: A Regional Overview of the Leeward Islands. In *Small Islands, Large Questions,* ed. K.F. Olwig, 73–99. London: Frank Cass.

———. 2000. The Appropriation of Lands of Law by Lands of Myth in the Caribbean Region. In *Lands, Law and Environment: Mythical Land, Legal Boundaries,* ed. A. Abramson and D. Theodossopoulos, 116–135. London: Pluto Press.

———. 2002. *Martha Brae's Two Histories: European Expansion and Caribbean Culture-Building in Jamaica.* Chapel Hill: University of North Carolina Press.

Bloch, M. 1996. The Resurrection of the House amongst the Zafimaniry. In *How We Think They Think: Anthropological Approaches to Cognition, Memory and Literacy,* M. Bloch, 85–99. Boulder: Westview Press.

Brodber, E. 1975. A Study of Yards in the City of Kingston. Working Paper 9. University of the West Indies, Mona.

Byron, M. 1994. *Post-War Caribbean Migration to Britain: The Unfinished Cycle.* Aldershot: Avebury.

———. 1998. Migration, Work and Gender: The Case of Post-War Labout Migration from the Caribbean. In *Globalised Identities,* ed. M. Chamberlain, 217–31. London: Routledge.

————. 1999. The Caribbean-Born Population in 1990s Britain: Who Will Return? *Journal of Ethnic and Migration Studies* 25 (4): 285–302.

Chamberlain, M. 1997. *Narratives of Exile and Return.* New York: St Martin's Press.

Chevannes, B. 2001. Jamaican Diasporic Identity: The Metaphor of Yaad. In *Nation Dance: Religion, Identity and Cultural Difference in the Caribbean,* ed. P. Taylor, 129–37. Bloomington: Indiana University Press.

Clarke, E. 1966. *My Mother Who Fathered Me.* London: George Allen and Unwin.

Davenport, W. 1961. The Family System of Jamaica. *Social and Economic Studies* 10 (4): 420–54.

Douglass, L. 1992. *The Power of Sentiment: Love, Hierarchy and the Jamaican Family Elite.* Boulder: Westview Press.

Eldemire, D. 1997. The Jamaican Elderly: A Socioeconomic Perspective and Policy Implications. *Social and Economic Studies* 46 (1): 75–93.

Eyre, L.A. 1997. Self-Help Housing in Jamaica. In *Self-Help Housing, the Poor and the State in the Caribbean,* ed. R.B. Potter and D. Conway, 75–101. Knoxville: University of Tennessee Press.

Foner, N. 1971. Social Change and Social Mobility in a Jamaican Rural Community. Chicago: University of Chicago.

————. 1978. *Jamaica Farewell: Jamaican Migrants in London.* Berkeley and Los Angeles: University of California Press.

Gibson, Thomas. 1995. Having your House and Eating It: Houses and Siblings in Ara, South Sulawesi. In *About the House,* ed. J. Carsten and S. Hugh-Jones. Cambridge: Cambridge University Press.

Goulbourne, H. 1998. *Race Relations in Britain since 1945.* Social History in Perspective. New York: St Martin's Press.

Henke, H. 1996. Mapping the "Inner Plantation": A Cultural Exploration of the Origins of Caribbean Local Discourse. *Social and Economic Studies* 45 (4): 51–75.

Higman, B.W. 1984. *Slave Populations of the British Caribbean, 1807–1834.* Baltimore: Johns Hopkins University Press.

Horst, H. 2004. *"Back a Yaad": Constructions of Home among Jamaica's Return Migrant Community.* PhD diss., University of London.

————. 2005. Landscaping Englishness: The Postcolonial Predicament of Returnees in Mandeville, Jamaica. In *The Experience of Return Migration: Caribbean Perspectives,* ed. R. Potter, D. Conway and J. Phillips. Aldershot: Ashgate.

Hudson, B.J. 1997. Houses in the Caribbean: Homes and Heritage. In *Self-Help Housing, the Poor and the State in the Caribbean,* ed. R.B. Potter and D. Conway. 14–29. Knoxville: University of Tennessee Press.

King, R., T. Warnes and A. Williams. 2000. *Sunset Lives: British Retirement Migration to the Mediterranean.* Oxford: Berg Press.

Klak, T. 1997. Obstacles to Low-Income Housing Assistance in the Capitalist Periphery: The Case of Jamaica. In *Self-Help Housing, the Poor and the State in the Caribbean,* ed. R.B. Potter and D. Conway. 102–19. Knoxville: University of Tennessee Press.

Lazarus-Black, M. 1994. *Legitimate Acts and Illegal Encounters: Law and Society in Antigua and Barbuda.* Washington, DC: Smithsonian Institution Press.

Marcoux, J.S. 2001. The "Casser-Maison" Ritual: Constructing the Self by Emptying the Home. *Journal of Material Culture* 6 (2): 213–36.

Maurer, B. 1997a. Fragments of Blood on Fragments of Soil: Capitalism, the Commons, and Kinship in the Caribbean. *Plantation Society in the Americas* 4 (2–3): 159–72.

———. 1997b. *Recharting the Caribbean: Land, Law and Citizenship in the British Virgin Islands.* Ann Arbor: University of Michigan Press.

Mintz, S.W. 1974. *Caribbean Transformations.* Chicago: Aldine Publishing Company.

———. 1985. From Plantations to Peasantries in the Caribbean. In *Caribbean Contours,* ed. S.W. Mintz and S. Price, 127–54. Baltimore: Johns Hopkins University Press.

Olwig, K.F. 1993. *Global Culture, Island Identity: Community and Change in the Afro-Caribbean Community of Nevis.* Reading, UK: Harwood Academic Publishers.

———. 1995. Cultural Complexity after Freedom: Nevis and Beyond. In *Small Islands, Large Questions,* ed. K.F. Olwig, 100–122. London: Frank Cass.

———. 1997. Cultural Sites: Sustaining a Home in a Deterritorialized World. In *Siting Culture: The Shifting Anthropological Object,* ed. K.F. Olwig and K. Hastrup, 17–38. London: Routledge.

———. 1999. Caribbean Place Identity: From Family Land to Region and Beyond. *Identities* 5 (4): 435–67.

Percival, J. 2002. Domestic Spaces: Uses and Meanings in the Daily Lives of Older People. *Ageing and Society* 22: 729–49.

Smith, R.T. 1988. *Kinship and Class in the West Indies: A Genealogical Study of Jamaica and Guyana.* Cambridge: Cambridge University Press.

Sobo, E.J. 1993. *One Blood: The Jamaican Body.* Albany: State University of New York.

Solien, N.L. 1959. The Nonunilineal Descent Group in the Caribbean and South America. *American Anthropologist* 61: 578–83.

Statistical Institute of Jamaica. 1997. *Jamaica Survey of Living Conditions 1996.* Kingston: Statistical Institute of Jamaica.

Thomas-Hope, E. 1995. Island Systems and the Paradox of Freedom: Migration in the Post-Emancipation Leeward Islands. In *Small Islands, Large Questions,* ed. K.F. Olwig, 161–78. London: Frank Cass.

Williams, B.F. 1991. *Stains on My Name, War in my Veins: Guyana and the Politics of Cultural Struggle.* Durham: Duke University Press.

Williams, G. 1990. *The Experience of Housing in Retirement: Elderly Lifestyles and Private Initiative.* Aldershot: Avebury.

CHAPTER 7

# Second-Generation "Returnee" Migration to Jamaica and Barbados
## Pursuing Happiness and Mobility

| Dwaine E. Plaza |

In 1981, we went to Jamaica to see how the land was lay. I was not making plans at that time to move back, I was just checking out the place to see what property was like, what jobs were around and I was seeing how the land lay. I remember thinking the prospects were good. I spoke to several lawyers to see how things were. I got the impression that said "come down", it will not be a problem. My family in Jamaica was supportive, my family in England were not happy. My step mother in the United Kingdom felt that was a very backward thing to do and that we would be back in England very soon. . . . And there was the issue of her grandchildren and she asked why were taking them away from her. She was very upset by this. My father in law actually went on a religious retreat to pray for us because he thought we were crazy to be going back to such a backward place. My aunts and other relations were also sceptical although they did not voice it in the same way. In general people felt that we were a bit fool hardy in what we were doing.
– *Jamaican respondent JR095 1A in the Economic and Social Research Council programme Population and Household Change*

## Introduction

The decade of the 1990s was very important in the history of post-war Caribbean migration to Britain. In the 1950s and 1960s, Caribbean migrants to Britain left their homelands in their late teens and early twenties. These same migrants were reaching retirement age in the 1990s. The subgroup of the Caribbean population in Britain of pensionable age doubled between the census of 1981 and 1991 from less than 6 per cent to over 11 per cent of the total. By 2000, this age group increased in size to nearly 50 per cent of the Caribbean-born population (Byron and Condon 1996; Byron 2000). Since the 1980s, researchers have identified a growing trend among retiring first generation Caribbean migrants to Britain – a desire to return "home", expressed as both a longing and a real aspiration (Fenton 1986). This desire would clearly fulfil what Thomas-Hope (1992) called the last step in completing the "migration circuit" – returning to the place of origin. Bhalla and Blakemore (1981), surveying the first generation immigrant population in Birmingham, noted that compared to members of the Asian population, African-Caribbeans were more dissatisfied with British life and showed more signs of wishing to live in another country, particularly after retirement. Peach (1991), comparing British census totals of people born in the Caribbean over the past three decades, shows that return migration and re-migration to North America has become a growing phenomenon. Peach further notes that over 50 per cent of future returnees (or about 48,000) would be destined for Jamaica, with Barbados receiving the next highest number (about 7,000).

Joining the group of retiring returnees to the Caribbean is a cohort of young second-generation British Caribbeans who are eager to find work and start new lives. These individuals were born in Britain of Caribbean parentage, or they migrated to Britain at a young age, or they arrived at a later time (usually before age twelve) and were reunited with parents who migrated earlier. These second-generation "returnees", as we might call them, experienced most of their formative socialization in Britain. Unlike elder retired returnees, the young returnees are likely to possess some kind of professional accreditation or university qualification. The young second-generation returnees are new to the Caribbean in the sense that many know the region only from early childhood memories, as occasional holiday destinations or through the nostalgic stories passed down from their parents. As a result, most of the second-generation returnees go back to their family's place of origin with the hope that they will experience a romanticized reconnection with kin, achieve a sense of belonging and find happiness. Ironically, however, once these individuals settle in their place of origin, they soon become aware that their imagined belief of the warm, welcoming island paradise does not really exist. Instead, they find societies stratified by "race", gender, skin colour and class politics. All of these factors hinder their smooth transition back into the society and culture of their parents.

Using qualitative interview data, this chapter explores the social history and cultural adjustments of twenty second-generation British-Caribbean returnees to Barbados and Jamaica. In order to accomplish this analysis the chapter is divided into three sections. The first section provides a description of the methodology used to undertake the research and a general description of the second-generation British-Caribbean returnees in this study. The second section examines the settlement and social adjustment issues young returnees faced while growing up in Britain. The experiences growing up and working in Britain ultimately played a key role in influencing these individuals to "return" to Jamaica or Barbados. The final section of the chapter uses qualitative interview data to examine the social, psychological and cultural adjustment experiences of twenty second-generation British-Caribbean "returnees" currently living in Barbados and Jamaica.[1]

## Methodology and Sample Characteristics

This chapter is based on life history interview data collected from an Economic and Social Research Council project entitled "Family Structure and Social Change of Caribbeans in Britain".[2] The project explored the transnational patterns of Caribbean-origin family, kinship, and households in Britain from the 1950s to the present.

Life history data was collected from a non-random sample of individuals who originated in Barbados, Jamaica and Trinidad and who had arrived in Britain since the 1950s. Initial contact with informants was made through island or community associations in Britain. Using a snowball technique from the initial contacts, a sample of sixty three-generation families was located. This sample can be considered a balance of gender, "race" and place of birth. Interviews were conducted between 1995 and 1997 in London, Birmingham, Coventry, Barbados, Trinidad and Jamaica. Typically, we interviewed the original migrant to Britain, one of their children and then a person identified in the Caribbean as a family member who never migrated but still stayed in close contact. These were considered as the typical elements of the sixty transnational three-generation Caribbean-origin families. Within the sample of interviewees we were also able to locate some family members who fell into the category of being second-generation returnees. In these situations we typically interviewed four members of the same family including the second-generation returnee son or daughter now living in Barbados or Jamaica.

By individually interviewing three generations from within the same family, we were able to capture the longer perspective of each family, which included its rhythm and cycle, as well as changes that have occurred. This method also allowed us to better understand how each transnational Caribbean family functions in response to such issues as the original migration, settlement, racism and discrimination, schooling issues, and support for return.

The interviewing took place using a structured interview schedule. The areas covered during the interview included a demographic profile of the family; an examination of the family household structures, living arrangements, social networks and transnational connections; and the factors contributing to the decision to migrate. All of the interviews were audio taped and took between two and three hours to complete. The interviews were transcribed and analysed using the strategy of the constant comparative method of analysis, a strategy of data analysis that calls for continual "making comparisons" and "asking questions" (Strauss and Corbin 1990). Interviews were coded and sorted according to emerging themes. These themes were then compared to each other for generalizablity. Categories which were relevant to the theme of this study, such as the decision to return or adjustment, were noted and further theorized.

## Characteristics of the Respondents

Fifteen of the interviewees were women and five were men. All twenty of the individuals had parents who were born in the Caribbean. Twelve second-generation interviewees emigrated to Britain while under the age of fifteen years. The rest were born in Britain. The oldest person interviewed was forty-four years old, while the youngest was twenty-seven. The average age of the returnees at the time of the interview was thirty-three. Seven of the interviewees were born in Jamaica and five were born in Barbados. Four had been living in the Caribbean ten or more years. The rest had "returned" in the last five years.

Two of the interviewees were born in the Caribbean but migrated to Britain after having spent a short time with relatives in the United States. All of the interviewees grew up in London, Birmingham or Coventry. With respect to the period of arrival, most of the interviewees born in the Caribbean (fourteen of twenty) arrived a few years after their parents. These individuals were left in the Caribbean to be raised by grandparents, aunts or other kin before being sent for. Two individuals came with mothers to be reunited with a father. The rest were born in Britain.

With respect to current occupations in the Caribbean, five of the interviewees were managers, four were accountants, three were lawyers, three worked in the education field (two secondary school teachers and a university instructor), two were nurses, two were computer systems analysts, and one was a journalist.

In terms of the highest level of schooling completed, all twenty had completed at a minimum a bachelor's degree, with some also having completed a professional accreditation, four had completed a master's degree and one had completed a doctorate. Everyone in the sample finished his or her post-secondary degrees in Britain.

Twelve of the women interviewed were not married and five were officially separated or divorced. Only three of the women were married to someone living in Jamaica or Barbados at the time. All of the men in the sample were married. Two of the men who indicated that they were married at the beginning of the interview revealed during later conversation that they were no longer living with their wives.

All of the men indicated having children either in Britain or in the Caribbean. Two of the men that were married had their children living with them, while the other men talked of their children and were in occasional contact with them. Six of the fifteen women had one or more children. Four of these women had their children living with them. Two women had left their children with a parent or family member to be raised in Britain.

All of the interviewees had made at least three holiday visits to the Caribbean before returning to live. This suggests the continued importance of maintaining a transnational link to family and kin still living in the region before making the decision to return. With respect to a continued ability to live in Jamaica or Barbados for the foreseeable future, only twelve of twenty felt that in the next five years they would still be there. Those who said they would not be in Jamaica or Barbados talked about moving to the United

States in pursuit of better opportunities. Some also discussed operating some sort of international business that would allow them to live part-time in the Caribbean and part-time in Britain.

From the above socio-demographic profile of the twenty second-genera-tion British-Caribbean returnees in the sample, it is apparent that this is quite a heterogeneous mixture of individuals who nevertheless had a common eth-nic Caribbean background, high levels of educational attainment and the experience of having grown up in Britain. As a consequence of the sample size being small and non-randomly selected, it is difficult to make strong claims of reliability in the findings that follow. The life experiences of these individuals can, however, give us a valid picture of the way twenty second-generation British-Caribbean returnees to Barbados and Jamaica rational-ized their return migration decision, adapted and negotiated a space for themselves once they migrated to the Caribbean.

The analysis which follows is based on the life experiences of these people. Although these individuals were part of complex family structures, only their voices and perspectives are used in the analysis that follows to under-stand the decision to return, settlement, adjustment and coping strategies. These life history interviews offer rich qualitative data on the particular indi-viduals, their perspectives on life, their cultural values and their social norms. However, they do not generate information which can be subjected to quan-titative analysis nor can they be used as a basis for making sweeping state-ments about more general conditions. The strength of these interviews is the fact that they offer us an exploratory view of the significance of the return migration phenomenon among a cohort of second-generation British Caribbeans and the transnational fields of relations to which such travel gives rise.

## Second-Generation Experiences Living in Britain

Caribbean migration to Britain effectively started in 1948, reached its peak in 1961 and ended by 1973, after which date the annual net-migration balance between the two countries amounted to only a few thousand people. The pattern of emigration from the Caribbean to Britain between 1951 and 1962 can be divided into three distinct phases. Intakes between 1952 and 1956 were stimulated by intense labour shortages due to post-war reconstruction.

The boom tapered off between 1956 and 1960. However, in 1961 intake increased to a new peak of 66,300, stimulated primarily by a large influx of immigrants trying to reach the United Kingdom before the passing of the 1962 Commonwealth Immigration Act (Hall 1988).

Almost all of the early pioneer migrants originally intended to go home after five years but this expectation for most did not materialize because resources were never quite sufficient. In most of the first- and second-generation interviews conducted with migrants in Britain, individuals revealed an initial resistance to establishing permanent roots or in admitting that they would be spending longer than five years.

It has always been possible to argue that the first generation of Caribbean immigrants to Britain have tended to occupy low status jobs and not experienced the "mobility dream" due to a combination of factors: a lack of knowledge about the social conventions of British society, a lack of employment networks, non-recognition of their qualifications, and structural and institutionalized discrimination. In many respects, the first generation has been prepared to accept their circumstances and taken whatever jobs they could find, however unsatisfactory, because they believed that their children would ultimately benefit in Britain through opportunities for better schooling and jobs.

One of the realities that Caribbean-origin people living in Britain have had to deal with is the overt discrimination and racism they encounter in their workplace and day-to-day activities. Although Caribbeans have come from societies where distinctions of social behaviour, speech and education play an important part in determining treatment, in Britain none of these fine distinctions were of much significance in relation to the more dominant issue of race and ethnicity. Learning to deal with the colour and race issue was difficult for some because it went against their constructed notion about Britain as the mother country, where all of her subjects are supposed to be equal and united under the Union Jack. Opportunities for mobility were supposed to be available to everyone so long as he or she was willing to endure sacrifice and work hard. The reality of the situation, however, is that a "colour bar" exists in Britain and it continues to be directed at those who are a dark skin colour (Goulbourne and Chamberlain 2001).

One of the effects of the long-term exposure to racism is that Caribbeans, particularly the second generation, have come to regard themselves as outsiders from British society (Chamberlain 1997). We gathered that our interviewees felt a consistent feeling of not belonging in British society. Coral, a thirty-five-year-old Jamaican-born woman, clearly articulates this sentiment of being a "foreigner" when she tells us about an incident which took place while travelling on a train from Birmingham to London. She says:

> No, I'm not an immigrant, I was born there. But what I'm saying to you is that I do not feel as if I belong. Let me tell you a story, I was on the train a few years ago, I sat by a big white guy, and the train was very, very full. And I was very polite. I was well-dressed. I was travelling back to London from Birmingham, I said, "Excuse me", and he looked me up and down, and grudgingly, grudgingly, moved across, and I sat beside him. And I looked him up and down, and I felt very aggressive. I could smack him up the face, because he tried to make himself so small so he didn't have to touch me. I felt angry, because I thought, "Who the hell do you think you are?" And for purpose, I got closer and closer, till there was nowhere for him to go. I wanted him to get up and say, "Excuse me", and move altogether. And he didn't do that. (JR 093 1A)

Many second-generation British Caribbeans responded to the feelings of alienation and disenfranchisement by latching onto a pan-Caribbean culture. Since the 1950s, the most dominant pan-Caribbean culture in Britain has been a Jamaican "roots" reggae subculture. Second-generation Caribbeans tended to be drawn to the "roots" aspects of Jamaican culture, language and music because it gave them a sense of belonging which they were denied when they tried to become "British". The dominance of Jamaican culture is not surprising, since this ethnic group comprised more than two-thirds of all Caribbeans living in Britain. Evidence of the Jamaicanization of Caribbeans in Britain came out in a number of our second-generation interviews. Denise, a twenty-six-year-old woman of Barbadian origin who grew up in Croyden, makes this point when she reflected on the socialization of her peer group:

> I think it was probably because, if you didn't speak like them, you didn't feel part of the group, and I think there was a lot of peer pressure. . . . The friends that I had, the Jamaican girls, okay, they were British, but . . . there was only about two that were actually born in Jamaica, and, like myself, came when they were small. The rest of them were English girls anyway, by birth, but their parents were Jamaicans, and, I mean, you'd thought they just landed from Jamaica. . . . To be Jamaican was, like, hip, you know. So I learnt how. . . . And, you know, without even really asking, I just got myself in. And then I got in trouble, like, at home, because my dad would say, "We're not Jamaican. Do not bring that in here." (BD 20 1A)

It is not surprising that our interviews revealed the most important issue in the lives of second-generation Caribbeans growing up in Britain as peer group acceptance. It was from this socializing agency that many individuals were made to feel wanted or unwanted as part of British society. Gaining acceptance and making long lasting friendships with their "white" counterparts was important in the psychological adjustment for our cohort of interviewees. For many, their white friendships tended to be short-term, superficial and one sided in the sense that they were always giving in and adopting to the so-called white world. Difficulty in finding true friendships within the British population was certainly the case for Lisa, a twenty-eight-year-old woman of Jamaican origin who grew up in South London. She told us that the barrier to "true long lasting" friendships was the parents of her white friends. As a result, Lisa felt that she never could feel very attached to her white schoolmates. Since she did not live in a neighbourhood with other people of colour, this added to her feelings of psychological alienation in British society:

> You knew at school they accepted you . . . but you also knew they never truly accepted you. I didn't have any of my white girlfriends stay over and sleep by me, but I could go and sleep with them. And at that time, I couldn't quite understand why their parents wouldn't allow my "best friends" to come and sleep at my house. . . . It took me a lot of years to understand why there were excuses, from a parents' point of view. From a children's point of view, the prejudice wasn't as great. But the influence of the parents, vis-à-vis the children, you don't do certain things. At school, it's okay. After school, well, it's not quite all right. (JR 35 1B)

Another notable barrier to a sense of belonging as reported by our second-generation interviewees was that of having to deal with the selective harassment by the police. This was a situation more commonly reported by the males in our sample. Black males consistently reported that they were systematically centred out and "criminalized" by the selective surveillance tactics of the police force. This practice was common in the early 1970s with the passing of the sus laws, but it continues into the present period. Many of our interviewees recalled the terror tactics they have been routinely subjected to when walking or driving on London streets. Glen, a thirty-two-year-old Barbadian male living in Brixton, told us about his frequent encounters with the police:

I was going to look for my friend and there was a police car, like, just waiting, and they was parked just after the turning that I was going to go into. So
I turned into the road to see my friend, and then, I mean, it was late, it was
about eleven o'clock, and then they, came up beside me, and they said what
am I doing out here? And I said, "Well, I'm gonna check my friend", you
know, "going to my friend's house", and they was asking me all these kind of
questions, "Who is your friend?" and all the rest of it, you know. But this
is an everyday thing, really, because there's so much police on the streets,
you just . . . you've got to be prepared to bump into them now and again.
(BR 20 1B)

## Factors Affecting the Decision to "Return"

The men and women in this sample who were able to overcome the odds
and go on to complete post-secondary schooling can be regarded as the
"cream of the crop" among the British-Caribbean second-generation population. This is especially so when one considers the low proportion of black
Caribbeans who actually make it through the school system to finish a post-
secondary programme. According to the 1991 census, only 5 per cent of black
Caribbeans between the ages of twenty-five and fifty-nine years have completed a university degree. This is compared to 10 per cent for white and 12
per cent for Asian groups in Britain (Jones 1993). This distribution seems to
reflect the low proportion of post-secondary schooling qualifications among
people of Caribbean-origin in Britain.

The group of second-generation returnees to the Caribbean therefore represent a significant reverse brain drain within the overall Caribbean population in Britain. Their decision to return to the Caribbean seems to be based
on a number of factors. Most importantly, individuals (fifteen of twenty) felt
that they would feel more "at home" in the Caribbean. This was a sentiment
quite similar to what Gmelch (1980) found among older returning migrants.
For many, the feeling of being at "home" in the Caribbean stems from them
having made numerous holiday visits and from them constructing an idyllic
notion of the Caribbean as a warm and welcoming place through the many
stories told by family and kin in Britain. Having an idyllic "homeland" to
return to allowed many to cope with the day-to-day struggle of living as a
"foreigner" in Britain. Angela, a thirty-one-year-old lawyer and returnee of
Barbadian origin, clearly makes this point:

> Growing up I had always come back with my mother to Barbados. Actually I came back five times before I moved back. We travelled all over the island when I was younger. I just love the feeling of it being a black country. These are people I can identify with, lawyers, doctors, pharmacists everyone was black and I could feel good about this and seeing these men and women doing these jobs. Blacks do these jobs in England, but they are so far and few in between that I don't feel the same way. Growing up there was no black role models as professionals I could look at and say that I want to be like them. (BH 074)

From our sample of respondents it seems that racism and discrimination experienced in Britain played a major role for some (fifteen) and a minor role for others (five) in their decision to return to the Caribbean. This response towards racism is similar to what Gmelch (1987) found in his research on returnees to Barbados. A large proportion of the interviewees in his study indicated that racism was indeed a factor in their decision to return. Gertrude, a thirty-four-year-old computer programmer and Barbadian returnee, decided that she would rather work in the computing field in Barbados because it offered a better quality of life for herself and her family. Her sentiment highlights for us some of the ambivalent responses to racism in Britain:

> The decision to return to Barbados had been made a long time ago; the second time I had been back to Barbados was 1978. At that stage I said to myself: "If I am in England in the next five years then something is wrong." I just thought that this is the place that I want to make a comfortable life. Part of it is that I believed that real change is possible. I cannot say that racism made me leave England. It was a fact of life but it's not something that I took on in that kind of way. It's not my problem. It's there and you have to cope with it. It's projected at you. I cannot honestly say that I left England because it was too much of a racist society. (BJM 127A)

Having children in Britain, for some professionals, was an important reason for returning to the Caribbean. Some individuals felt that the school system was better in the Caribbean and the way of life superior for raising young black children. Another reason for Vanessa, a thirty-three-year-old Jamaican-born returnee lawyer, was the fact that she felt that her children did not need to grow up in an environment that was hostile to young black children. Her sentiment echoed the group who felt that racism was a major factor in their decision to return:

> When I had the children, I felt that it was not a great place to bring them up. My son, who is now going to be fourteen, if he were back in England, I would be fretting because that's the age they start to become "targets". Because you are a black man on the streets. If there are more than two of you on the street then that is trouble. I did not also want to sacrifice my children to the inter-city school system in Britain. (JRRI 150A)

The decision to return to the Caribbean for our sample of interviewees seemed to be very gender specific. Women returned in much higher numbers than did men: fifteen of our interviewees were professional women in Barbados or Jamaica. When asked to comment on this phenomenon, many of our interviewees had different answers as to why there was a skew. A common sentiment among the women was that they were more willing to take risks than were their male counterparts back in the United Kingdom. The women were not afraid of failure or having to return to Britain after a period of time and admitting that they were not successful. The men, on the other hand, appeared to be cautious and conservative in terms of losing face and having to return to Britain as a "failure". The men in our sample appeared to be willing to return only when they had a guarantee of a permanent, well-paying job. Edmond, a thirty-six-year-old Barbadian returnee manager, had the following reflection to offer as to why he felt the proportion of women was so much higher than men:

> It is mostly women who are returning that's what I am seeing. The men seem to be afraid of failure, more afraid of looking bad and having to return to England with their tail between their legs. That's what I see makes women more adventurous, they don't have to worry about looking bad or failing because that's what everyone expects of them to do anyway. (BM 1161A)

Another possible explanation for the phenomenon of a higher proportion of young women returnees compared to men is provided by Nanton (1997). He notes that the official inter-censal estimates indicate a considerably higher percentage of intermarriage between younger males of West Indian descent and white British females, compared with older males of West Indian descent and white females. Older West Indian male heads of households born outside the United Kingdom averaged only 15 per cent for the years 1985–88, while younger West Indian men averaged 40 per cent for the same period. This pattern suggests that the proportion of second-generation men of Caribbean-origin able to follow an uncomplicated return migration path would be considerably less likely, since these men would also have to make preparations for their white British partners who would obviously experience a significant culture shock. Intermarriage trends also create new levels of social bonds and networks in Britain for the men. This undoubtedly makes it more difficult for them to return even if they desired to. For British-Caribbean women, on the other hand, their transition to their country of origin would likely be less complicated, since they do not seem to be as inter-ethnically partnered as their male counterparts. One can speculate that these factors help explain why we found a disproportionate number of women in our sample of second-generation British-Caribbean "returnees".

## Settlement Reception and Adjustment

In the next section of the chapter, we examine the adaptation to life in Jamaica and Barbados for our cohort of second-generation "returnees". For most of our interviewees, the least complicated aspects of returning were the ease with which they found work, the relaxed work atmosphere and the weather. Almost all of the men and women in this sample had arranged work before they migrated to the Caribbean. The jobs they obtained were on par or a little higher in status compared to what they had left in Britain. The relaxed atmosphere in the office was commented on by most of the interviewees. Most found it to be refreshing, although others found that tardiness and the lack of respect for deadlines was difficult to get accustomed to. Karen, a thirty-six-year-old Barbados-born returnee manager had the following to say about her adjustment:

> It's probably been the weather. A lot of people have complained. Even my father, when he comes down, he complains, saying how hot it is. But that's never been my thing. Yes, I seem to get used to some extent of the laid-back aspects, even though they may have a negative connotation. Some of the laid back aspects, maybe they feed on your kind of inner desire not to be so . . . disciplined. (BJ 076 2A)

One of the most difficult aspects of returning was getting accustomed to the awkward response when the returnee told others about his or her reasons for moving back. Many Caribbean people continue to have the idea that North America and Britain are the land of opportunity and that anyone can find a pot of gold on every street corner. Therefore, when some people hear that a young person is returning from the land of plenty to the Caribbean territories where life for most people is hard, they wonder about the individual's mental state or their abilities. This was certainly the case for Sandra, a thirty-nine-year-old returnee from Jamaica:

> Sometimes at work they call me "English lady".... At first people would say you like a foreigner, I would say: "Yes I was born not bred here." I could understand it you know.... I am "home", I leave it at that. Many people also ask me: "Why you come back, why you not try America or Canada instead?" The idea that young people have failed if they return to Jamaica is quite prevalent. Some people find it difficult to think that I was in the First World and then I left to come back. (JR093 2A)

The sentiment about being crazy for returning was also voiced by Erlinda, a thirty-two-year-old returnee to Jamaica. She was assumed to not be ambitious for the decision that she took to return to Jamaica in 1995 when she had a decent job in Britain:

> I find that most Jamaicans assume, if you're coming to Jamaica at our age, mid-thirties or whatever, then, somehow, you are either mad, which the English are supposed to be.... Or you come back and you have lots of money, otherwise, why would you come back to Jamaica? ... You've got a visa, you've got a passport and your young so what the hell are you doing in Jamaica? (JRRI 150A)

Despite the overall ease with which many described their adjustment period, there were still a number of aspects about Caribbean society, culture and organizations that presented adjustment difficulties. One of the difficult aspects of returning was becoming accustomed to the disparity between the wealthy and the poor. This was especially the case in Jamaica, where poverty and the crime rate were always "in your face". Although social conditions were poor, many of our Jamaican returnees had psychologically prepared themselves for this. Previous holiday return visits allowed most to cope with the disparities. Felix, a thirty-two-year-old manager and returnee of Jamaican origin, had this to say:

> The crime and social breakdown in Jamaica is the same as everywhere. I am aware of it. I just pray that it does not affect me personally. You are aware of the crime, poverty and violence, but it does not consume me. It happens in the

United States and Britain, so it's nothing new. I do take precautions like not parking my car in a secluded place or checking my yard before opening the front door. One cannot be too lax with those sorts of hit and run crimes in Jamaica which are common but at the same time one cannot run their life always in fear. (JK 031 1A)

Leaving family and friends behind in England was a sadness that most of the interviewees commented on. Most understood that by returning they were essentially cutting the close ties which they had established between family, kin and friends. The high cost of transatlantic travel meant that regular visits from family and friends in Britain were more than likely not going to happen. Loneliness in Jamaica and Barbados was compounded by the reality that, for most, making new friends was a difficult prospect. According to our interviewees, the local population appears to be happy and to welcome one as an annual visitor, but their attitude changes once one expresses intentions to live permanently on the island. Many of the women in our sample were very clear about the difficulty they had encountered in making new friends in either Jamaica or Barbados. Many of the new friendships these women formed were with other "foreigners" living on the island. This was a sentiment found in Gmelch's (1987) research on elderly women returnees to Barbados. Most expressed a feeling of being treated like an outsider or in "competition" with the local women for men. In commenting on her own experiences, Lauren made the following point:

> I have one very good Jamaican friend. I don't have that many Jamaican friends. I have friends that I've known since before I came, who live in Jamaica. And where we are not as close as we used to be, because people live very different when they're at home to when they're abroad. Most of the people I know, actually, are like myself, from England. (JRRI 150A)

The difficulty in becoming adjusted to the work culture in the Caribbean was an important consideration that came up in virtually all of our interviews. For some, this was the most difficult aspect of becoming accustomed to Jamaica or Barbados. For others, however, they noted that it took some getting used to but overall they welcomed the more relaxed office atmosphere. Michelle, a thirty-four-year-old Barbados-born bank manager noted that her initial frustrations eventually gave way to tolerance:

> One of the things about being from England, you are treated slightly differently. Some people are annoyed at you because you seem to work in a differ-

ent way, you are a bit more organized and more efficient, and you could be seen as a know-it-all. But they also value you because you will actually do the work. You will actually do it when they want you to do it, no procrastinating. Most people from England have not had a problem actually doing the work, and doing over and above it. Their problem is dealing with the quirks of the bosses, the individual quirks. (BG 091 1A)

For others it was shocking to find out how important social and business networks were in the Caribbean in terms of promotion, hiring or just getting little things done in the society. Lauren noted that without the right network connections, upward mobility is limited. She had learned, over years of living in Jamaica, that while it was necessary to rely on one's qualifications or credentials, one also had to go out and make social links in order to get ahead. This was very much like Britain, but in the Caribbean she felt more at an advantage in terms of knowing some of the right people. In Britain, her social circles were limited and chances of improving them were nil:

> I don't have too many networks so I am now having to build them. I feel at a disadvantage, since Jamaica runs on networks. I am not in the in-crowd. That puts me at a disadvantage here. I don't have the right name, have not gone to the right school or have the right parents to take advantage of that here in Jamaica where that's all important. All I have is that drive that I had from the UK and my qualifications. I have to develop networks in Jamaica. (JRRI 150A)

Coming to terms with the class and colour issues in Jamaica and Barbados was quite sobering for our sample of interviewees. Most had constructed an image of the Caribbean as being devoid of colour stratification issues in terms of socializing, hiring or promotion practices. However, the legacy of colonialism and class hierarchies which formed after emancipation (circa 1834) still remains very much entrenched in the psyche of the local population (Marshall 1982). Learning to accept and work in a class-conscious atmosphere was difficult for our interviewees. Many had an idealized picture of a meritocracy in the Caribbean that would not be based on class hierarchies. When most realized that, just like in Britain, "race", class and gender inequalities were very much interwoven into the fabric of Caribbean society, many felt a sense of being let down. Tracy, a forty-year-old Jamaican-born accountant, makes an important comment when she talks about the class issue:

> The class thing is a serious issue, because a working-class person in England is very different from a working-class person in Jamaica. A working-class person in Jamaica, basically, expects you to give them orders, they don't expect you to ask for their opinion. They're not meant to be party to decision, so you're supposed to tell them what to do, which is quite difficult. I think, for a lot of us from England we use a language which conveys a message that is not necessarily an order, even though we want them to do something. We are not ordering them, we're just asking them. And we also say "please" too often, we say "thank-you" too often. We say too many words in a sentence for most Jamaicans. We have a strange accent, and we have a funny colour. The accent they don't associate with the colour on the face, so we have a problem with that. (JE 016 1A)

The final area that seemed to come up in a great number of our interviews as being difficult for the returnees to contend with was the male/female dynamic in the Caribbean. This parallels Gmelch and Gmelch's (1995) study which found that a significantly large number of single, elderly women returning to Barbados faced particular cultural readjustment issues in terms of male/female roles and dynamics. Since the majority of our sample were women returnees, it was not surprising that the same issue emerged as being important in their adjustment to Caribbean society. According to Tiffany, a thirty-eight-year-old Jamaican-born computer programmer, it seems that Caribbean society is not ready to tolerate platonic male/female relationships. The range of male and female relationships that she and others were accustomed to in Britain was not easily replicable in the Caribbean. For many of our interviewees, this was frustrating because they were accustomed to having "men friends" and not worrying about what others thought about the relationship. Tiffany's reflection about life in Jamaica provides us with some insight into the negotiation for second-generation women returnees:

> The relationship between men and women here has been different. . . . I am accustomed to very close platonic friendships with men in the UK, here in Jamaica they are a problem. Men and women seem to relate in very distinct ways . . . actually one or two ways, there is not the diversity that I am accustomed to . . . so that tends to make me feel a little outside of the mainstream. . . . I am also perceived as "English". In some ways they are impressed and attracted by this, but in other ways it scares them. (JR 093 2A)

## Coping Strategies for Adjusting to Life
## in Jamaica and Barbados

In the final section of the chapter, we examine the coping strategies put into place by our sample of second-generation British-Caribbean returnees. Most of our interviewees had innovative strategies they used to "maintain sanity", as Arlene puts it. Her coping strategy is unique, but it highlights for us the extreme measures taken by second-generation returnees in order to avoid feeling frustrated. They often try to meld their own "British quirks" into the local pattern of activity. In Arlene's case, she is someone who likes to be efficient in her day-to-day activities. Given the "inefficiencies" of life in Jamaica, Arlene was quite maddened when she first arrived. In order to cope with the situation, Arlene came to realize that the only way to maintain her perception of efficiency was to come up with innovative strategies for circumventing the exisisting culture of "slowness", as she put it:

> I am still learning how to live in Jamaica. Actually, I have nine bank accounts because I hate to waste time and wait in line. I have narrowed it down to which bank can get me in and out in the shortest time. I have four hairdressers and five supermarkets depending on what time of day. I try to make life based on my lifestyle in which I don't like to waste time. Jamaicans can at times be so slow and inefficient. (JE 016 1A)

For others, developing a more laid back attitude towards their day-to-day activity was the solution. Letter writing, email and telephoning friends and family back in England was sometimes found to be a source to vent frustration. This also allowed some individuals to "maintain a level perspective" according to Dan, a thirty-two-year-old Barbadian-born manager. What did come out in every interview was the fact that individuals maintained a strong link with Britain. This transnational link was mainly in terms of return visits to see family – visits to settle matters related to investments or property, or to seek out health-care. In commenting on his own situation, Dan notes the importance of his transnational link:

> I go back to England every year. Every year I go home. Oh yeh. Yeh, I keep in contact. Barbados is so small you need to get off the island. And because I'm the only one here I feel lonely sometimes. My two sisters are there. I don't have that sibling contact you know? And to me, it's important, because you have

friends, but there's nothing like your family. And as I said, when we were growing up, we were very close. So it's important for me to see them, and to see the nieces and nephews. (BF021 1A)

The transnational link was also revealed quite strongly in terms of feelings of nationalism towards Britain. Although most second-generation returnees felt very anti-Britain before migrating, almost all developed a much greater tolerance for Britain since living in the Caribbean. This tolerance was attributed to the fact that individuals came to realize just how "British" they really were in terms of cultural socialization and mannerisms, as well as likes and dislikes. Cheryl, a Jamacian-born thirty-two-year-old, reflected on her identity before and since migrating and made this point quite clearly:

> Before I left Britain I probably would not have said I was Jamaican per se, but I wouldn't necessarily be extolling the virtues of being English and British. But it's when you come here, and you realize how you behave. Even in a work setting, things that I would never have thought of in England, just in terms of turning up on time, your expectations of how meetings will go, the fact that you'll have a meeting and people will agree to do things, and they will actually go away and do it. . . . We were in England for a substantial period of time, it formed your life, and that's it, and there's no running away from it. I think some of us were running away from it. I'm not sure I was running away from it, but maybe aspects of it. But the reality is that it's part of you. That's what you are. (JRO93 2A)

## Conclusion

This chapter began with a sentiment by Arlene, reflecting on her family's reaction to her decision to take her family and return to Jamaica. Her sentiment highlights the fact that despite concerted efforts to be accepted as a Jamaican she was considered to be making a step backwards in the eyes of many members of her family and the Jamaican host population. Returning as a young, working-age person to the Caribbean – particularly when one does not have to – is regarded as being a "failure" by many residents in Jamaica because the traditional historic flow of young bodies is outward from the region in order to make a better life for oneself and to create new opportunities for family left behind (Marshall 1982; Thomas-Hope 1992). The local

population and culture is conditioned to be more welcoming and understanding of the elder generation of returnees who move back after twenty-
five or thirty years of being away. This group is acceptable because they have
followed the traditional "culture of migration" pattern – they went away,
they worked hard, they sent back remittances to family and kin, and then
they returned when they reached old age (Marshall 1982). For the cohort of
second-generation returnees in this study, however, the action of moving
back while still young represents an unnatural event because it breaks the
culture of migration cycle. By returning to work, and therefore using up
scarce resources, second-generation British Caribbeans are inadvertently
making it more difficult for local young people to get access to the limited
supply of good jobs. As a result, young, skilled second-generation British-
Caribbean returnees are often regarded more as a threat to the local population than an asset. It is, therefore, of little surprise that the second-generation
returnees in this sample all ironically reported feeling like foreigners and
unwelcome in the place they regarded as their "home".

As a result of being treated like outsiders, the idyllic reconnection with
the Caribbean that many second-generation returnees dreamed about has
not really materialized according to plan. The mobility opportunities and the
society have been greatly affected over the last decade by the new factors of
structural adjustment and globalization. The island paradise that many
recalled from childhood memories, earlier holiday visits or family stories was
quite different once they moved there permanently. The issues of "race",
gender, skin colour and class politics linger below the surface in both Jamaica
and Barbados and prevent many second-generation British Caribbeans
from making a smooth transition into their "home" societies. For a second-
generation returnee who has parachuted into this milieu, these realities can
be overwhelming and shocking, to say the least.

Undoubtedly, most people that we interviewed were glad that they had
lived out one of their life ambitions, that is, returning to and living in the
only place they considered "home". Having lived in the Caribbean, these
individuals seem to come to a new understanding of Britain and their own
"Britishness". Some of our interviewees are considering returning to Britain
or moving to the United States. Most are making long-term plans to live a
transnational lifestyle. This involves having a business or occupation which
allows them to function in either the Caribbean or Britain at various times of
the year.

## Acknowledgements

An earlier version of this chapter, entitled "In Pursuit of the Mobility Dream: Second Generation British Caribbeans Returning to Jamaica and Barbados", was published in the *Journal of Eastern Caribbean Studies* 27, no. 4 (2001).

## Notes

1.  All primary references, unless otherwise stated, are interview data collected in the Economic and Social Research Council research programme on Population and Household Change. The project is entitled Family Structure and Social Change of Caribbeans in Britain. The data tapes are deposited with the Economic and Social Research Council Qualidata Resource Center at the University of Essex. The tape reference is divided into three parts. First, the letter refers to the place of origin of the respondent: J is for Jamaican and B is for Barbados; second, the number refers to the family code; and third, the last numbers are the tape number and the side (A or B) of the tape where the quote was taken.
2.  This Economic and Social Research Council-funded project was led by professors Harry Goulbourne and Mary Chamberlain. Dwaine Plaza was the post-doctoral research fellow and David Owen was a research partner on the project.

## References

Bhalla, A., and K. Blakemore. 1981. *Elders of the Minority Ethnic Groups.* Birmingham: AFOR Press.

Byron, M. 2000. Return Migration to the Eastern Caribbean: Comparative Experiences and Policy Implications. *Social and Economic Studies* 49 (4): 155–88.

Byron, M., and S. Condon. 1996. A Comparative Study of Caribbean Migration from Britain and France: Towards a Context-Dependent Explanation. *Transactions of the Institute of British Geographers* 21 (2): 91–204.

Chamberlain, M. 1997. *Narratives of Exile and Return.* London: Macmillan Press, University of Warwick Caribbean Studies Series.

Fenton, S. 1986. *Ageing Minorities, Black People as they Grow Old in Britain.* London: CRE.

Gmelch, G. 1980. Return Migration. *Anthropol* 9 (1): 135–59.

————. 1987. Work, Innovation and Investment: The Impact of Return Migrants in Barbados. *Human Organization* 46 (2): 131–40.

Gmelch, G., and S.B. Gmelch. 1995. Gender and Migration: The Readjustment of Women Migrants in Barbados, Ireland and Newfoundland. *Human Organization* 54 (4): 470–73.

Goulbourne, H., and M. Chamberlain. 2001. *Caribbean Families in the Transatlantic World.* London: Macmillian, University of Warwick Caribbean Studies Series.

Hall, S. 1988. Migration from the English-Speaking Caribbean to the United Kingdom, 1950–1980. In *International Migration Today,* vol. 1, ed. R. Appleyard, 45–72. Paris: UNESCO.

Jones, Trevor. 1993. *Britain's Ethnic Minorities: An Analysis of the Labour Force Survey.* London: Policy Studies Institute.

Marshall, D. 1982. The History of Caribbean Migrations. *Caribbean Review* 11 (1): 6–19.

Nanton, P. 1997. The Caribbean Diaspora in the Promised Land. In *London: The Promised Land? The Migrant Experience in the Capital City,* ed. A. Kerstein, 246–81. Aldershot: Averbury.

Peach, C. 1991. *The Caribbean in Europe: Contrasting Patterns of Migration and Settlement in Britain, France and the Netherlands.* Research Paper in Ethnic Relations, no. 15. Coventry: Centre for Research in Ethnic Relations, Warwick University.

Philpot, S.B. 1973. *West Indian Migration: The Montserrat Case.* London: Athlone Press.

Strauss, A., and J. Corbin. 1990. *Basics of Qualitative Research: Grounded Theory Procedures and Techniques.* Newbury Park, CA: Sage.

Thomas-Hope, E. 1992. *Explanation in Caribbean Migration.* London: Macmillan Press.

CHAPTER 8

# Maximizing Migration

## Caribbean Return Movements and the Organization of Transnational Space

| Elizabeth Thomas-Hope |

## Introduction

Caribbean migration has always been associated not only with the movement of people but also the circulation of capital. This is a critical issue that is often subsumed, namely that it is in the movement of people as bearers of various forms of capital that the transnational space is configured. Thus the space is characterized not simply in terms of the shape of the space, of which the parameters are the locations of the movement, but also the texture of the space, containing tangible resources and social capital as personal socio-cultural, economic and political networks variously extend over more than one country. For while the movement is certain to involve people, it also involves the transfer of money, goods and services, information, and ideas so that systems of circulation become established and perpetuated by the recurrent movements of people and all forms of capital flows. The transnational space is therefore textured by the networks and the value or meaning ascribed to those networks by the migrants as they make decisions to move within and establish transnational livelihoods. The extent to which the return is part of the maximization of the migration is, therefore, the extent to which the migrants are strategic in the ways that they relate to the challenges and opportunities provided by their transnational space.

Who moves outwards, like who returns, is determined by factors of selectivity that originate in international and national relationships and, at the same time, in community, family and individual livelihood strategies. Neither the outward nor the return moves are confined to one type of person or carried out for a single purpose. On the contrary, persons of all ages, male and female, in all professions as well as the unemployed, dependents and students have been and continue to be engaged in the outward and return migration processes (Thomas-Hope 2002a).

This chapter illustrates the nature of return migration as an essential aspect of the circulation that defines the parameters of individual and shared transnational space. Further, it highlights the ways in which this space is constructed and used strategically, in the sense that it is negotiated by migrants in an effort to maximize the value of their migration.

## From Labour Migration to Transnationalism

The demand for labour in metropolitan projects located in the Caribbean region provided the opportunities for migration in the late-nineteenth and early-twentieth centuries. These were in railway engineering, the Panama Canal construction, fruit company operations, as well as the expansion of sugar, oil and tourist industries. Later opportunities came in the United States, the United Kingdom and, from the mid-1960s, in Canada as well.

The labour migrations associated with these projects formed the basis for the establishment of linkages that ultimately evolved to produce the transnational networks between and within countries in the Caribbean as well as between the Caribbean and countries of North America and western Europe. These networks provided the social capital that facilitated the movement of other persons. The linkages that were maintained between members of households and families across national boundaries were critical for providing the opportunities to return periodically or permanently. It has become common for migrants to return to their Caribbean country of origin for occasional or regular visits over a prolonged period of time after which some return to reside indefinitely while others continue to circulate. At the same time, the networks have provided the means whereby migrants return to their home country without losing their base abroad and therefore their access to those countries and other places in the future. In addition to the movement of persons, an important feature was also the movement of all forms of capital – social and material – between household and family members abroad and those in the Caribbean.

Throughout the last three decades of the twentieth century, the return movements from the United Kingdom and North America increased dramatically, as also did the circulation and dual residency of persons or households straddling more than one country. This circulation provided a new trend in the Caribbean migration pattern. Livelihoods became increasingly based in more than one country simultaneously as well as sequentially. The livelihoods of these transnational persons invariably involved working in one place and context, maintaining their families in another, and socializing, making purchases of goods and services, investing, and engaging in leisure pursuits that spanned at least two countries. The individual could thus live in one place but rely upon another for current and future support and rewards. The livelihood of the individual became defined by the total space, not just one segment of it that approximated, or was confined to, national boundaries – not even to their country of citizenship or principal country of residence at any particular period of time (Thomas-Hope 2002b). The transnational aspect of the lives of the returnees developed and was sustained by the transnational pattern of their personal movements, as well as from their generation of social and economic capital.

These new transnational livelihoods and identities formed the basis of new elements in Caribbean cultural construction and new meaning to the idea of locality and "home". Above all, transnationalism has always been dynamic; it changes and will continue to change in various ways and it is perpetuated by the extent and value of the movements that occur within the fields or spaces of migration.

Despite the evidence of significant return and reciprocal moves of people between Caribbean countries and migration destinations in North America and western Europe, the migration process itself has persistently been regarded by scholars and policy makers as a series of linear flows from points of origin to destination – return migration being the move from destination to origin – with migration viewed solely in terms of population displacement. Yet, when Caribbean international migration is examined in its entirety, activities at places of migration origin and destination are seen to be intrinsically linked. The presence of migrants abroad, as also their pattern of return, is seen to be part of the wider transnational system of outflow, interaction, circulation and feedback of various types as well as being viewed as the transnationalization of social capital (Thomas-Hope 1986, 1988; Georges 1990; Schiller, Basch and Blanc-Szanton 1995).

The networks transmit both multilateral and bilateral interactions. The motivations for the perpetuation of the connections are variously political, social, domestic and emotional, as well as economic and market-driven. The dynamic of this phenomenon is generated by interactions and linkages at all levels: regions and nations, organizations and institutions, as well as communities, families, households and individuals.

On returning to their country of origin, migrants develop strategies at various levels for coping with the demands of more than one place and, to greater or lesser extent, must be able to adjust and readjust within such an international environment. Their lives remain closely linked to the country abroad in which they had previously resided before their return. They retain connections through their social networks and financial and welfare benefits and through their pattern of investment.

## Return Migrants to Jamaica

The experiences of return migrants are represented in this chapter by thirty-seven migrants selected from a group of fifty-eight professionals who returned to Jamaica between 1996 and 2000.[1] They comprised a distinctive group of returnees on the basis of their demographic, occupational and educational qualifications. They were all participants in the Return of Talent programme, a scheme sponsored by the Government of Jamaica with the assistance of the International Organization for Migration that provided financial supplementary support for a period of two years, during which time the returnees were obliged to take employment in the public sector (IOM 1998).

Because of the nature of the programme's selectivity, the return migrants were all active in the workforce, not retired as are many persons at the time of their return. More than two-thirds of the group were between the ages of thirty-one and fifty and the rest over fifty when they returned, having initially migrated between ages twenty-five and thirty-five either to take up employment or pursue studies. They were all professionals – the group included senior directors, administrators and project officers in government ministries and agencies, university lecturers, engineers, architects and medical personnel. Again, consistent with the nature of the employment gaps they were intended to fill, all had tertiary education, with 42.9 per cent holding a master's degree and 20 per cent a doctorate. In a number of cases (45.7 per cent), the returnees had received at least part of their tertiary or professional education in Jamaica.

Men comprised 62.9 per cent of the sample population and women 37.1 per cent. The majority (51.4 per cent) had returned to Jamaica from the United States of America; 14.3 per cent each from Canada and the United Kingdom; 17 per cent from locations in the Caribbean; one person from having lived and studied in Poland. Most persons interviewed had returned between 1995 and 1996, two had returned between 1993 and 1994, and six in 1997. Some persons in the group had already returned to Jamaica and were in the process of taking up employment prior to knowing about and later being accepted into the Return of Talent Programme. Others had made the decision to return and then took the opportunity of applying to the programme so as to gain the financial benefits it offered (Thomas-Hope 2002b).

## Maximization of Migration through the Return

From the outset, all migrants, to a greater or lesser extent, share some common objectives of migration. In the Caribbean, migration has provided expanded environments of opportunity, but for most people its success is based on the relationships maintained with the place of migration – the "homeland". For the homeland provides the psychological support and a sense of belonging that is only, in a minority of cases, superseded or replaced by attachments generated abroad.

The key to establishing successful transnationalism and thus the ability to maximize the migration experience is conditioned by the nature of the organization of personal and collective space within which the migrants function. The maximization of the return becomes possible chiefly through the migrants' development of transnational networks and livelihoods around which their transnational space is constructed and organized:

1.  The return ensures the freedom to circulate between countries of migration origin and destination and, in so doing, maximizing the benefits of both countries and minimizing the constraints of each.

2.  The return allows the migration effort to be valorized in the country of origin.

3.  The return permits reincorporation into the country of origin and therefore the reclaiming of "home". At the same time, the returnee can retain rights of entry and even citizenship in the country of former residence.

Full incorporation of the return migrant requires their adjustment to the home society – a process that demands their strategic negotiation of the culture and conditions of the renewed place of residence. Success in maximizing migration through the opportunities of the return varies considerably. In some cases the migrant becomes a well-adjusted transnational person able to optimize the potential of the return, while in other cases the migrant finds the challenges of negotiating the space too difficult and reverses his or her situation by going back or retreating to the previous position of living abroad.

### Construction of Transnationalism for Maximizing Freedom

Migrants at their destinations abroad seek freedom from the constraints of their home country. These constraints include the limitations of small size and, therefore, of opportunities for work, career development and the rigidities of the accepted channels of upward mobility and recognition. In the Caribbean, migration provided the freedom from economic limitations and social rigidities but rarely an emotional substitute for "home". One returnee indicated the following: "I'm home in the place where I feel comfortable. When you live in the USA or Canada, the question of colour always seems to come up. I've never felt that I ought to remain in either country and be regarded as a minority." Another of the returnees explained that he was now in receipt of a Canadian state pension and held a senior advisory position in the public sector in Jamaica – a job that gives him "satisfaction and a sense of belonging". He claimed however, that he had not made a "wholesale return" (author's personal interviews with returnees 1999–2000).

One return migrant indicated that all her children were in Canada and made this point: "You do become part of that society. And I had lived in Canada for a longer time than I had lived in Jamaica." Yet, as she explained, incorporation into society at the migration destination had also been difficult: "As a black person living in a Euro-dominated society, you always have to prove yourself. Though even in Jamaica this feeling sometimes exists; women are not treated well in Jamaica. It is like pushing against the tide."

The objectives of migration are therefore maximized through the return where the acknowledged success vindicates the effort and even the sacrifices that were made in migrating. Home reinforces the sense of legitimacy and belonging. Upon return, the migrants "escape" the economic pressures, social rigidities and racial marginalization that restricted full incorporation at the destination. At the same time they ensure that the economic security and access to the country of residence abroad are not lost in the process. Migrants spoke of moving away from the racism that they encountered in the country abroad and of their enjoying the sense of being "home". Nevertheless, in many cases total reincorporation was difficult. The aim had to be to negotiate between the positive and negative aspects of both places and to adjust to living within that context. Efforts to do so were based upon maintaining access to more than one place and developing livelihoods based on multiple locations, maintaining dual citizenship or work and residence permits, or through the transfer of their way of life at former migration destinations abroad back to Jamaica.

## Multi-location Accessibility

The access to more than one country is maintained through personal circulation as well as the social networks and economic linkages that characterize the organization of the transnational space of the returnees.

### *Personal Circulation and Social Networks*

A considerable amount of personal transnational circulation continued throughout the migrants' lives. The majority of return migrants returned periodically (many annually) to the country of their previous residence, reflecting a strong tendency to spend vacations in familiar places abroad and usually reinforcing social and family connections at those places.

Networks of family members and friends always spanned at least two countries. Family members (invariably adult children) and friends resided in the country of their previous residence and remained part of the interactive space of the migrants on their return. The social networks of most of the returnees were primarily based in a country overseas or equally overseas and locally in Jamaica. Only a small percentage of migrants participated in networks of friends who were mostly or almost entirely Jamaica-based after their return. The social networks of the returnees comprised some persons whom they had known prior to migrating from Jamaica and others whom they had met since their return. There was, therefore, quite considerable continuity or reconnecting with the social networks that had existed prior to migrating, but to an even greater extent was the establishment of new social connections since the return.

The social networks were truly transnational in nature, comprising a combination of persons whom the returnees had met prior to migrating, while living abroad and since returning. Generally, however, when comparing these three components of the returnees' social networks, the largest group of current contacts had been developed while the migrants were based overseas.

## Flows of Financial Capital

Contrary to the general pattern observed for returning migrants that had retired, persons returning to work did not tend to remit substantial sums of money. Some even sent money back from Jamaica to the country abroad to support family members, in particular children who had not accompanied them on their return.

Almost half the number of persons in the sample population would be entitled to social security payments from the country of their former residence and/or state pensions when they reached retirement age. A small number, upon retirement in Jamaica, would also be in receipt of company pensions from their previous place of work abroad. The sense of financial security was largely supported by the external country to which they had previously migrated. This money would in due course be remitted to the migrant in Jamaica, provided that they had not re-migrated before retiring.

In terms of the purchase of goods, the majority of returnees did most of their shopping for personal and professional goods outside of Jamaica. Overall, therefore, the orientation in terms of the acquisition of goods remained largely external.

Despite the emphasis on consumer purchasing overseas, the pattern of investing was different. The majority of returnees currently tended to invest in Jamaica more than they did abroad. Although any investment of the money earned in Jamaica remained in the country, at the same time, as indicated above, income earned abroad was usually left there and not repatriated. Maintaining income abroad was regarded to be of great importance to ensure financial security at the overseas point of their migration space. Only in a few cases, where the migrants had only just entered their professional life prior to returning, did a return migrant close the prospect for keeping investments or savings in the country of previous residence.

With respect to health insurance, some persons or their dependants no longer had any health insurance in a country abroad and thus relied totally on health care in Jamaica. Nevertheless, a significant proportion did still retain access to health care facilities overseas and were very conscious of the fact that in the event of requiring these services, they would immediately return to that country to avail themselves of them.

So global in scope were the livelihoods and livelihood strategies of the return migrants that they not only spanned more than one country but actually depended on more than one country for what they regarded as a satisfactory livelihood and lifestyle. These were associated with identities that have no fixed cultural reference. Besides, they were predisposed to remain in a state of continuous transit with a sense that there were future movements still to come. The fact that a total displacement of the migrants did not occur among the skilled returning nationals in this study, but that there was a strong persistence of the role of places of previous migration destinations in their lives demonstrated the transnational character of their livelihoods. As in the outward phase of the migrations discussed above, so in the return phase, work and a range of social processes incorporated more than one location that extended across international boundaries based on the migration process.

In addition to organizing the infrastructure of the transnational space on the basis the various networks established and social capital generated, the migrants also retained transnational identities that permitted them to feel part of and gain access to more than the one country.

## Transnational Identity and Citizenship

The return migrants negotiated their transnational space so that they could reclaim their identification with home and the legitimacy of belonging while at the same time retain their rights of access to their former country of residence abroad. As the geographic parameters of action and the boundaries of livelihood changed, so did the migrants' citizenship options and relationships. The negotiations between two national states became complex. The migrants themselves were forced into a repositioning of self in relation to the former place of residence abroad through which they experienced a transition of consciousness, a transition in being and a transition in the very sense of self.

It was evident among the returnees to Jamaica that just as in the initial emigration, so in the return moves, the negative factors were generally minimized in the minds of those who wanted to move and had the opportunity of doing so. However, prior to returning, the migrants all ensured that they had established their residency or citizenship status in their country of destination abroad. The majority had dual citizenship and held a passport of another country as well as a Jamaican passport. Many also had residency entitlements in another country in addition to Jamaica. This was the "safety valve" that their transnationalism provided, should they decide to leave Jamaica again for short or long periods of time at some later date. Many returns were, therefore, tentative in nature. Above all, the returnees were clearly disposed towards further movement abroad of varying duration. Nearly three-quarters of the sample felt that they might or definitely would be going abroad to live and work again before reaching retirement. Most would return to the country in which they had previously lived, though there were some who felt that they would not necessarily return to their previous place of residence. This showed a penchant for future mobility, even to new destinations.

The returnees held a Jamaican passport mainly because of their sense of, and commitment to, "being Jamaican". Yet although most of them had a strong sense of Jamaican identity, there was some ambivalence among others. Besides, the situation was complicated by the weaker commitment to Jamaica on the part of non-Jamaican born spouses; there was a clear commitment in fewer than half the cases in the study population. The commitment to Jamaica of the children of the returnees was weaker still. For transnational persons who returned to their country of birth, the experience of belonging and yet not belonging was a profound and persistent aspect of their transnational identity.

## *Sense of Identity*

The sense of "being Jamaican" was of major importance to most persons and was associated with the significance placed upon "belonging". This surpassed the negative feelings that emerged after returning. It was stated by one returnee that, despite everything, "Jamaica is home and I am glad that I returned, even though I did not have any bad experiences abroad."

The intensely unsettling emotion resulted from the conflict of feelings experienced in being connected to place as part of the intrinsic reality of "home" and, at the same time, the difficulty or inability encountered in the relocating of self at "home". The result was that returnees kept all options open and thus the return was reaffirmed consciously and subconsciously as merely a stage in the process – not an end in itself. As put by one of the returnees: "Despite the problems, I am glad to be back home, where my navel-string is, and any plan to return to the United States will be due primarily to my depleted financial status." Yet another declared, "I do keep my Jamaican passport, because it is my identity."

Nevertheless, a strong sense of a Jamaican identity was not seen to conflict with the feeling that they would necessarily remain in Jamaica, since they were able to maximize their migration through the freedom of having the choice to circulate within a transnational space. As one returnee stated:

> I am Jamaican from head to toe but travelling enables me to enjoy various cultures and see things in a broader perspective. . . . I definitely intend to go abroad again to live, though I am not quite sure where. I hold dual citizenship. Readapting to Jamaica had its hitches. . . . After two years you tend to get back to a decision-making state of mind – do I stay, do I go back? . . . I am not necessarily happy with the direction some things are going or have gone [in Jamaica] and I could honestly say that if I had not returned, economically I would have been better off. But here is Yard. Here is home.

There were others whose nationalism within the transnational context was not so clear. One of the migrants, a doctor, had left Jamaica when she was in her teens. She had returned to do voluntary work in Jamaica for two years but then got married and took advantage of the Return of Talent programme to obtain the financial benefits being offered. She felt herself to be "half and half" Jamaican and Canadian.

## Reconstruction of the Culture of Home

The transnational space is also organized so as to create the conditions that are deemed desirable to exist in the home country to which the migrants had returned. As part of the strategy of readjustment on the return, the migrants consciously or subconsciously attempted, in various direct and indirect ways, to create in Jamaica the kind of system, organization and ethic of the work environment so that it would be more like that to which they had become accustomed abroad. This invariably involved the returnees working much harder than they would have abroad in order to achieve the same work objectives in Jamaica.

In terms of adapting to Jamaica, one return migrant from the United Kingdom explained, "I think it is good to separate adapting into two categories: social and professional. Socially it really was not a problem. But professionally it's a bit different, because in Jamaica the way that the professional activities run is different from abroad. Professionally there is a big difference."

In many cases attempts were also made by the return migrants to reconstruct the material environment of their houses. The significance of the way that the space of the returnees was constructed or organized is highlighted by the conscious efforts made by other migrants to avoid falling into an old pattern. This was pointed out by the person who, on returning, brought back very little furniture and household equipment because, she explained, "I do not believe in creating Canada in Jamaica."

The migrants' attempts on their return to construct the kind of environment that they regarded desirable also extended to the wider community and nation. Indeed, part of the perceived achievement of migration was to be able to make an impact upon the community and country. This was seen by the return migrants as a desire to contribute to Jamaica's "development" and they became frustrated when they encountered no wholehearted demand for, or receptiveness to, such change at the local level. Nevertheless, there was strong belief that the values and conditions of the place of previous residence should be transferred to Jamaica. This was evident in the migrants' views that migration provided a "value added" dimension to whatever might otherwise have been possible had an individual not had the experience of working and living abroad.

## Valorization of Migration

### *Making a Contribution to Jamaica*

The view of many return migrants in the Return of Talent programme was that it was a good programme since, from an individual point of view, it provided the opportunity to make a contribution to the "home" society. From the local society's point of view, the belief was that benefits were obtained from those who returned. There was absolutely no doubt in any of the returnees' minds other than, as stated by one person, "experience abroad definitely counted for a lot . . . almost anything that took place in Jamaica could benefit from return migrants in the sphere of knowledge and experience". This was reinforced by others: "I think that my experience abroad is very valuable. It gives me another perspective. . . . the whole aspect of bringing comparative approaches and comparative analysis."

Most of the migrants felt that the position to which they had been posted could not have been adequately filled without recruitment. This view was expressed in various ways as in the case of the individual who believed that there were "benefits in bringing nationals back home even in cases where vacancies could be filled locally". She was of the opinion that "educated Jamaicans abroad should return to assist". Another returnee's view was that "a local person could not have filled the position I currently hold because of the absence of a certain level of expertise. I therefore feel that there is an advantage in bringing Jamaican nationals back home even for vacancies that could be filled locally."

Other ideas of how Jamaicans abroad could assist in a material way to improve the situation in Jamaica were expressed thus: "In terms of access to resources . . . my being here provides a direct link to a wider base of resources abroad that I can tap into and that benefits what I'm doing here." It was further maintained that "we are in positions that can influence decisions and public policy abroad that can benefit Jamaica". In similar vein another returnee stated the following: "I feel very positive about the fact that I've come back to my own country to serve the way I want to in the field of education."

Further views of how overseas Jamaican nationals could help were indicated, as in the words of one of the returnees: "I would say send money home. The country badly needs it." Another opinion was that "every national abroad should have a money account in the country of his birth". Also vehemently expressed was the opinion that "there needs to be a common thread that binds all Jamaicans worldwide together, and if we harness it, it becomes natural for them to want to contribute to the country".

## Negotiation of the Transnational Space in the Migrants' Adjustment on Their Return

The professional persons returning to Jamaica were aware that to maximize the benefits of their migration they had to negotiate their way around the constraints of the system.

Undoubtedly, the present-day first-time Caribbean outward migrant traverses a transnational space that has been created by previous movement. Yet the individual invariably enters that space without really appreciating its full complexity. Certainly the outgoing first-time migrant was generally unaware that they and their identities would be changed by the migration experience and that this would make difficult the later reincorporation into their country of origin. Some migrants had become aware of this during their residency abroad and realized that it was only through maintaining close contact with Jamaica while they were away that they would be able to readjust fairly quickly on their return. The return migrant was much more aware of the nature of the space and felt confident to both traverse and reorganize it.

### Adjusting to Living in Jamaica

All return migrants in the study were acutely aware of the need to adjust in order to become fully incorporated into society. They were facilitated in many ways but also confronted by a number of challenges.

The circumstances that chiefly facilitated the adjustment process were based primarily on the personal support of family and friends. But some migrants knew that to adjust they themselves had to actively engage the situation. The experience of one of the returnees was that it was fairly easy for him to readapt to living in Jamaica: "While still in the US, I was mentally preparing myself for my return. This has to be done to adjust to Jamaica. It included expecting the electricity to be off, expecting water lock-offs, expecting the phones not to work. If you do not psyche yourself up for these things, you will have problems."

The living conditions were in most cases regarded as being very favourable, but many returnees recorded their dissatisfaction with the social aspects of life that they found in Jamaica on their return. Others were aware of the need for improvement but did not feel unduly dissatisfied about the situation. There were more negative feelings about the economic aspects of Jamaica. Though there were some also who had no complaints, there were others who felt that although there was room for improvement, the situation did not prevent their level of readjustment.

There were various factors that presented challenges to achieving the comfort level to which migrants aspired. For some it was based primarily on what was described as "the negative nature of the work ethic as well as the country's social problems". This person regarded the social conditions in Jamaica as "very unsatisfactory, and the economic conditions as even worse". Some of the areas of social decay to which he referred were the poor standards of public service, the treatment and care given to children and the elderly and the poor quality of medical care. Other negatives were "the level of crime . . . and the lack of professionalism on the part of public sector workers".

There were further areas of frustration voiced in terms of aspects of life reflecting the bureaucracy. One of the return migrants maintained that "there are some impediments to returning to Jamaica – the customs, for example. I think I had to spend two days trying to clear my stuff". Further views expressed were that "[in Jamaica] you have systems that are a blockage"; and yet another person expressed a similar observation: "in Jamaica, the bureaucracy is stifling".

There was much greater ease in relating to local practices and culture. Although some migrants found some practices frustrating as expressed for instance, in comments such as the following: "I hate waiting in long lines, for example, at ATM machines, and I only wait in these lines when I absolutely have to."

## Adjustment to the Work Environment

In terms of work, well over half of the returnees in the programme had definitely or largely retained their former patterns of work and found readjustment to Jamaican work patterns very difficult. This was repeatedly expressed in terms such as that of one person who said, "I have to work harder in Jamaica than I did in the US because the level of the support staff is not as high." Many carried on through their determination to succeed in their objectives. For example, one returnee felt that he was "able to work as effectively in Jamaica as abroad because of my determination and the availability of key basic facilities".

Although the work environment did not generally provide an incentive to return to Jamaica, most kept trying to maintain the work patterns and aspirations developed abroad. The effort to adjust to local work patterns thus produced a great source of frustration for many. It was as though their motivation to achieve and their orientation towards identified goals could not be easily compromised or abandoned because it had become so intricately linked to their self-assessment of success versus failure, their *raison d'être* and, therefore, their sense of themselves. Thus the option of re-entering the work environment of the country of previous migration or elsewhere was frequently considered by many in the group.

## Balancing between Cultures as
## Part of the Strategy of Adjustment

Transnationalism is necessarily associated with the complexity of merged cultures giving rise to variants of a hybrid culture. Those who are able to balance the bi- or multiculturalism of their transnationalism are then best able to adjust. They become incorporated into the home society, thus enhancing the process of maximizing their migration. The success in achieving this was expressed by one returnee: "I am a balanced bi-cultural person." Another of the returnees expressed his sense of cultural hybridity in terms of being part of a global culture stating the following: "I regard myself as a global individual, not restricted professionally or otherwise. I am glad to be back in Jamaica because this is where I need to be at this time."

Some persons remained in a state of perpetual motion in terms of place. Consequently they were in an ongoing state of ambivalence about staying in Jamaica. The options were always consciously kept open and periodically considered. A number of the return migrants stated that they were aware that the decision to reside abroad again, as one person put it, "will be an issue to be dealt with in due course". The balancing is difficult for many return migrants thus fuelling the sense of not being grounded in any particular locality within the transnational space. This situation was, however, itself a way of adjusting and using that space as a means of facilitating a fluidity of commitment – the commitment being to the overall space rather than any one locality within it. The sense of centrality and marginality became blurred and sometimes they even changed dramatically.

## Interpretations of the Return as Maximizing Migration in the Context of Transnationalism

Conceptualizations of return migration as a component of transnationalism raise several theoretical issues, including the following:

1. The ways in which the return can be characterized as circulation defines the parameters of the transnational space;
2. Transnationalism is associated with the sense that centrality and marginality are blurred so that their significance to migration is removed (Guarnizo and Smith 1999);
3. The return is critical in determining the nature and organization of the transnational space;
4. Transnationalism reflects a weakened nationalism with the movements effectively occurring between borderless states.

Transnationalism may be interpreted as a form of resistance "from below" and the means of personally negotiating the benefits of migration from the perspective of, and managed by, the migrants themselves. These benefits are derived partly in the locality of migration – the destination country or countries overseas – and also in the home country where the major material gains of the migration are seen to be maximized. This material enhancement is invariably through lifestyle enhancement upon return.

From a non-material standpoint, the gains of migration are based on the status determined by qualifications and professional levels achieved. Negotiating the existing structures is required to avoid the frustration of the migrant and the negation of the benefits they could bring to any particular work or social situation.

New economic relations derived from transnational business operations, multipositional identities and dual- or multicultural lives (referred to elsewhere as "hybrid cultures") permit strategies of escape from the control of the societal systems of both states. The return migrants/transnational persons avoid racism, social exclusion and other possible negatives at the destination while enjoying the economic, experiential and training benefits of work in the centres of global capital. Furthermore, the transnational person returns to the locus of emotional security and comfort levels of "home" while at the same time retaining the citizenship status and access to a country elsewhere and its benefits.

Migration is not simply the movement of people between places, but the relocation of individuals in relation to the social space that they occupy and within which their identities are fashioned and livelihoods developed. A new identity and relationship of "self" and "other" thus defines the mechanisms and methods of reincorporation into both or all the localities with which the individual relates. In the metropoles, they are transient and therefore not impacted in the same way by circumstances there, including the exclusivities of race and nationality. In the Caribbean, they have the freedom of returning to the former place of residence though citizenship or other residency facilities.

The emancipatory character of transnationalism is usually if not always counter-hegemonic but they are not always resistant (Guarnizo and Smith 1999). Studies have shown that transnational practices and livelihoods can be used for purposes of capital accumulation as effectively as for the purpose of contesting hegemonic narratives of race, ethnicity, class and nation (Mitchell 1993 and Ong 1999) .

Transnationalism introduces new aspects of cultural construction that incorporates the local with the global in the value of Caribbean migration and diaspora. Transnationalism also suggests that, in conceptualizing migration, local sites of global processes do matter. The social construction of place is an important part of the migration process; migration alters the meaning of place as the migrants become part of the space, even central points in the transnational space and transnational flows. This process also plays a role in class restructuring within the migrant community and social transformations in the localities that are major points or centres in the transnational networks.

## Conclusion

Transnationalism is dynamic. The processes involved and the space it defines change and will continue to change in various ways, perpetuated by the extent and value of the movements within the migration fields. Further, transnationalism is a multifaceted process with parameters that are multi-local. It may be conceptualized as significantly influencing power relations, cultural constructions, economic relations, and in a general way, the social organization at the level of the household and family as well as the local community.

The individual is invariably forced to experience and develop a new identity and sense of identity at each new location within the transnational space. The transnational space contains the experiences, memories and bonds that relate to the various locations that form part of the space, and therefore the social capital that is generated. Some of these locations have reflected dramatic shifts in both livelihood and identity, others only minor changes, but all changes of location reflect some form and degree of change. Above all, while at one location one never loses the experience of the previous locations; nevertheless, their relevance changes and their dominance and roles in the total livelihood of the individual is characterized by a new dynamic with each move made (Chambers 1994).

Transnational space has no centre or periphery. The relationships and networks exist in relation to the individual at any point in that space. The source of migration becomes the destination and vice versa. It is not a case of balancing pluses against minuses or "pulls" against "pushes". They are both part of the reality and the strategy is to negotiate them effectively. The space is constructed of negatives and positives and the migrant positions him or herself in relation to these, usually negotiating between them – sometimes more successfully than at other times. Sometimes they shift financial capital, at other times they themselves move; they relate to social networks that incorporate more than one country and invest selectively in one or another place, differently at different times.

Migrants assume a sense of having earned the right to negotiate the transnational spaces associated with their migration experience. This does not simply imply the avoidance of negative circumstances but sometimes even the engagement of those negatives in order to maximize the individual's migration situation.

The return migrant learns to negotiate this space in order to maximize the migration experience. Some are more prepared for the challenges involved in readjustment of livelihood and identity. There are therefore various levels at which the migration is maximized through the return. For some persons the balance is never achieved while the locus of residence is in the Caribbean and they re-migrate to another locality.

To maximize migration, the transnational space becomes organized in such a way that relative freedom from the negative circumstances of both systems is facilitated and access to the opportunities and positive conditions of each system is enhanced. This does not mean that the result is a stress-free relationship with the various places that delineate the space. There is still the need for migrants to negotiate their livelihoods. However, the individual becomes the centre through which the space is engaged, and transnationalism the means of the strategic organization of the space. Within this context, the return takes place, largely in the quest to maximize the benefits of the migration

## Note

1. A study conducted by Elizabeth Thomas-Hope in 2001–2 on Experiences and Implications of the Return of Talent Programme. This was a programme sponsored jointly by the Government of Jamaica and the International Organization of Migration. Of the total number of fifty-eight migrants who participated in the programme, thirty-seven persons were interviewed. The information collected forms the basis of this chapter and the personal experiences and views quoted have been selected from the personal stories recorded in the study.

# References

Chambers, I. 1994. *Migrancy, Culture, Identity.* London: Routledge.

Georges, E. 1990. *The Making of a Transnational Community. Migration, Development and Cultural Change in the Dominican Republic.* New York: Columbia University Press.

Mitchell, K. 1993. Multiculturalism or the United Colors of Capitalism? *Antipode* 25: 263–94.

Ong, A. 1999. *Flexibile Citizenship: The Cultural Logics of Transnationality.* Durham: Duke University Press.

Guarnizo, L.E., and M.P. Smith. 1999. The Locations of Transnationalism. In *Transnation-alism from Below,* ed. M.P. Smith and L.E. Guarnizo, 3–34. New Brunswick, NJ: Transaction Books.

International Organization of Migration (IOM). 1998. Key Issues Relating to Migration in Jamaica. Typescript. Kingston, Jamaica.

Schiller, N.G., L. Basch and C. Blanc-Szanton. 1995. From Immigrant to Transmigrant: Theorizing Transnational Migration. In *Migration and Transnational Social Spaces,* ed. L. Pries, 73–105. London: Ashgate.

Thomas-Hope, E. 1986. Transients and Settlers: Varieties of Caribbean Migrants and the Socio-economic Implications of Their Return. *International Migration* 24 (3): 559–70.

———. 1988. Caribbean Skilled International Migration and the Transnational Household. *Geoforum* 19 (4): 423–32.

———. 2002. Transnational Livelihoods and Identities in Return Migration to the Caribbean: The Case of Skilled Returnees to Jamaica. In *Work and Migration: Life and Livelihoods in a Globalizing World,* ed. N. Nybergg Sorensen and K.F. Olwig, 187–201. London and New York: Routledge.

# Episodes of Return Migration in Tobago

## A Phenomenological Study

| Godfrey C. St Bernard |

## Introduction

The majority of Caribbean countries are net losers of population as a result of net migration. Notwithstanding this fact, there is evidence of in-migration and, in particular, that which assumes the form of return migration. Lewis (1958) noted that Caribbean countries have been characterized by an unlimited supply of labour. This is a feature that still persists in a number of Caribbean countries where levels of unemployment and underemployment have been indicative of social problems that prompted highly skilled and professional workers to seek employment in greener pastures overseas. In this regard, Trinidad and Tobago is no exception, having lost highly skilled workers in a number of fields including health care, education, information technology and construction. Moreover, the escalation of criminal activity targeting the entrepreneurial class has been threatening investment prospects in Trinidad where there has been evidence of capital flight to distant lands as a means of escaping the clutches of domestic criminal elements. Despite the net loss of the population at national levels, the situation in Tobago is much more critical insofar as Tobago has been losing considerable proportions of its domestic skills and expertise through internal migration to Trinidad. Notwithstanding such losses, Tobago has been the target of in-migration for a number of European settlers, Germans in particular. Tobago has also been targeted as the primary destination for a number of return migrants principally from European countries. This is interesting and warrants further investigation as a considerable number of such returnees have exhibited the potential to invest in business undertakings or make civic contributions to social development initiatives on the island.

This chapter assumes the form of a phenomenological study that strives to examine the experience of return for returnees who have chosen Tobago as opposed to Trinidad as their primary destination. Except for De Souza (1998) and St Bernard (2005), there have been no known studies examining the phenomenon of return migration in the context of Trinidad and Tobago. This chapter examines the meanings and experience of return migration from the standpoint of returnees to Tobago. While some of the returnees are retirees, others are still actively participating in the island's labour force, making substantial contributions as entrepreneurs. Interestingly, a considerable number of them were born and bred in Trinidad as opposed to Tobago and chose Tobago as the site for their retirement or entrepreneurial ventures. Given that Tobago has been known to lose some of its best minds to Trinidad and elsewhere due to the forces of migration, the study is interested in examining the nature of returnees' Tobagonian sojourn and the extent to which it is likely to foster or hamper social development prospects for Tobago, given migratory trends from Tobago to Trinidad and elsewhere in the world.

## The Phenomenological Tradition

The phenomenological tradition is geared towards gaining insight into the lived experiences of a set of individuals with respect to a given phenomenon. It strives to elicit from such experiences the meanings that individuals associate with the phenomenon. Such a process hinges upon the premise that the phenomenon is shared by a wide cross-section of individuals. In 1907, Husserl (1859–1938) articulated some essential principles that underlie the principal tenets of phenomenology. At that time, he argued that attempts to understand physical phenomena hinged upon the use of methods that were not amenable to understanding human thought and action (1964). In more recent times, Schutz (1962, 1964, 1967, 1970) has built upon the ideas articulated by Husserl making substantial contributions to disciplines such as psychology and anthropology. Moreover, phenomenology has been acknowledged as a research paradigm in a number of disciplinary arenas including nursing (Oiler 1986; Nieswiadomy 1993), psychology (Moustakas 1994) and the social sciences (Denzin and Lincoln 1994; Miles and Huberman 1994). Creswell (1998) endorses phenomenology as one of a number of qualitative traditions used in the conduct of research. Altogether, phenomenology is considered to be the qualitative tradition that strives to gauge reality through the eyes of another.

## Some Relevant Studies and the Experience
## of Return Migration

In the context of Caribbean societies, studies of return migration are inevitable given phenomenal levels of emigration that were evident in the pre-independence era and persisted though at lower rates in the post-independence era. According to Stinner, de Albuquerque and Bryce-Laporte (1982): "Migrants to the metropole and to other societies within the region do return and this return conveys important demographic, socio-economic and political implications for the original sending society and the migrants themselves" (xxxix).

The dynamic character of return migration has been captured in a number of studies targeting myriad Caribbean societies. From a historical standpoint, Marshall (1987) makes reference to the repatriation of West Indians from places such as the United States and Cuba during the period of 1920 to 1940 and highlights levels of discontent that arose upon their return to their homelands due mainly to their overall exposure to higher living standards during their overseas sojourn. Based on fieldwork done during the 1960s, Philpott (1973) has cited cases in which Montserratians had returned to the island to become petty entrepreneurs investing in "rum shops", transportation and agriculture. Although such decisions enhanced their social status in domestic spheres, several of them eventually returned to the metropole, deeming the Montserratian economy to be incapable with respect to assuring them a sustainable livelihood.

With reference to more recent waves of return migration, Byron (2000) highlights return migration that has been characterized mainly by a return of elderly persons from Britain, especially during the 1970s and 1980s. She also made reference to the return of younger returnees due mainly to the internationalization of industries such as tourism, retailing and high-tech sectors. Plaza (2002) examines the adjustment experiences of second-generation

British-Caribbean returnees in the labour markets of Barbados and Jamaica. De Souza (1998) provides a qualitative account of the factors motivating return to Trinidad and Tobago. While De Souza's work has focused primarily upon the experiences of returnees who returned to Trinidad, there is no equivalent study targeting the dynamics that have unfolded in Tobago where additional antecedent factors are likely to be at work. This is especially important given that some returnees who had been born in Trinidad have opted to return and settle in Tobago.

## The Research Setting: Tobago

Tobago is the smaller of the two islands that form the twin-island state of Trinidad and Tobago. It is a tiny island covering a total land area of three hundred square kilometres and has a population of about 54,084[1] residents or approximately 4 per cent of the national population (estimated to be in the vicinity of 1.3 million). A little more than 90 per cent of Tobago's population is of African descent. During the decade of the 1990s, in particular, there have been increases in the proportion of East Indians and persons of mixed origin in the population of Tobago. Tobago has a relatively young population. As much as 60 per cent of the population are below the age of thirty-five years and about a quarter (24.5 per cent) are under fifteen years. It is worth noting that the population aged sixty-five years and over represents 6.8 per cent of the island's population and constitutes a greater share of Tobago's population when compared with the corresponding situation in most of the other Caribbean islands.

According to indicators of living conditions in Tobago, households in eastern Tobago are poorer than those in western Tobago (Policy Research and Development Institute 1999). Approximately three in every five persons aged fifteen years and over are part of the island's labour force. Traditionally, the economy of Tobago has been primarily dependent upon agriculture – a legacy of slavery on the island. In the past three decades, however, tourism has become one of the major economic sectors and, along with the public sector that is manifest through the activities of the Tobago House of Assembly, it employs the largest proportion of the island's labour force. During the late 1990s, just under a half of the labour force were employees of state enterprises or the government (between 46 per cent and 50 per cent). The private sector accounted for just under 40 per cent of the labour force (between 37 per cent and 40 per cent) while own account workers accounted for just over 10 per cent. The majority of Tobago's labour force were employed in the following industries: community, social and personal services (37.7 per cent), transport, storage and communication (23.7 per cent), and wholesale and retail trades, including restaurants, hotels and construction (20 per cent).

## Methodological Issues

### *Data Collection*

The main focus of this study is the return migration experience of returnees who settled in Tobago during the 1990s. A sample of eight returnees was selected based upon the principles of theoretical sampling.² A semi-structured interview schedule was developed and administered with the eight returnees. From July to August 2003, in-depth interviews were conducted with the eight subjects and this permitted the collection of qualitative accounts of return migration experiences. The interview schedule sought to obtain responses to issues such as the subjects' reasons for returning, their aspirations upon return, the essence of their return experiences and their prospects of remaining in or leaving Tobago as a result of their experiences. In general, the interviews were of variable length lasting between forty-five and ninety minutes. There were four male and four female subjects, none of whom was born in Tobago.

### *The Subjects*

*Jasmine:* A female born in rural Trinidad and as a child lived in very humble surroundings. She emigrated in the early 1970s to escape poverty and pursue socio-economic advancement. She always wanted to return to Trinidad and Tobago as she considered herself Trinidadian. She claimed that she was forced to return prematurely because of an ageing parent who was also terminally ill. While she preferred Trinidad as her home base, her European husband preferred Tobago despite his reluctance to leave his homeland when she first mooted the idea of establishing a greater presence in Trinidad and

Tobago. To him, Tobago was ideal as he did not have to travel far to enjoy his fishing hobby. Settling in Tobago was critical in obtaining her husband's support and accompaniment in making the migratory move back to the Caribbean. Her husband is a skilled tradesperson who could transmit vocational skills in Tobago but feels that he will be linguistically challenged if he has to communicate in English. Nevertheless, as a good tradesperson, he gets jobs and hires a local to assist him. She thinks that the frustration associated with doing business in Tobago would be the only thing to discourage her from remaining in Tobago, and the alternative would be to move to Trinidad. For the moment, however, Tobago is likely to be the family's home.

*Delia:* She is a second-generation Tobagonian who was born in England but has roots in Tobago. Though born in England, she never felt a connection with English culture and responded negatively to the ethnic division and racism that she deemed to be characteristic of her life experience in England. She yearned for a new life in a new setting and chose Tobago, the place of her father's birth. She has a professional career and continues to live in Tobago with her husband and children. She has expressed tremendous joy having returned to Tobago and claims that she has absolutely no desire to ever leave Tobago. She has also attempted to ground with locals at the community level in order to eliminate perceptions of status differences that exist between locals and returnees.

*Arnold*: He was born in Trinidad and grew up in the outskirts of the city of Port of Spain. He was nurtured in a working-class environment and as a young man went to England where he studied and spent many years working in a professional capacity. Married to a European woman, Arnold is now retired and lives in Tobago with his wife. In retirement, Arnold and his wife are financially secure and independent of any form of public assistance. While acknowledging that there are some negative aspects of life in Tobago, Arnold has absolutely no regrets about choosing Tobago as the site for his retirement and at the time of the interview had no intentions of leaving Tobago to go elsewhere.

*Andre*: He was born in Port of Spain, Trinidad. He has been living abroad since the 1970s and has been mainly engaged in work-related activities. Married to a European woman, they decided to return to Trinidad and Tobago and chose to settle in Tobago as opposed to Trinidad. In Tobago, he is actively involved in a business venture and has not expressed any desire to leave Tobago to settle elsewhere. In addition, Andre's wife is fond of the tropical climate that is characteristic of Tobago and prefers to remain in Tobago rather than return to Europe. Generally speaking, he feels that the positive and negative aspects of life in Tobago are inter-related. He has yearned for the slower pace of life that is characteristic of life in Tobago but this has also spawned a number of problems that impact negatively upon his business interests.

*Cassandra*: She was born in a town in east Trinidad and lived abroad for a number of years. While abroad, she worked in locales similar to Tobago providing a range of services consistent with her training in the hospitality sector. Her husband is European and, in keeping with their quest to initiate a business venture, they chose Tobago because she is a citizen of Trinidad and Tobago. They also took advantage of the fact that Tobago's economy was oriented towards tourism. Generally speaking, they worked tirelessly in their establishment and were happy with the quality of their product and the returns on their investment. Despite their successful business venture, they indicated that they may not continue to live in Tobago. In Tobago, they felt that they were unable to overcome the disequilibrium that was characterizing their life experiences resulting from their engagement in business.

*Gordon*: He was born in a rural village in South Trinidad. His father was a professional who migrated to England in the 1950s in response to a job offer. During the early 1960s, the family was reunited in England at a time when he had begun attending secondary school in Trinidad. In England, he completed his education, got married and started a family. Between leaving and returning home, he lived the entire period in England. Now retired and still relatively young, he is currently living in Tobago, extremely happy to be there and would not have it any other way. It is worth noting that his desire to return to the Caribbean, and Tobago in particular, was so great that he did so despite constantly being discouraged by some of his West Indian colleagues in England. Upon reflection, Gordon's humility was manifested in his passionate connection with his rural past and the culture that characterizes rural spaces.

*Louis*: He was born in Port of Spain and grew up in a suburban district of Port of Spain. He migrated to England in the 1980s in response to a job offer. He never had any interest in remaining in England indefinitely, a feeling that was so great that he returned home. He continues to maintain physical contact with his son and they take turns visiting one another across the Atlantic. For Louis, Tobago has had a great appeal, and he now lives a quiet life that includes working in his field – a field that revolves around the aquatic culture that is characteristic of Tobago. He has indicated that he wants to make a profound contribution in his field that would impact positively upon Tobagonian pride. In general, he is very satisfied with his destination upon his return home. He feels that the good outweighs the bad, despite the fact that there are shortcomings. He claims that he is a returning resident and that Tobago is his last port as a returning resident.

*Marjorie*: She was born in Port of Spain. Her European husband visited Tobago and as fate would have it, they met, eventually got married and she migrated to Europe. She spent a major part of her adult life in Europe and decided to return to Tobago upon her husband's retirement. In fact, her husband sought Tobago as the ideal destination for his retirement insofar as he had grown to love and know Tobago as a result of experiences linked to his frequent trips to the island. In particular, her husband was fond of Tobago's climate, and that was a major consideration in his decision. She trusted her husband's judgement and opted to follow him to Tobago, especially since her prospects for employment were under threat by the imminent closure of the establishment that employed her. They also felt that they had the financial means to live comfortably in Tobago. On arriving and settling in Tobago, the couple became aware of a number of problems that had not been previously envisaged. First of all, they thought that the island was not sufficiently developed intellectually and infrastructurally. The couple also appears to have a penchant for participating in voluntary initiatives and assuming membership in associations. These initiatives were usually poorly supported and often collapsed. Marjorie considered such outcomes to be functions of xenophobic tendencies among Tobagonians and the overwhelming tasks that had to be pursued without pay. Generally speaking, Marjorie and her husband have been dissatisfied with their experiences but currently still continue to live in Tobago. For the couple, it is either Tobago or the European country where her husband was born. They have absolutely no desire to live in any other countries.

# Thematic Accounts: Returnees' Experiences in Tobago

## Challenging Working Experiences

Both Jasmine and Cassandra claim that they have had to work harder than expected to the extent that vacations are scarce. The core-periphery character of business activities across the two islands has constituted a major challenge to returnees who have established business ventures in Tobago. In particular, the inter-island transportation services have frustrated the efforts of returnees such as Jasmine and Andre, both of whom have business interests in Tobago. They have complained about the inadequacy of flights between the two islands, the inefficiency of the inter-island ferry service (especially with respect to obtaining space to accommodate their private vehicles) and the hassles associated with obtaining car rentals on the two islands. These experiences thwart business initiatives, causing them to be less efficient to the extent that some returnees have considered relocating to Trinidad despite their love for the Tobagonian ambiance. There is also a shortage of skilled tradespersons, such as masons, carpenters and plumbers, to support investment initiatives that are to be undertaken by returnees.

The work experiences of returnees engaged in the provision of professional services have not been encouraging, and there are reports that many have since returned to the metropole. The situation has been so critical that such returnees would rather face racism, the threat of terrorist attacks and other metropolitan atrocities than the indignities that they have associated with being a professional in Tobago. In the case of Cassandra, long hours of work have taken a toll on her social life because she has been unable to obtain reliable assistance within the local community.

## Variable Work Ethic

Jasmine and Andre operate business interests in Tobago and have had problems getting locals to perform tasks at acceptable levels. Andre believes that the problems impacting negatively upon the island's work ethic are associated with the slow pace of life on the island, a characteristic feature that has attracted those who yearn for a stress-free life. For returnees who have business interests, however, the slow pace of life has been observed to be a source of stress. Based upon her experiences, Jasmine noted,

> They wouldn't do their work right. If they come you have to be around, you have to be around all the time. You can't tell them: "Well this is what I want done" and you go your way and do your work, because when you come back everything will be in a mess but they gone. They don't want to work eight hours a day, they just want to work for a couple hours but get a lot of money. They come very lazy. I know when I came here in 1989 they seemed to be very motivated, willing to work and so, but now not at all. And they do very bad work.

As a business woman, Cassandra also reports on her experiences that are similar to those of Jasmine:

> They want a job, but not to work. It is like a crisis, you just can't get people to work. They would come out – they would come today and just not show up the next day. Their dishonesty is terrible and a lot of people have that same complaint. And we need people to work, we need people to train. Look, we are about to leave Tobago right now and nobody knows what we are doing. We just can't get through to them. This would have been a lucrative business for anybody to buy over, if they could have done the product, because the market is here, and we have done the hardest part, we capture the market, we already have the market, we just need to produce and keep selling, we don't need to do anything else.

Cassandra's sentiments also deal with the elements of distrust that are evident in Jasmine's coverage of her experiences. Cassandra also alludes to her willingness to prepare a local to continue the business and the extent to which his or her work ethic may have militated against such an outcome.

Local entrepreneurs have also alluded to the poor work ethic that they have observed, especially among young Tobagonian males. The following account provides ample evidence:

> I have a friend. . . . Her brother has a mechanic shop, he said he took three young men to work there, and two of them worked for two days, the Monday, the Tuesday, they came back the Friday for pay. They had all kinds of excuses, they never called, they never showed up, but they knew that the Friday is pay-day. It is really bad, you really don't know what you could do to motivate them to know that they have to work, or they have to learn a trade or something so that later on they can survive.

Louis feels that local authorities could at times be too "laid back" in the delivery of critical services within communities. Gordon has also expressed similar sentiments referring to the wastage of water due to ruptured pipelines that are left unattended for relatively long periods by the Water and Sewerage Authority. The following comments reflect Louis's feelings with regard to such matters:

> Admittedly things could be a little laid back sometimes. Certain times you would like a little bit of service. For instance you would go into a local authority, for instance like the Trinidad and Tobago Electricity Commission [T&TEC] – I would call T&TEC numerous times to come and cut some bush down that is covering some electrical lines, they are taking their time, they will come, but I hope they will come in time when the trees have not overgrown. These are some of the things that could be a little negative factor but they will get it done in time.

Unlike the other returnees, including those who have engaged in business ventures, Gordon seems supportive of the commitment of Tobagonians to diligence in the provision of labour services in private capacities. He also considered Tobagonians to be friendly and sought to get along well with the majority who crossed his path. Gordon's image of Tobagonians was different from that of other returnees and could in part be due to his extremely humble and warm disposition coupled with the fact that he has rural roots and would spend time in his rural village and in Tobago whenever he visited Trinidad and Tobago while living in England. He also demonstrated a willingness to eschew metropolitan values and lifestyle when he chose to return to the Caribbean, a decision that was incomprehensible from the standpoint of many of his West Indian colleagues who chose to remain in the metropole. His humility and compassion is reflected in this statement that supports a more positive orientation towards the work ethic among tradespersons in Tobago.

> The guy I had as the builder we had a rapport; we got along well; he knows that I am a person who pays a fair day's pay for a fair day's work. I believe in paying a fair pay for a fair day's work. I say that to everyone, I am giving you what is the top of the pay of what a carpenter gets, a mason gets, what a steel bender gets, so I expect a fair day's work for my money. And if you give me a fair day's work, you are getting a fair day's pay. I am not trying to short pay. And I think, with that understanding from the outset, it works. There were

people who came and gave me a day's work for nothing because they have been treated so good.

I know a lot of people who say you can't get Tobagonians to work. That is something I have heard, that's a common occurrence in Tobago, but that's not my experience. I am not saying that that does not happen. It probably does happen, but every circumstance is different, and how those people treat their workers is probably why they go. I have had a couple trainees come on here, and that was like throwing money away because they are not giving you the service, but I have billed that into the cost of building the house – a certain amount for a trainee to come in, learn a trade. The guy who did some of the building for me . . . he is learning the job, we are paying him an apprentice wage. That's fine, I have had two of them. That's a cost that I had to put in, but that is using local people and giving the local people an opportunity to spread that money around. It is all about spreading the money around anyway. They are good workers. I know that I have heard from neighbours that you will get scorched, you will get burned, but that has not been my experience.

## Petty Theft

Some returnees have been the targets of thieves whether in the context of their private homes or their business ventures. As Jasmine states,

> We have maids who work with us and they steal, they steal the people's things, and if this continues people are going to tell other people and then I would not have a business. I need people now to help me with the garden, to trim the trees, but I am just scared to death, because I cannot stay here twenty-four hours a day, and as soon as you turn your back, they keep their eyes opened and they look all over and they are going to try to steal something. I had a problem about two years ago with the break-ins. Tonight this house, tomorrow night the other.

Arnold also notes that there have been recent increases in the prevalence of petty theft that he attributed to the tourism thrust that has been gaining momentum in Tobago. Andre, on the other hand, claims that Tobago is relatively crime-free and believes that any apparent escalation in crime is more likely to be perpetrated by Trinidadians than Tobagonians.

## *Insularity*

Despite the fact that Trinidadian returnees regard themselves as citizens of Trinidad and Tobago, there has been evidence to suggest that some have had life experiences that led them to believe that Tobagonians respond differently to them purely on the basis of their place of birth.

> Well, yes. The people are very nice, but you know when you are a Trinidadian living over here you are still considered a foreigner. If you were not born and grown up here, they don't really consider you a Tobagonian. But that does not mean that they show you bad face, but you get that feeling, because they would start talking about Tobagonians, Tobagonians all the way up. I don't know who started it, but that's the way it is.

## *Poor Environmental Awareness Standards*

With regard to the disposal of waste, there has been some evidence pointing towards poor environmental awareness standards among locals. This is especially evident in private areas, some of which host tourists who come from relatively pristine environments and expect to witness local efforts to uphold similar standards when on vacation or sojourning in a different locale. Some returnees have observed a wanton disregard for the environment and have documented cases where children appeared to have been influenced and encouraged by adults, including parents, to sustain less than acceptable standards for the disposal of waste. Such experiences are documented in the following sentiments expressed by one of the returnees:

> Not because we are a Third World country you have to be this way. You see too, what gets to me is the dumping. You see a vacant lot there, they have cuttings from their garden, they take it and dump it here. People come all the way in here, they leave . . . gardens and come all the way to a little lonely place, look around and when they see nobody they dump their stuff. I mean how does that look, the coconut branches, the bougainvillas; they dump it right on the side of the road where the grass is. I had a gardener cut there and we could park there. They dump and before it gets real dry it gets smelly, and you have the tourists walking by. I don't know why they don't see this as untidy.
> When you turn in to come in here, there is a vacant lot there, the house is right next door, they go and they dump their stuff there. It is right in front of

where they are living. And you tell them hundreds of times. They even have children doing it, taking the stuff and throwing it there. Now they get to the point when the children see me they would just stand still until I pass by. So you see where I am coming from. If they are teaching the children, they must be telling the children it is okay to do that, and I stopped and I told the boy, one was only nine, the other is about eleven, and I said you know it is wrong to dump trash on other people's land. He said, "Everything is going to go down there." I said, "No, no, you are not correct, that is being untidy, and it is not good for the environment." He looked at me as if he really did not think so; he thought it was okay to do that. And then I pass time and time again and I see them out there and they are doing that, only he would not throw it when he sees me, he would wait until I go by.

The returnee also alluded to the prevalence of "fires" that could be avoided if individuals were more sensitive to the environment. They often deem these fires to be a source of atmospheric pollution that impacts adversely upon the respiratory health and personal comfort of residents and their guests. The returnee indicated that waste from her household is not burnt. Instead, the returnee's spouse usually drives to Studley Park – a waste disposal site – in order to get rid of household waste. There is no cost for the disposal of waste at the site where one can dispose of items such as old stoves, refrigerators, building materials, everything.

## Perceptions of Returnees' Social Status

In general, returnees expressed the view that Tobagonians associated their overseas sojourn with greater wealth and, in many cases, extended favourable reception and support with a view towards benefiting in cash or kind. The returnees spoke about overt acts of acceptance and support that greeted them upon arrival and relatively short periods thereafter. Whether from relatives or associates, returnees felt that such enthusiasm usually waned when it was discovered that benefits in cash or kind might not be forthcoming. The returnees feel that there is an inflated opinion of their social well-being and status abroad despite the fact that they enjoy superior living standards when compared with the average Tobagonian. Returnees have also alluded to similar experiences in professional settings whether in the capacity of voluntary or non-voluntary initiatives. There have also been feelings among returnees that their Tobagonian counterparts might perceive their professional activities as threatening and, therefore, they have been experiencing some amount of resentment.

### Ancestral Ties and Familial Bonding

Delia alluded to the delight associated with walking the streets and terrain traversed by her deceased father. She also expressed tremendous joy in the thought that her children are currently living in premises that had once been occupied by their fore-parents. This sentiment was vividly expressed as follows:

> Watching my children grow up in my grandmother's house and my father's land; it is exciting to see the cousins all about. Whether they like me or not I don't care, they are still my cousins they can't stop that. I am overwhelmed and that continues to grow because that is why I came back. I wanted to be with my people and work for my people.

For Delia, the importance of ancestral ties and family bonding were further expressed as follows:

> So that is unique for me, and that is why here is exactly where I belong, it is where I am supposed to be and where I came from originally. That experience of the cycle of return of meeting people of my father, walking where he walked, living in my grandmother's house – there is no price I can put on that. I can't even explain to you. I couldn't feel that anywhere else in the world. And that has been my personal and priceless gift. If I should die tomorrow, I am a hundred times happier than I was before. You could not make me happier by giving me a million dollars, you know.

### A Deep Sense of Patriotism

Delia also expressed her desire to work against the odds to contribute towards the social development of Tobago. She recognizes her professional capabilities and thinks that she possesses other innate talents that she could use to develop the island that she now labels "home". In the process of building Tobago, however, she laments the fact that there appears to be cleavages on the basis of skin colour among blacks in Tobago. This experience was most disappointing and inconsistent with the unity that she witnessed among blacks in England. To capture such sentiments, Delia remarked,

> In England we as black people stick together, and here black man pulls down black man; we destroy ourselves, we commit suicide here. And that is the hardest thing about coming home: realizing that we really are against one another. And even the colour grading. It is like South Africa: "oh you nice and fair". What's nice about red? I was horrified about that. And even some people wanting to call me white, after suffering all that racism in England coming home as a favourite son, it was horrible. So that lack of unity of black people here as compared with what we had in England was the most surprising thing, and the most disappointing thing, and still remains so.

Delia also claims that it is very painful to watch Tobago destroy itself or struggle when it doesn't need to do so. When Delia was asked if she thinks that she will ever leave Tobago to live elsewhere in the world, her reply was as follows:

> It has to be something very serious like Tobago is uninhabitable, education-wise, literally, land-wise. I don't think even an invasion would keep me out, I would stand up and fight. Tobago is my country I would be the last person to turn a new life. I have fought so hard to come home, I would have to be crazy. I would have gone by now. It is ten years since I am home. I am now starting to flip my wings, I ain't begin. If my country is in danger, it is my country. I am not saying that I would not send away my children, or if there is some terrible disease – there has to be something life threatening. But I would only run away to come back again for my commitment to Tobago is total.

Gordon also expresses a deep sense of patriotism in justifying his decision to return to Trinidad and Tobago. Moreover, he exhibits a nostalgic connection to his rural "beginnings" by drawing an analogy between his childhood rural village and Tobago. Gordon's thoughts are encapsulated in the following comment:

> I think it has to do with something like, "this is my home, this is where I was born". I have never regarded England as my home. When you are reaching a stage where you are near finishing your working period, even though I was quite young still, I wanted to come back home before I was too old to set myself back up in Trinidad and Tobago. Because if you leave when you are

too old, the change would have been too dramatic for me, I think. You have to do it before you reach that change in your mind set, because it is two completely different worlds. This is always where I was coming back. I was not going to die in England for I would be dying in a foreign country. A lot of people thought I was going crazy.

## Island Paradise

Delia, Andre and Arnold felt that Tobago was relatively crime-free when compared to Trinidad and saw this as a definite advantage. They attributed such an outcome to the impersonal nature of events that unfold in small island settings such as Tobago. There was also reference to the absence of atmospheric pollution that was prevalent in some of the major international cities. This also made Tobago an attractive option especially with respect to the preservation of health. The island paradise context deemed to be characteristic of Tobago is succinctly captured in one of Delia's statements:

> A lot of things tie in with one another that makes it right – from the environment to the country aspects of it – the fact that it is rural, the fact that it is simple, it is not too sophisticated, the fact that we still have a lot of Christianity it is very important for me; community feeling, I mean everything. All these you cannot put a price on, and all these things were hard for me to find outside.

The island paradise conception of Tobago was uppermost in Arnold's mind when he was making his decision to return home upon retirement. While he identified the peaceful character of the island as ideal for retirement, his wife revelled in the thought of being close to the sea and being able to swim. Gordon, on the other hand, remembers his mother referring to Tobago as "paradise on earth" and visited Tobago for the first time in the early 1980s. Since then, he visited Tobago every time he came to the Caribbean to the extent that it was his natural choice when he was considering a place to spend his years in retirement. Gordon's conception of Tobago as paradise is best captured as follows:

> The first time I came to Tobago in 1980, just to see what the place was like, I fell in love with Tobago after that. So whenever I came back down to see the family in [small Caribbean island of his fore-parents] and in Trinidad, I used to take a week to come and spend in Tobago. So I was coming to Tobago nearly every year since 1990. So I made the decision then that in Tobago I

could get the country feel that I wanted like [small rural village of his child-hood]. But I also had the convenience of the airport three or four minutes down the road, and it is convenient for everything. This is my ideal place to live really. And that is why I made the decision for Tobago. Not that we had any family ties in Tobago, we have none. I mean I might as well have gone back to live in [small Caribbean island of his fore-parents]. I was not born [there] so I never felt that [it] was the place I wanted to go back to.

In fact, Louis and Gordon shared similar views of Tobago as an idyllic paradise. Louis visited Tobago regularly while abroad and knew exactly that its setting was conducive to the type of lifestyle that he had envisaged upon his return home. When asked about his return to Tobago, Louis states,

> It is very laid back or relaxing. I do work, I can earn myself enough money to live. I enjoy the nature most of all, the naturalness of the island. I also enjoy the food here, I enjoy the beautiful atmosphere. I live by the sea. . . . I love the sea.
>
> For instance, I mentioned to you earlier about the turtles coming up on my beach. Some would pay whatever to see that. And this is what I appreciate – the natural environment. I appreciate the lovely clear marine water. I love it here. It is very relaxing. It is what I want personally. As far as experiences here, you get a variety of different experiences.

In expressing his preference for Tobago over rural Trinidad, Gordon continues,

> Not like in Tobago, perhaps I would have had to go and live somewhere up north in Trinidad or on the east coast and the waters there are not the best. And you know the situation, there is a different type of situation here. In Tobago, we don't have that heavy crime rate. I can leave my front door opened and go to sleep. In Trinidad, you cannot do that. . . . Look at what happened recently in Moruga, innocent people were getting hurt, because bandits obviously assumed that the drugs that were washed up on the beach were in their houses.

## Substandard Customer Service

In Caribbean societies, the majority of returnees return home from countries such as the United States, England and Canada where consumers have power and can determine the fortunes of business establishments. This means that business establishments have to assure that all dimensions of their service delivery, including customer service, attain the highest standards, a characteristic feature that many returnees have grown accustomed to during their sojourn abroad. Marjorie and her husband greatly value the quality of service that they receive as customers. Having returned to Tobago, they have been evaluating the quality of customer services in a wide range of business establishments and have expressed utter disgust about their experiences. They recounted numerous instances when clerks, cashiers and even store managers were obnoxious towards them during business transactions. This has been a major source of the family's dissatisfaction with its return experience, especially given its knowledge of equivalent service standards that persist in Europe. Marjorie was very passionate in expressing her displeasure with several episodes involving clerks, cashiers and even store managers. The following is an account of scenarios and experiences that reflects some of Marjorie's encounters:

> But how often could you go in a shop in Tobago, you want to buy something, and the woman who is there to serve you is sitting down reading the newspapers, or eating their lunch, or holding a big conversation, and they look up at you: "Are you getting through?" That is a very common question they ask you – this is not a way to treat a customer. The customer is the one who is going to place their hard earned money on something they want. The same thing goes for many of the people employed in the public offices.
>
> If you go to a supermarket, you pick out your things from the shelf, by the time you get to the cashier, if you are the only one, she yawning: "Way [Why] you come with a whole basket of stuff to wake me up for." She has not looked at you yet, and she will punch in the eighty things you have in your trolley and she has not looked at you as yet. And you would pay her and she would just drop your change in mid air. She will not look at you.
>
> I went to get a fan for our son, who has just opened a little [business] at Pigeon Point, because after opening we noticed that the place was a little hot. I don't know if you know the —— family who has a lot of stores around, very rich people, just like the Penny Savers family. We went to get this fan and he had quite a few for demonstration, and I asked if I can have one demonstration, and the answer was, "Yes, if you want." And I said, "Yes, I want." He called a service lady and she fumbled and fumbled with fan after fan because half of them that were displayed weren't working, and so I said, when we did find one that was working, and I asked her all the questions that I wanted to

ask her, I asked, "Is there any warranty on these fans?" Then he jumped, the owner of the establishment: "No, lady, you see all of them displayed there, we don't have to lie to nobody, you know." This is his attitude – you see them displayed. So I said, "I just went somewhere else and they were also on display and there was a three month warranty on them." Well, "We don't give warranty because you test it in the shop and it working. The others, you ain't sure if it working that is why they giving you three months warranty." I said, "Isn't it so that any electrical equipment that you buy . . . because it is quite a bit of money that I am going to pay for it that there should be some sort of warranty, let us say eight days?" He said, "No, lady, so if you don't want it left it nah, I would prefer you to go and buy your thing somewhere else. If you don't want to buy here go and buy it elsewhere."

This is how this guy is arguing with me, the customer who is coming to buy something for two hundred and something dollars. "If you don't want it go and buy it somewhere else." And this is the third time that it has happened to me in his shop. And I said to him, "You are so damn ugly and so rude, that there should be a law against people like you." But I needed the fan, and it was a closing time on a Saturday and I couldn't get to Scarborough, so I bought the fan, but I vowed that that would be the last penny that I am spending in his establishment. I am not going there again.

I went into another one of their family's establishment – a fabric store to buy some fabric. I bought three hundred dollars-odd in material and this is to send back to [European country] to my daughter. I gave the girl exact money. One five-cent piece had some corrosion, one side of it. She said, "That ain't good." I said, "It is money, it is only corroded." She said, "It ain't good." I said, "It was given to me, dear, and if it was given to me, I can give it to you." She watched me and stupsed, she take the five cents she went with the bill and came back, stamped the bill noisily, the draw flew out, she shoved the money in, she ripped off the bill, and she just dashed it at me, and it landed on the floor. That was the service that I got for my three hundred dollars. She took my five cents and threw it into a bin in front of me and *stupsed*. That's the service you get.

Marjorie and her husband feel that Tobagonian police officers are limited in their capacity to deliver service to communities because of interpersonal familiarity that is associated with the island's small population. They have relied upon the services of the local police a few times and had some really bad experiences to such an extent that they feel that the police are ineffective. On one occasion, Marjorie claimed that they were very disappointed because everything that the police officer wrote down or happened to do was misplaced. She seems to have lost confidence in the local police officers and expresses her preference for officers from Trinidad:

> Police in Tobago are just men in uniforms who are there for a sure salary, and the small benefits – nothing else. These are harsh words, but they should send the whole bunch of them to Trinidad, and let Trinidadians perform here where they have no ties. You look shocked. I don't know if you heard that before too.

## The Home Experience Revisited: Some Reflections and Implications

Based upon the accounts of the eight returnees, the decision to return to Tobago is predicated upon conceptions of Tobago as the ideal Caribbean paradise when compared to Trinidad. To these returnees, Tobago is synonymous with tranquility, beauty, the absence of atmospheric pollution, isolated petty crime that is not as violent when compared with Trinidad and a stress-free life. In the eyes of some returnees, Tobago has been likened to a desire to abandon metropolitan ideals and artefacts and return to a place where humankind and nature abound free of any interruption. The ideal paradise concept was further complemented by the climatic conditions that prevail in the Caribbean when compared to the North Atlantic. In all cases, the returnees consisted of individuals who had either been citizens of Trinidad and Tobago by birth or descent and have had the option of choosing Tobago as their destination upon return. Interestingly, some of the returnees opted for Tobago on the insistence of their spouses for whom Tobago generally meant an "island paradise". In all cases, there was some amount of familiarity with Tobago as the returnees and/or their spouses had visited the island repeatedly while living in the metropole.

Returning home meant that returnees had made that ultimate decision to reside in rather than visit Tobago. It meant that they had to gainfully participate in the island's labour force and/or consume goods and services on a routine basis. It meant that returnees had to interact with a wider range of individuals, institutional organs and infrastructural artefacts than if they had been visiting for a relatively short stay. For the majority of returnees in the study, the return experience exposed them to threats that challenged the idyllic notion of Tobago as a tropical paradise. There were reports of challenging work experiences that severely interrupted their social lives or threatened their capacity to operate their business ventures optimally. Returnees such as Jasmine and Andre alluded to the hassles associated with obtaining raw materials and transportation to and within Trinidad. Cassandra spoke about the burden that she bore as a result of many long hours spent ensuring that her products were of an acceptably high standard. Although Tobago has constituted a viable site for their productive ventures, these returnees have at times weighed the challenges impacting upon their work experiences against the relevant "pull factors".

Some of the returnees have been reacting negatively to the work ethic of the locals. Invariably, returnees who pursued business ventures were sceptical about the commitment and diligence of their employees. Among such returnees, there was also evidence of vindication when other persons expressed similar views about the problems they encountered with regard to the attitudes of the local work force in the delivery of services whether in business or on a personal level. Despite their intention to continue residing in Tobago, Jasmine and Andre have reflected upon the worthiness of their investments in Tobago, this being especially the case when evaluated alongside inherent burdens linked to their work experiences. Gordon on the other hand has had more favourable experiences with workers who he has occasionally hired on a more personal level. He stated that he has always informed workers of his willingness to pay them a fair day's pay for a fair day's work and done the requisite research to ensure that he was paying them at the top of their scale. Despite a few disappointments with some workers, Gordon has been extremely delighted with his experiences since returning to Tobago and has no intentions of leaving, irrespective of the status of the public services and infrastructure. As such, he recognizes that such problems extend beyond Tobago and are national rather than island-specific insofar as they are also prevalent across Trinidad. He states that he will continue to live in Tobago until he is put to rest in Buccoo Cemetery.

In some quarters, perceptions of substandard customer service may be linked to the perceptions of poor work ethic gleaned from the eyes of some of the returnees. Such perceptions have been evident in the public service, the public utilities and even within the private sector such as in restaurants and merchandizing. Marjorie and her husband have been very passionate in articulating their experiences. Having defined customer service in accordance with North Atlantic ideals, the couple is profoundly offended by the local practices with regard to customer service. In accordance with their observations, such poor standards are also meted out to locals who they perceive to be indifferent about such treatment. The couple believes that high standards of customer service are consistent with a viable business ethos and have clearly stated that they will desist from doing business with such service providers. These experiences have been by far the most disgusting experienced by Marjorie and her husband. The couple has also expressed dissatisfaction with the levels of voluntarism that they have perceived as being relatively low. They yearn for higher levels of voluntarism as a vehicle to empower institutions and development processes across the island. Despite their disgust, this couple has invested substantially in Tobago and seems prepared to continue living there, tolerating the numerous shortcomings that also appear to have eroded their conception of Tobago as an island paradise.

Poor environmental awareness standards constitute another factor that has been a source of annoyance for returnees. Marjorie, her husband and Jasmine have made such observations in their specific residential settings and expressed a desire for locals to improve their physical surroundings. They have interacted with children and adults in order to treat the situation and reported virtually no success in their efforts. They have defined the problem as endemic and suspect that it will be sustained as parents and even the schools do not appear to be having a positive impact. Interestingly, these observations were associated with those returnees who lived in Europe but not in England. Most of the returnees alluded to their knowledge of cases of petty theft in Tobago. Notwithstanding such cases, they generally felt that Tobago was relatively free of the violent crime that was evident in Trinidad and were generally satisfied with their levels of personal safety. They also noted that Tobago possesses a community spirit that quells the prospect of criminal tendencies, a sentiment expressed in the comments of returnees such as Gordon, Louis and Arnold.

In Caribbean societies, it is customary to believe that the social status of returnees is elevated due principally to their lengthy stay in metropolitan areas in the North Atlantic and perceptions of living standards in such areas. Returnees are usually conscious of their social status and at times have experienced differential treatment, sometimes with positive and at other times with negative consequences as a result of their perceived status. Despite their desire to offer voluntary support in their fields of competence, returnees have expressed a desire for more egalitarian orientations and practices in public and private spheres. Delia, Arnold and Louis in particular have sought to ground with the masses despite their metropolitan exposure and acquired competencies. In general, they have expressed the desire to be viewed as residents of Tobago rather than as any special category that experiences differential treatment because they are returnees. In essence, they seek simple livelihoods and strive to promote and facilitate activities that would impact positively upon social development processes in Tobago.

Ancestral ties and familial bonding have played a critical role in the decision making process to return to Trinidad and Tobago. It was family bonding and, in particular, the desire to be at her mother's side that precipitated Jasmine's interest in returning home, though it was her husband's preference for Tobago that influenced their ultimate choice to settle in Tobago. For Delia, her return to Tobago was a response to escape the social inequities that were characteristic of her experiences in England. It permitted her to seek comfort through bonding with relatives who shared her ancestral past. She has described her return experience as a "priceless gift" and has been overwhelmed by the nostalgia associated with her return to her ancestral home or, more specifically, her ancestral space. A deep sense of patriotism was evident among the majority of returnees who expressed interests in empowering Tobagonians and enhancing capacity within key institutional arms of Tobagonian society. Interestingly, none of the returnees was born in Tobago. but the vast majority demonstrated patriotic tendencies.

The island paradise conception has been the major "pull factor" enticing returnees to return to Tobago. Notwithstanding some unfavourable experiences, all returnees – with the exception of one – had no immediate plans to leave Tobago and it is quite likely that they may never leave the island to live elsewhere. In making their migratory move, the returnees have all yearned for the ideals associated with the ideal paradise concept – peace and tranquility, unspoiled natural environment, a stress-free zone, a manageable pace of life and its aquaculture. On settling, the returnees have acknowledged experiencing problems of one kind or another and as one stated, such problems have largely been functions of the ideal paradise conceptions; in particular, the slow, carefree pace at which business is pursued. The latter has been a principal concern especially for returnees who have established business operations on the island. Nonetheless, the island paradise conception stands out as the principal exogenous factor that precipitated returnees' desire to return and their subsequent exposure to unfavourable experiences whether with respect to a substandard work ethic, stressful and arduous work routines and the lack of voluntarism. Notwithstanding these experiences, the returnees have generally been indicating that they are prepared to remain in Tobago, a response that is likely to be due ultimately to the ideal paradise conception as the major factor shaping their decision and major experiences. A bit of nostalgia and the desire to fulfil some philanthropic ideals appear to be additional factors that would strengthen their commitment to remain in Tobago.

## Notes

1. This is a preliminary estimate based upon the Trinidad and Tobago Population and Housing Census 2000 (Central Statistical Office 2001).
2. Creswell (1998, 65) suggests that in the context of phenomenological studies, data collection should target no more than ten cases. In Tobago, there may not be many returnees and from a qualitative standpoint, the sample used may in fact be approaching saturation.

## References

Byron, M. 2000. Return Migration to the Eastern Caribbean: Comparative Experiences and Policy Implications. *Social and Economic Studies* 49 (4): 155–88.

Central Statistical Office of the Republic of Trinidad and Tobago. 2001. *2000 Population and Housing Census: Preliminary Report.* Port of Spain: Central Statistical Office.

Creswell, J.W. 1998. *Qualitative Inquiry and Research Design: Choosing among Five Traditions.* Thousand Oaks, CA: Sage.

Denzin, N.K., and Y.S. Lincoln. 1994. *Handbook of Qualitative Research.* Thousand Oaks, CA: Sage.

De Souza, R.M. 1998. The Spell of the Cascadura: West Indian Return Migration. In *Globalization and Neo-Liberalization: The Caribbean Context,* ed. T. Klak, 227–53. Lanham, MD: Rowan and Littlefield.

Husserl, E. 1964. *The Idea of Phenomenology.* Trans. W.P. Alston and G. Nakhnikian. The Hague: Martinus Nijhoff.

Lewis, W.A. 1958. Economic Development with Unlimited Supplies of Labour. In *The Economics of Underdevelopment,* ed. A. Agarwala and S. Singh, 400–449. London: Oxford University Press.

Marshall, D. 1987. A History of West Indian Migrations: Overseas Opportunities and Safety Valve Policies. In *The Caribbean Exodus,* ed. B. Levine, 15–31. New York: Praeger.

Miles, M.B., and A.M. Huberman. 1994. *Qualitative Data Analysis: A Sourcebook of New Methods.* 2nd edition. Thousand Oaks, CA: Sage.

Moustakas, C.E. 1994. *Phenomenological Research Methods.* Thousand Oaks, CA: Sage.

Nieswiadomy, R.M. 1993. *Foundations of Nursing Research.* 2nd edition. Norwalk, CT: Appleton and Lange.

Oiler, C.J. 1986. Phenomenology: The Method. In *Nursing Research: A Qualitative Perspective,* ed. P.L. Munhall and C.J. Oiler, 69–82. Norwalk, CT: Appleton Century Crofts.

Philpott, S.B. 1973. *West Indian Migration: The Montserrat Case.* London: Athlone Press.

Plaza, D. 2002. The Socio-Cultural Adjustment of Second Generation British Caribbean "Return" Migrants to Barbados and Jamaica. *Journal of Eastern Caribbean Studies* 27 (4): 135–60.

Policy Research and Development Institute. 1999. *Tobago Survey of Living Conditions Report 1997.* Tobago House of Assembly.

Schutz, A. 1962. *The Problem of Social Reality.* The Hague: Martinus Nijhoff.

———. 1964. *Studies in Social Theory.* The Hague: Martinus Nijhoff.

———. 1967. *The Phenomenology of the Social World.* Evanston, IL: Northwestern University Press.

———. 1970. *On Phenomenology and Social Relations.* Chicago: University of Chicago Press.

St Bernard, G. 2005. Return Migration to Trinidad and Tobago: Motives, Consequences and the Prospect of Re-Migration. In *The Experience of Return Migration: Caribbean Perspectives,* ed. R. Potter, D. Conway and J. Phillips, 157–82. Aldershot: Ashgate.

Stinner, W., K. de Albuquerque and R.S. Bryce-Laporte. 1982. Preface. In *Return Migration and Remittances: Developing a Caribbean Perspective,* ed. W. Stinner, K. de Albuquerque and R.S. Bryce-Laporte, ix–lxvii. Washington, DC: Research Institute for Immigration and Ethnic Studies, Smithsonian Institution.

# Sequence of Emigration and Return

## The Jamaican Experience

| John Small |

Among the English-speaking Caribbean countries, Jamaica has had the largest outflow of its citizens than any other island since migration began in earnest in the early 1950s. Over the last fifteen to twenty years, a significant number of those early migrants have been returning. However, return migration to Jamaica is not a recent phenomenon; it has always been an accompanying feature of both the country and the Caribbean region. Against this background, the phenomenon of return migration to the Caribbean in general and Jamaica in particular can best be understood through an examination of the sequence of emigration and the interlocking nature of outward flows and returns to the home country. This should also be accompanied by an analysis of those intervening variables, which arose from the dynamics of the process. Some of these factors are the push and pull determinants which feature in the initial decision to go or to stay and, after a period in the receiving country, to stay or to return to the sending country. Return migration therefore should not be viewed as an isolated phenomenon operating within discrete boundaries, but as interconnected processes which are operating across borders and in which the dynamics have positive and negative implications for sending and receiving countries. These implications go beyond the immediate individual and extend into future generations.

This chapter briefly examines the interlocking dynamics of emigration and the causes for the flow of Caribbean people to the United Kingdom, Canada and the United States of America as well as the return flows to Jamaica. The chapter construes the experiences of the migrant and adjustment issues in the receiving country as critical variables in the decision to return. Data on return migration to Jamaica are presented with particular emphasis on the return flow from the United Kingdom. The activities of returnees and the process of readaptation to the homeland are also examined, as are migration policies, currently of major concern for Jamaica and other countries of the region as they respond to the return flow and the needs of the receiving countries to replace those migrants who have returned to the home country.

## Some Underpinning Theoretical Considerations

Migration is generally explained at micro and macro levels. At the micro level of explanation, the migrants are dominant, responding to prevailing conditions at home and taking action to maximize the quality of life by the removal of geographical obstacles through international migration. By being able to conquer the "tyranny of space" the migrants experience gains. If they do not obtain greater rewards for their labour, they will return to the homeland as "return failures" or after a period of productive employment and accumulating savings in the receiving country, they return to the sending country with feelings of success. Successful returnees may become agents of change by the use of their capital, experiences and skills acquired in the receiving countries thereby resulting in an increased level of economic activity and economic growth in the home country (Appleyard 1992; Massey et al. 1993). However, other writers on the subject have drawn our attention to the limitations of the rational maximizer and point to the fact that there are other variables which cause migration (Fisher, Martin and Straubhaar 1997). As Tilly (1990, 75) pointed out it is "not people who migrate but networks" and Cohen (1986) indicated that migrants are not "atomistic flies", implying that the process of migration and return includes primary and secondary ties with several individuals. The macro-level explanation holds that migration can best be understood if the movement is seen within the historical perspective, which takes into account the broader structural transformation. Migration within this framework exacerbates regional imbalances and it reproduces in the sending country the same structural forces that created surplus labour which forced people to migrate in the first instance. The micro and macro levels of explanation assume the existence of "push" and "pull" factors but they cannot adequately explain migration in general, nor migration from or return flows to the Caribbean. The explanation therefore seems to be somewhere between both.

## Sequence of Caribbean Migration to the United Kingdom Setting the Stage for the Return

Caribbean people have always been migrants either inter-regionally or internationally (Thomas-Hope 1998; Koslofsky 1981). But it was not until after World War II that the number of Caribbean migrants increased substantially. Post-war Britain began an economic expansion which saw many British workers moving up the occupational ladder, creating vacancies at the lower levels to be filled by Caribbean and other migrants from the former colonial countries. The movement of people from the Caribbean was a direct link of Caribbean labour to the region's colonial history. There was also a sense, among migrants, that higher wages could be obtained in the mother country. Migration to Britain was largely a response to demand for labour. In Davison's sample in 1962, a number of West Indians were asked why they were going to Britain. They were provided with four possible responses: to seek employment, to join relatives, to study, or any other reason. The majority responded that they were going to Britain to seek employment. The British Labour Party Leader Hugh Gaitskill said in 1961 that there exists "an almost precise correlation between the movement in the number of unskilled vacancies . . . and the immigration figures. Immigration rose and fell according to the demand for labour from year to year . . . when demand fell away as it did between 1957 and 1959 there was a corresponding decrease in West Indian immigration" (Hiro 1973, 9). During this period, Britain had an "open-door" policy that resulted in about 17,000 West Indians migrating to Britain in 1954. The Commonwealth Immigration Act of 1962, however, triggered the "beat-the-ban" movement and caused up to 34,000 people (Goddard 1976) to arrive prior to the 1962 Act. The 1962 Immigration Act gave rise to family-based migration from the Caribbean and became a watershed in migration flows into Britain, thereby giving Caribbean migration a distinguishing feature by becoming very selective, primarily women and children. Davison (1962), in his study, found that 98 per cent of the children of early West Indian migrants were left behind. This would suggest that the early migrants did not have permanent settlement in mind, so the stage was already set for the return phenomenon. The majority migrated when they were between thirty and forty years old. Peach (1998) has shown that the Caribbean population in the United Kingdom has grown from approximately 28,000 in 1951 to 559,000 in 1991 and of this total about 264,591 were born in the Caribbean and 326,424 were born in the United Kingdom.

By 1970, the flow slowed drastically due to the principles that were set out by the Home Secretary in the House of Commons debate on 21 February 1973, which ushered in the concept of "minimum" entry:

> The first principle in recognition that Britain is a crowded island with a labour force which, for the moment at least, appears ample for her needs, and, therefore there must be restriction on all permanent immigration to what I described in my statement on 25th January as the "inescapable minimum" and we must have the establishment of effective controls to achieve this. The second principle is to recognize, within the overall need, a continuing responsibility to those . . . entitled to United Kingdom citizenship. . . . The third principle is the recognition that it is both right and natural to give easy access to Britain to all those with close and recent family ties with this country . . . (House of Commons 1973)

When the unrestricted flow to the United Kingdom came to an end, the flow to the United States accelerated and this was amplified by re-migration and return to the home country. Since the movement to the United States began, figures from the Immigration and Naturalization Service show that over 400,000 legal immigrants entered the United States from Jamaica alone.

## Phases and Flows of Migration to the United Kingdom

The flow of migrants from Jamaica to the United Kingdom can be divided into several phases:

1. 1948–55: The 1948 Immigration Act gave right of entry and settlement that did not exist before. It facilitated the free movement of labour from the Caribbean to meet the shortage of labour in the United Kingdom. The people who migrated during this period were the skilled and semi-skilled.

2. 1955–62: In the early period following 1955, emigration was stimulated by chain migration but this was overtaken by the effect of the pending

legislation to restrict entry to the United Kingdom. Consequently, skilled, semi-skilled and unskilled workers dominated the flow. The Immigration Act of 1962 created the mass movement of people from the Caribbean to Britain and brought forward planned and unplanned family reunification.

3. 1962–71: This period consisted mainly of the selected flow; it is characterized by family re-unification that included skilled, unskilled and semi-skilled workers as well as children under eighteen years old.

4. 1971–2003: Select migration and visitors. This period also represents the commencement of return migration, circular migration and re-migration of some Caribbean people from the United Kingdom to Canada and the United States.

## Attitude Towards the Caribbean Population in Britain: A Factor in the Return Process

The Caribbean population obtained menial jobs that the white working-class population in Britain did not want. These jobs were poorly paid and often dirty. Most jobs provided a poor working environment and required long, antisocial hours. At the same time the only available housing was in areas that were designated for slum clearance. The Caribbean population at that time was faced with triple jeopardy, lack of adequate housing, low-grade jobs and serious health risk (Rose, Deakin and Abraham 1969). This situation was reinforced by the negative attitude of a part of the British population towards them.

Two days after the arrival of the SS *Empire Windrush* in 1948, a Labour member of parliament wrote to the Labour leader Clement Attlee calling for a ban on immigration. "An influx of colored people domiciled here is likely to impair the harmony strength and cohesion of our public and social life and to cause discord and unhappiness among all concerned," he said. Also, following a debate on the matter, the Labour government set up a Cabinet committee in 1950 to review "the further means which might be adopted to check the immigration into the country of coloured people from the British Colonial territories" (James and Harris 1993, 56). A Cardiff newspaper at the time summed up the general attitude to the arrival of West Indians into Britain:

> The Government ought to declare it to be a part of the national policy that this country is not to be regarded as an emigration field, that no more immigrants can be admitted and that immigrants must return to where they came from. This must apply to black men from the West Indies as well as the United States. (Hiro 1973, xx)

Twenty years later Daniel (1968) found massive discrimination against the black population, which has more recently been reconfirmed by Macpherson in 1999.

## Experiences in Britain: A Return Push Factor

During the early phase of arrival in Britain, Caribbean migrants faced many challenges arising out of the process of migration and adaptation to a country that was sometimes hostile towards them. The adaptation process involved issues relating to separation from the familiar and attachment to the unfamiliar (Foner 1998, 2001). These challenges were sometimes very difficult to overcome because of structural forces in the society which militated against the drive among the Caribbean population to settle, achieve and return. The Caribbean migrant resolved and continues to resolve issues of adaptation, assimilation, incorporation, segregation, integration, cultural transformation, together with racial and cultural identification (Gilroy 1987). They had to learn the ways of the host community in order to secure a path that would lead to success thereby providing the base for a successful return to the homeland. A central variable in the path to success is employment which would provide adequate income, but this was retarded because of factors that were operating in the society. Glass (1960) found that 55 per cent of new arrivals from the West Indies underwent job downgrading when they arrived in Britain. This had a detrimental effect on those who were professionals. On arrival they had created new structures to cope with individual and collective failures in the host country while at the same time safeguarding traditional values. These values were often the primary source of their strength in an unfamiliar environment and in some instances operated as push and pull factors in the return process.

What are some of the return push factors? The welfare state has failed to support Caribbean migrants. A larger proportion of the black population is

concentrated in lower-paid occupations (Modood 1997). There are a disproportionate number of black Caribbean children in the care of the state and
they are less likely to be reunited with their own families or be placed with
substitute black families. Many of these children are placed inappropriately
in transracial settings. Daycare facilities provided for black children are very
poor. Black women are more likely to be home workers or casual employees
than white women. The schools have failed the Caribbean family causing
an over-representation of black boys in school exclusion figures and a
greater percentage are underachieving educationally (Grant and Brooks
1996). Proportionately more black children are placed in educationally
subnormal schools. Black people are more likely to become homeless, particularly those between the ages of sixteen and twenty-four, and they are more
likely to be affected by changes in social security benefits. There is an
over-representation of Caribbean people in psychiatric hospitals (Fernando
2002; Nazaroo 1997). Financial institutions apply more rigid criteria for
assessing the status of black people for private housing loans. Black people in
Britain have levels of unemployment twice that of the white population. In
confronting these challenges, the Caribbean population has used a number of
adaptive mechanisms, such as collective identities, to create solidarity and
coordinate action. Also, other possible measures have been geographical segregation as well as returning to the home country or moving to another country. The move to another country caused a snowball effect and set off another
process of chain re-migration and family unification in other countries, such
as the United States or Canada (Gilroy 1987).

## Trends in the Present Caribbean Population:
### A Return Reduction Factor

Modood et al. (1997) found that two-thirds of the Caribbean population in
the United Kingdom arrived before 1964 and that only a small percentage of
the children were not born there. Approximately one-third of the Caribbean
population came to Britain as children. Currently most Caribbean adults
were born in Britain, therefore new births are the second British-born generation. Fifty per cent of British-born Caribbean men and one-third of the
women have white partners. Two-thirds of Caribbean men are in mixed
relationships. Two out of every five children with a Caribbean mother or

father has a white parent. Salt (1996) analysed the census data on migration and showed that approximately two-thirds of the Caribbean population was born in Britain and only a very small portion of the elderly had been born in Britain. It is no longer accurate, therefore, to describe the Caribbean population in Britain as a migrant population. The Fourth National Survey of Ethnic Minorities in Britain (Modood et al. 1997) found that 96 per cent of the Caribbean population aged zero to fifteen were born in Britain, of those who are in the working age group of sixteen to fifty-nine, 53 per cent were born in Britain and those sixty or over constitute only 2 per cent (Warnes 1996). Against this background, and if present trends continue, it can be predicted that within the next forty to fifty years the Caribbean population in Britain will be totally transformed or disappear and return migration to the Caribbean will be reduced to the bare minimum.

## Comparative Pension Transfers: A Pull Return Factor

The flow of remittances to Jamaica is indicative of potential return because it is a conscious decision by the Jamaican migrant to save or invest at home rather than in the United Kingdom. It is also an expression of interest in the welfare of members of the family and support for communities and institutions to which they are bonded back home. The flow of British state pensions and related benefits to the Caribbean in general and Jamaica in particular represents a significant source of foreign exchange for these countries. Table 10.1 shows the extent of pension transfers to several Caribbean countries. Jamaica had the largest number of pensioners (24,000) resulting in pension flows and related benefits amounting to fifty-four million sterling in 1997, followed by Barbados with 3,083 pensioners and flows of £5,828,614. St Kitts and Nevis had 460 pensioners and benefits totalling £729,823; Grenada had 1,140 pensioners and benefits of £1,925,391; St Lucia had 1,120 pensioners and benefits of £2,018,100; St Vincent had 634 and benefits of £1,014,121; and Antigua had 338 pensioners and pension flows of £567,125. Britain has a reciprocal social security agreement with Jamaica and other Caribbean islands which means that British state pensioners who are residing in these countries are able to receive their pensions with relative ease. The pension flows and related benefits from the United Kingdom constitute a steady source of income and financial security for returnees, and are also

**Table 10.1**    UK State Pensions Transferred to Pensioners in Jamaica and the
Eastern Caribbean Countries, 1997

| Country | Number of Pensioners | Total Transferred (£) |
| --- | --- | --- |
| Jamaica | 24,000 | 54,000,000 |
| Barbados | 3,083 | 5,828,614 |
| St Kitts/Nevis | 460 | 729,823 |
| Grenada | 1,140 | 1,925,391 |
| St Lucia | 1,120 | 2,018,100 |
| St Vincent | 634 | 1,014,121 |
| Antigua | 338 | 567,125 |

*Source:* UK Pensions and Overseas Benefits Directorate 1999.

critical variables in the volume of remittances from overseas which are received annually in these countries. The portability of pension funds acts as a push factor in the return process.

## The Transnational Nature of Return Migration to Jamaica

Outward migration and return to the homeland has been a survival strategy of the people of the Caribbean. Marshall (1982) is of the view that there is a culture of migration in the Caribbean. Essentially, people from the Caribbean are transnational migrants. Periods of "bust-and-boom" in the receiving and sending country have pushed and pulled Caribbean people in both directions. These forces together with other factors created the phenomenon of multiple movements. The dynamics of the process over time generated social and economic relationships which link migrants and non-migrants into transnational communities, which in turn become the major force that sustains the outward flow and return to the homeland (Gemelch 1987; Levitt 1997; Massey, Goldring and Durand 1994). They support not only migration flows and family unification but also events back home, and in some instances they also support other directed forms of behaviour such as the drug trade (Dreher, Shapiro and Stoddart 1997; Griffith 1997). The network process becomes self-perpetuating by the evolution of structures and relationships which sustain the reciprocal flows. The network pulls together individuals, families, communities and friends into a complex web of inter-connections and interrelationships with multiple dimensions, political, economic, social, religious and cultural (Massey, Goldring and Durand 1994). Networks energize the return migration impulse by the provision of infor-mation, as well as financial, psychological and other forms of support rele-vant to the decision to return. It was these networks that pulled Caribbean migrants to certain areas in Britain thereby causing the geographical distri-bution of the Caribbean population in areas such as Greater London, Manchester, Birmingham and Sheffield (Peach 1998), and it is networks which have pulled returnees to certain geographical areas in the home country.

## Interdependencies between Emigration and Return: The Search for a Caribbean Typology

Every departing Caribbean is a potential returnee. Migration is indeed a complex process with a multitude of variables that influence the decision to go or to stay. Many theoreticians (King, Strachan and Mortimer 1983) have proposed several hypotheses to explain the return phenomenon: disappoint-ment theory, target income theory, network theory and circulation theory, but no single theory can explain return migration. Against the background of these theories, writers on the subject of return migration have developed several typologies. Not surprisingly, they all have overlapping features. These include: temporary or permanent worker migrants; student migrants; seasonal worker migrants; settlers; long-term circulators; transients; early returnees and late returnees. Return ideologies include short stay, long stay, voluntary and involuntary ("forced" or "free"), commuting, and recurrent (Byron and Condon 1996; Byron 1999; Gmelch 1987; Thomas-Hope 1985). It is clear from the typologies that Caribbean migration does not involve an ini-tial move with a final end, neither can return migration to the region be seen as the final stage in the process, since some return migrants will leave and return to the sending country a number of times during their lifetime thereby establishing multiple residences. Some migrants clearly choose to belong to more than one country at the same time. The typologies are used to identify the gains that the returning migrants have experienced in three major areas: educational advancement, human capital assets and capacity to remit resources to the country of origin (Goulbourne 2002). Although this approach is useful it is somewhat limited in terms of a comprehensive understanding of the contribution that the returnees can make to development. A more useful approach would be to examine the characteristics of the returnees, the reasons for their return and the timing of their return. These factors will determine to a large extent the contribution that returnees can make to the development of the particular society and will also have implications for government policy directed towards returnees.

## Return Migration to Jamaica: Types of Return Migrants to Jamaica

Returning residents to Jamaica fall into a number of distinct groups:

- Those who have reached retirement age
- Those who have been made redundant because of restructuring or downsizing in the private as well as public sectors
- Those who have taken voluntary severance or early retirement
- Some are in search of employment
- Some have returned to establish themselves as owners or managers of a business
- Some have achieved their objectives
- Some have returned to provide care and support for elderly relatives
- Others have become tired of living in the United Kingdom, Canada and the United States
- Some are searching for their identity and to know the country of their parents or grandparents
- Some have returned to fulfil their deep desire to contribute to the development of Jamaica
- Some have failed
- Some are "multiple returnees"
- Some have been deported back to Jamaica from the United States, Canada and the United Kingdom

## Economy and Society: The Returnees' Contribution

The contribution that the returnee can make to Jamaica will depend on a number of factors (Small 2002, 2003):

- The stage of the life cycle of the returnee
- The reasons for the return
- Whether the return is temporary or permanent
- The quality of the experience of the returnee in the receiving country and the country of origin
- The financial capital that has been accumulated in the receiving country
- The educational level of the individual
- The commitment and emotional bonding to the country of origin and the host country
- The health status of the returnee

The age profile will suggest the types of resources that will be necessary to provide services to meet the needs of the returnees. On the other hand, those who have retired represent a guaranteed source of foreign exchange flow into the country to which they have returned.

## Magnitude of the Volume and Flows of Returning Residents to Jamaica

Table 10.2 shows the number of returning residents to Jamaica from 1993 to 2001. The United Kingdom has the largest number of returning residents overall with 919 in 1993. In this same year there were 988 from the United States, 278 from Canada and 174 from other countries. The flow peaked in 1994 for all three countries, with the United Kingdom accounting for 1,145 (and in this and subsequent years became the country accounting for the largest number of returnees), the United States accounting for 999, Canada accounting for 333 and other countries accounting for 110. Since 1995, there has been a progressive decrease in the number of returnees, to the extent that in 2001 the returnees from the United Kingdom numbered 531, the United States 427 and Canada 144. Within the nine-year period, the United Kingdom accounted for 7,800 returnees in total whereas 6,837 came from the United States, 2,138 from Canada and 983 from other countries. The total number of returnees for the period was 17,758.

There may be many reasons for the progressive decline. Many potential returnees may have decided to remain in the host country because of adverse reports that they have received about Jamaica, health reasons or to be close to

**Table 10.2**    Number and Origin of Returning Residents, 1993–2001,
Originating Country

| Year | UK | USA | Canada | Others | Total |
|------|-----|-----|--------|--------|-------|
| 1993 | 919 | 988 | 278 | 174 | 2,359 |
| 1994 | 1,145 | 999 | 333 | 110 | 2,587 |
| 1995 | 1,007 | 905 | 288 | 153 | 2,353 |
| 1996 | 995 | 863 | 296 | 114 | 2,268 |
| 1997 | 995 | 762 | 244 | 91 | 2,092 |
| 1998 | 821 | 715 | 211 | 128 | 1,875 |
| 1999 | 793 | 677 | 212 | 83 | 1,765 |
| 2000 | 594 | 501 | 132 | 55 | 1,282 |
| 2001 | 531 | 427 | 144 | 75 | 1,177 |
| Total | 7,800 | 6,837 | 2,138 | 983 | 17,758 |

*Source:* Planning Institute of Jamaica 2002.

their children and grandchildren. Others may have re-migrated to the
United States. As indicated above the larger number of returnees from the
United Kingdom may be due to the early flow between 1955 and 1962, and
some of these people have reached retirement age within the last twenty
years. Geographical proximity may also be a factor in that those Jamaicans
who are living in the United States are able to make regular visits to Jamaica;
consequently, they are more in touch with developments in Jamaica, so there
is not the pressing need to return home.

It is noteworthy that the return flow of Caribbean migrants currently represents the major movement of the Caribbean population between Britain
and the Caribbean. Table 10.3 shows the number of returnees who fall
within the category of deportee from the United Kingdom, United States of
America and Canada. Within the period 1990 to 2002, Jamaica received
21,779 deportees of which about 50 per cent were deported for drug-related
reasons, the others as a result of having committed other forms of crimes or
who were on visitor visas and remained in the country beyond the period
that is permitted. Over the period of thirteen years, there has been a progressive increase in the number of Jamaicans who have been deported back to
Jamaica. The United Kingdom has deported 3,625 persons; United States,
14,388; Canada, 2,912; and 854 have been deported from other, unknown
countries. In respect to the United Kingdom, there has been an astronomical

**Table 10.3**    Number and Origin of Deportees, 1990–2002, Originating Country

| Year | UK | USA | Canada | Others | Total |
|------|------|--------|--------|--------|--------|
| 1990 | 22 | 614 | 48 | 2 | 686 |
| 1991 | 83 | 624 | 66 | 39 | 812 |
| 1992 | 66 | 788 | 120 | 5 | 979 |
| 1993 | 41 | 796 | 182 | 12 | 1,031 |
| 1994 | 96 | 872 | 399 | 67 | 1,434 |
| 1995 | 120 | 1,018 | 382 | 62 | 1,582 |
| 1996 | 115 | 1,193 | 392 | 65 | 1,765 |
| 1997 | 119 | 1,238 | 277 | 65 | 1,699 |
| 1998 | 250 | 1,483 | 325 | 103 | 2,161 |
| 1999 | 242 | 1,533 | 227 | 69 | 2,071 |
| 2000 | 243 | 1,252 | 150 | 52 | 1,697 |
| 2001 | 767 | 1,410 | 203 | 151 | 2,531 |
| 2002 | 1,461 | 1,567 | 141 | 162 | 3,331 |
| Total | 3,625 | 14,388 | 2,912 | 854 | 21,779 |

*Source:* Planning Institute of Jamaica 2002.

increase in the number of deportees per year to Jamaica, moving from 22 in 1990 to 1,461 in 2002. Within this period, the British government introduced restrictive immigration measures. The number from the United States increased from 614 in 1990 to 1,567 in 2002. Canada deported fewer Jamaicans than the other two countries overall. However, Canada accounts for 48 in 1990 but increased to 141 in 2002. Canada also recently introduced more restrictive immigration regulations. The difference in the number of deportees from each country may be explained simply in terms of the number of Jamaicans who settle in each country and/or the number who have been given temporary visas. The deportee phenomenon has caused transnational criminal networks to flourish. The number of persons who are being deported because of crimes related to the drug trade suggests the need for measures to be taken to stem the demand for drugs and at the same time to stop the supply (Dreher, Shapiro and Stoddart 1997). Dealing with deportees represents a new challenge in terms of the need for additional resources for new crime fighting and security measures.

Special skills and programmes are also required to respond to the needs of deportees. Many of them have lived overseas for a considerable period of time and have severed their links with their relatives in Jamaica. Often on their return they become isolated and alienated and exist on the periphery of society. The need is even more obvious because of the age group of the deportees, the majority being twenty-five to thirty-five years of age.

## Characteristics of Returnees

The data presented consist of 460 participants who attended a national conference in Kingston, Jamaica in 2002. The participants came from all fourteen parishes throughout the island. All the participants were required to complete a conference form which sought such basic information as date of birth, year they migrated, country to which they migrated, year of return, country they returned from and why they returned. The participants in the conference who were not returnees were removed from the sample leaving a total of 365. The data must be viewed with considerable caution because participants at the conference had been self-selected, perhaps because their interest would be represented at the conference, or the speakers or the theme of the conference attracted them. These factors may explain why there were no returnees below twenty years of age in the sample. It may also explain why there were a greater number of females in attendance.

Table 10.4 shows the number of returnees who attended the conference and the country of origin of the returnees: 61.7 per cent (225) from Britain, 19.2 per cent (70) from the United States, 12.3 per cent (45) from Canada, and 6.8 per cent (25) from other countries. The data confirm, as in table 10.2, that Britain continues to dominate the return flow. This may be related to the fact that the majority of Jamaicans went to Britain during the early phase of the outward flows from Jamaica. Many of these people reached retirement age several years ago and have returned to Jamaica. The outward flow to the United States and Canada came at a later stage and may have included a younger population who may not yet have reached retirement age.

Table 10.5 shows the age distribution of the male returnees. Of the 160 male returnees, 134 (83 per cent) were forty to sixty. Twenty-seven (16.8 per cent) aged forty to forty-nine, and a similar percentage aged fifty to fifty-nine. Those sixty and over constitute the largest group of male returnees with eighty (50 per cent). Overall percentages in the three age groups constitute approximately 84 per cent. Clearly, the majority of returning males in the sample are retirees. Only twenty-six (16 per cent) are aged twenty to thirty-nine. This may be a reflection of bias in the data but it gives a glimpse of the pattern of the age group of returnees.

Table 10.6 shows the age group distribution of female returnees. Of the 205 females, twenty-three (11.2 per cent) are aged forty to forty-nine, forty-one (20 per cent) are aged fifty to fifty-nine and 123 (60 per cent) are over

**Table 10.4**    Conference Attendees by Country of Origin

| UK | USA | Canada | Others | Total |
|----|-----|--------|--------|-------|
| 225 | 70 | 45 | 25 | 365 |

*Source:* Author's tabulations.

**Table 10.5**    Gender/Age Distribution and Percentage of Returning Residents, Male

| Age Group | Number | Per cent |
|-----------|--------|----------|
| Under 20 | 0 | 0 |
| 20–29 | 8 | 5 |
| 30–39 | 18 | 11.25 |
| 40–49 | 27 | 16.87 |
| 50–59 | 27 | 16.87 |
| 60+ | 80 | 50 |
| Total | 160 | 100 |

*Source:* Author's tabulations.

**Table 10.6**    Gender/Age Distribution and Percentage of Returning Residents, Female

| Age Group | Number | Per cent |
|-----------|--------|----------|
| Under 20 | 0 | 0 |
| 20–29 | 6 | 2.9 |
| 30–39 | 12 | 5.9 |
| 40–49 | 23 | 11.2 |
| 50–59 | 41 | 20 |
| 60+ | 123 | 60 |
| Total | 205 | 100 |

*Source:* Author's tabulations.

sixty. There is a similar pattern in the age group of male returnees in that the majority is at least forty years of age. Only eighteen (8.7 per cent) are aged twenty to thirty-nine.

When the two groups are compared, 5 per cent of male returnees are twenty to twenty-nine years of age compared with approximately 3 per cent of females of the same age group. Of returnees aged thirty to thirty-nine, 11 per cent are male and approximately 6 per cent are female. Of returnees aged forty to forty-nine, approximately 17 per cent are male compared to 11 per cent female. Returnees aged fifty to fifty-nine are approximately 17 per cent male compared to 20 per cent female; returnees aged sixty and over are 50 per cent male and 60 per cent female. The females dominate in the age group of fifty and up. The difference may simply be a reflection of the retirement process in Britain where females retire at sixty and males at sixty-five. Also, perhaps more females returned home than males due to the death of the husband or the female returned first to pave the way for a smooth resettlement while the male remains overseas to conclude family matters before the total move.

When a comparison is made with the pattern of retirees from the United Kingdom who have returned to the Eastern Caribbean, a similar age distribution exists. Of the total number of retirees in the Eastern Caribbean the pattern is as follows: Antigua, 37 per cent; Dominica, 52 per cent; Montserrat, 61 per cent; St Kitts and Nevis, 55 per cent; St Lucia, 42 per cent; and St Vincent, 47 per cent, demonstrating that considerable proportions are retirees (CARICOM 1991).

Table 10.7 shows the number of years that returnees in the sample remained overseas. The majority of males as well as females remained overseas for between twenty and forty years. From the sample, ten males (3 per cent) remained overseas for between fifteen and twenty-four years compared with thirty-four females (16.5 per cent). Of returnees aged twenty-five to twenty-nine, there are ten males (6.2 per cent) compared with twenty-seven females (13 per cent). For returnees aged thirty to thirty-four, there are twenty-seven males (16.8 per cent) compared with forty females (19.5 per cent). For returnees aged thirty-five to thirty-nine, there are fifty males and fifty-five females (31.2 per cent and 26.8 per cent respectively). Of those aged forty and up there are sixty-three males (39 per cent) and forty-five females (21.9 per cent). Males remained longer overseas in percentage terms than females. The data are suggesting that the majority of returnees are now over

**Table 10.7**   Number of Years Returnees Remained Overseas

| Number of Years | Male | Female |
| --- | --- | --- |
| 0–5 | 0 | 4 |
| 5–9 | 0 | 0 |
| 10–14 | 2 | 4 |
| 15–19 | 1 | 10 |
| 20–24 | 7 | 20 |
| 25–29 | 10 | 27 |
| 30–34 | 27 | 40 |
| 35–39 | 50 | 55 |
| 40+ | 63 | 45 |
| Total | 160 | 205 |

*Source:* Author's tabulations and Mohood et al. 1997, 20.

seventy years of age, which is indicative of the types of policy and services that will have to be put into place by the government to meet the needs of this group of returnees.

## Adaptation Strategy and the Impact of Returnees on the Home Country

Return to the home country has been the dream of most Caribbean migrants. Many Jamaican migrants indicated that their initial intention was to remain overseas for a maximum period of five years but, as can be seen from the data, the majority have spent more than thirty years overseas. Many returnees have experienced difficulties in the readaptation process because of long separation from Jamaica and irregular visits causing them to be out of touch with events at home. In addition, many of them have internalized the norms, values, attitudes and culture of the receiving country – in some cases imperceptibly. These changes are sometimes in conflict with those of the home country. The majority of the returnees would have grown up under colonial rule with its rigid centralized command which was characteristic of plantation society and economy during that period (Beckford 1972). However, during the period overseas, they have acquired the attitude of the population of the host country and have become forceful in challenging bureaucracies and demanding their rights as citizens in a democratic society. While this approach is considered desirable in the host country, in some service areas in Jamaica it is often resented by those without the migration experience, thereby causing negative responses, which in turn can be very frustrating for the returnee. In some instances returning to the homeland represents the last phase of the life cycle. Although many returnees feel more secure than prior to migrating by virtue of their improved lifestyle, financial security and the experience of living in First World countries, nevertheless, they need to learn new survival strategies because the society has gone through major changes in contradistinction to when they first migrated. Many returnees feel that they are treated like strangers and are sometimes resented.

## Reintegration and Readaptation: The Organizational Response

In an effort to cope with the many challenges, the National Association of Returning Residents was founded in 1993. There now exist thirty chapters of the association throughout the country with at least one chapter in each of the fourteen parishes on the island. The nature of the association is summed up in the preamble to its constitution:

> Necessity gave birth to the National Association of Returning Residents. Many Jamaicans have travelled abroad, worked under adverse conditions, made tremendous sacrifice and saved for the return home. Many have succeeded; others have not . . . those who have returned experienced great difficulty with Government and other agencies. Some are exploited, treated like strangers and feel isolated. Returning residents have contributed and are contributing, and will continue to contribute to the development of Jamaica and must be offered the courtesy, rights, duties and responsibilities as true citizens of Jamaica. It is against this background that the national association was formed, its main aim being that of supporting returnees in the re adaptation process. (NARR 2002)

The association performs a number of functions. It acts as a pressure group; provides support and counselling for its members; offers a channel of communication between groups and returnees; establishes links with other groups overseas and with governments and voluntary organizations in countries from which its members have returned in order that unfinished business in the host countries can be dealt with expeditiously; and represents returnees and brings to national attention the contribution of returnees to the society and economy.

The association crafted a strategy for change which had three elements. First, to attract the attention of the society through a high profile programme of activities which policy makers and opinion formers could not ignore. Meetings were held with policy makers, senior civil servants, financial institutions and key politicians. Annual conferences were organized. The list of speakers at various conferences included the governor general; the prime minister and other key members of parliament; members of parliament from the United Kingdom and Canada; and key representatives from the United States Embassy together with ambassadors from other countries where Jamaicans have settled. The themes of the conferences captured the interest of all sections of the media. Themes included "The Role of Returning Residents in Social and Economic Development", "Crime, Poverty and the Economy", and "Together We Are Making a Difference". In addition, the association designed a programme whereby annual financial contributions are made to a variety of voluntary organizations.

The second strategy was to concentrate on measures to legitimize the organization in the eyes of its members and the society. Papers were presented at important events such as a seminar of chief executive officers of the fifty largest companies in Jamaica. Factual data regarding the effect of remittances on the economy and society and how returnees can use their skills to contribute to the development of the country were prepared and disseminated. The association presented a report to the government which contained recommendations for action in key areas of the economy and society. The recommendations were discussed at a round table with senior members of the government.

The third element of the strategy was to coordinate action that was in the interest of both returnees and all Jamaicans. An example of this was the lead role taken by the association in negotiating with the government to secure the savings of returnees and all Jamaicans at the time of the collapse of a major commercial bank during a financial meltdown in Jamaica in 1996. The organization joined with a depositors group and was able to negotiate and obtain agreement from the government to secure the savings of all depositors. Another element of the strategy was lobbying for a debate in the Senate focusing on the role of returnees and the Jamaican population overseas. A resolution was passed for the government to give more attention to both returnees and Jamaicans overseas. This debate and the subsequent resolution resulted in the establishment of an Overseas Department in the Ministry of Foreign Affairs and a national conference on the Jamaican diaspora. The association also established a weekly radio programme where returnees would talk about their experiences and the public would participate by phone calls to the host of the programme. Parliamentary representatives and private sector individuals were interviewed on topics that were of interest not only to returnees but also to the society as a whole. Members of the association were also encouraged to join neighbourhood associations and put themselves forward to be nominated as local and central government representatives. The strategy resulted in the association becoming a powerful pressure group which influenced the direction of certain policies.

## Policy Implications of Return Migration and the Role of Government

The role of government in emigration and return migration is a critical one. In recognition of this, the government created the "Returning Residents Charter" in 1993. The charter recognized the value of returning residents which is summed up as follows: "The Government of Jamaica regards Jamaicans resident overseas as an integral part of the country's assets and developmental resources. In order to address these and other concerns, the government intends to enact a Charter for Long-Term Returning Residents." A returning resident is defined as "a Jamaican national who has attained the age of eighteen years and has been residing overseas for not less than three consecutive years and is returning to Jamaica to reside permanently" (Ministry of Foreign Affairs, 1993).

On the basis of the charter, the government has pursued policies aimed at returning residents and the Jamaican community overseas. These include duty-free imports of personal and household effects; an information pack for returning residents and Jamaicans overseas; the creation of a commissioner of customs for returning residents; the establishment of a skill bank; and the development of investment programmes directed to attract returning residents and Jamaicans overseas such as the establishment of foreign exchange accounts with interest paid in foreign exchange. All this is in the interest of encouraging Jamaicans overseas to return home.

## Return Migration and Migration Policy

The dynamics of emigration and return forces us to examine the relationship between sending and receiving countries in terms of migration policy. The dynamics have raised issues regarding the loss of population from the sending country and concerns in the receiving country. Questions are often raised about employment, health, housing and educational resources in the host country. In some countries, migrants are no longer seen as assets but economic migrants fleeing from the adverse conditions in their county. Attitudes have therefore developed in some sections of the host country about the use of scarce resources to meet the needs of people who are considered as aliens. As a consequence of the flow between countries, questions of governance arise because migration has become problematic, primarily as a result of the absence of well thought out social and political responses to the phenomenon. This is evidenced by the double response to migration where migrants are seen as "external enemies" who are likely to become the "enemy within". This perception creates the view that the population must guard itself against the newcomers. The other response is that migrants are used as scapegoats for all the social ills in the society, a mechanism that can be used to divert attention from the structural factors which underpin the migration process and which spawn migration movements in the first place. These perceptions produce xenophobia and other forms of moral panic in the host population. The construction of a migration policy is the responsibility of the state but pressure groups and other interested parties such as trade unions and business enterprises have key roles to play in determining the direction that the migration policy should take. Globalization and the open market economy require the free movement of labour and capital, which brings into focus conflicting views about a migration policy. There is tension between control and security and whether economic gains should dictate the extent of the inflows to the country. This tension tends to produce two types of migration policies, the institutionalized which is highly regulated, and the unwritten or open door, such as that which was in operation before the Immigration Act of 1962 in Britain.

Migration has implications for the society and economy. It is against this background that the National Association of Returning Residents pressured for discussion and development of an international migration policy, which would provide a framework for guidance and regulation of migration flows in line with Jamaica's socio-economic development. This need is even more critical and urgent for foreign policy as vital areas of domestic policy and the nation-state are contracting under globalization.

## Conclusion

A final observation is necessary. Although this chapter analyses the interconnections of the dynamics of Caribbean return migration in general and Jamaica in particular, it also explores the migration process and issues from a broader perspective with the inevitable consequence of not dealing in depth with some of the peculiarities of return migration to Jamaica. The chapter starts from the neo-classical economic perspective of the push-pull model, where the rational actor is influenced by events at home and in the host country, which feature in the decision to go or to stay. However, this approach diverts attention away from other interlocking dynamics of the process which operate independently of the push-pull forces. Against this background, Caribbean return migration cannot be seen as a linear process but as a spatial, multidimensional phenomenon where those who move and those who stay constantly adjust their lives to take advantage of opportunities as they arise, This, in turn, determines just who stays or who goes.

The colonial linkages are essential to our understanding of Caribbean migration and return. But economic, social and political forces were in operation before the onset of migration which was generated by the colonial links. Once migration commenced, individual's families and communities developed their own strategies and these became the dominant factors in the decision to go or to stay and subsequently affected the volume and flows. The Caribbean population experienced harsh and unpleasant working conditions during the early period of settlement in the United Kingdom. This situation forced them to develop varied survival strategies, including viewing returning home as "success" or "failure" or moving to another country. The process caused transnational networks to develop which became a self-sustaining force for Caribbean migration flows. Caribbean migration followed distinct phases; an initial response to the demand for labour which subsequently became self-feeding; a further phase which became relatively independent of economic forces at home and in the host country; a subsequent selective phase largely determined by events in the receiving country; and a final phase of decline in the inflow and commencement of outflow in the form of return migration.

A prevailing view is that migration is of benefit to both the sending and receiving country. However, it is often argued that it is in the interest of the most economically powerful countries and that ultimately it is those countries that determine the volume and flow of migration. From this perspective it is further argued that outward migration creams off "the best and the brightest" to meet the shortage of labour in the host country and to fuel development there, and that the sending country seldom experiences gains by the acquisition of new skills so "the gain capital abroad is a myth" (Bohning 1984, 186). Bohning argues further that return signifies failure. If the migrant is successful, ties in the sending country are discontinued, remittances are reduced or terminated and efforts are made to settle in the host country. In this regard, return results in failure to take risks and often retirement, so development is not enhanced by the return. While there is evidence to support both sides of the argument, what is needed is not further justification for the competing positions but a framework which will allow us to take all of these variables and analyse them at the macro, micro and meso levels, and arrive at conclusions regarding the full effect of export and return labour on the economy and society. As indicated earlier, a decision to return to the homeland may be taken several times within the life cycle of the migrant; consequently, attention should not be so much on return but on those intervening variables which feature in the decision to go or to stay and the objective conditions of the returnees.

Return migration to Jamaica is selective. It is not a return of failure but largely a return for retirement. The return flow to Jamaica draws our attention to the role of linkages which sustain the return process thereby giving us a glimpse into the causes for the decision to go, to settle or to return. The data allows us to draw some general conclusions about the people who return in contradistinction to those who settle permanently.

Finally, the changing structure of the Caribbean population overseas, particularly in the United Kingdom, begs the question as to whether in the not too distant future the Caribbean population will be totally absorbed into the British population, thereby making return migration a phenomenon of the past. In view of globalization and the demand for cheap labour in developed countries, increasing poverty in developing countries and the role of remittances in the labour exporting countries such as Jamaica and the wider

Caribbean, we may be entering a new phase and type of international migration. In this new form of migration, the governments of the region may have to establish programmes to train their people for export in areas in which these countries will be able to compete confidently with developed countries as against their current incapacity to compete in other areas of trade. This new international migration flow may be characterized by temporary and circular migration to the benefit to both sending and receiving countries.

# References

Appleyard, R.T. 1992. Migration and Development: A Critical Relationship. *Asian and Pacific Migration Journal* 1 (1): 1–19.

Beckford, G.L. 1972. *Persistent Poverty.* Oxford: Oxford University Press.

Bohning, W.R. 1984. *Studies in International Labour Migration.* London: Macmillan.

Byron, M. 1999. The Caribbean Born Population in 1990s Britain, Who Will Return? *Journal of Ethnic and Migration Studies* 25 (2): 285–301.

Byron, M., and S. Condon. 1996. A Comparative Study of Caribbean Return Migration, from Britain and France: Towards a Context-Dependent Explanation. *Transactions, Institute of British Geographers,* new ser., 21 (1): 91–104.

CARICOM. CARICOM Regional Census Office. 1993. *Commonwealth Caribbean Population and Housing Census, 1991.* Port of Spain: CARICOM Regional Census Office.

Cohen, R. 1986. Some Theories of Migration: A Synopsis and Comment. In *Themes and Theories in Migration Research,* proceedings from an International Seminar on Migration Research, September. Rungstedgaard: Danish Social Science Research Council.

Daniel, W.W. 1968. *Racial Discrimination in England.* London: Penguin.

Davison, R. 1962. *West Indian Migrants.* London: Oxford University Press.

Dreher, M., S. Shapiro and A. Stoddart. 1997. Drug Consumption and Distribution in Jamaica: A National Ethnographic Study, Executive Summary mimeo.

Fernando, S. 2002. *Mental Health: Race and Culture.* London: Palgrave.

Fisher, P., A. Martin and R.E. Straubhaar. 1997. Should I Stay or Should I Go? In *Migration, Immobility and Development,* ed. T. Hammar et al., 49–90. New York: Oxford University Press.

Foner, N. 1998. Towards a Comparative Perspective on Caribbean Migration. In *Caribbean Migration,* ed. M. Chamberlain, 47–60. London: Routledge.

————. 2001. *Island in the City.* Berkeley and Los Angeles: University of California Press.

Gilroy, P. 1987. *There Ain't No Black in the Union Jack.* London: Hutchinson.

Glass, R. 1960. *New Comers: The West Indians in London.* London: George Allen and Unwin.

Gmelch, G. 1987. Work, Innovation, and Investment: The Impact of Return Migrants in Barbados. *Human Organization* 46 (2): 131.

Goddard, L.L. 1976. Social Structure and Migration: A Comparative Study of the West Indies. PhD thesis, University of Michigan.

Goulbourne, H. 2002. *Caribbean Transnational Experience.* London: Pluto Press.

Grant, D., and K. Brooks. 1996. Exclusion from Schools: Responses from the Black Community. *Pastoral Care in Education* 14 (30): 20–27.

Griffith, I.L. 1997. *Drugs and Security in the Caribbean: Sovereignty under Seige.* University Park: Pennsylvania State University Press.

Hiro, D. 1973. *Black British, White British.* London: Penguin.

House of Commons Debate, Col. 598. 21 February 1973. Cited in *New Community* 11 (2): 160.

James, W., and C. Harris. 1993. *Inside Babylon: The Caribbean Diaspora in Britain.* London: Verso.

King, R., A. Strachan and J. Mortimer. 1983. Return Migration: A Review of the Literature. Discussion paper in geography, no. 19. Oxford Polytechnic, Oxford.

Koslofsky, J. 1981. Going Foreign? Causes of Jamaican Migration. *North American Congress on Latin America Report* 15 (1): 2–32.

Levitt, P. 1997. Transnationalizing Community Development: The Case of Boston and the Dominican Republic. *Nonprofit and Voluntary Sector Quarterly* 26: 508–26.

Macpherson, W. 1999. *The Stephen Lawrence Inquiry.* Report of an Inquiry by Sir William Macpherson of Cluny, Command of Her Majesty, Com. 4262–1. London: HMSO

Marshall, D. 1982. The History of Caribbean Migration: The Case of West Indies. *Caribbean Review* 11 (1): 6–9, 52.

Massey, D.S., et al. 1993. Theories of International Migration: A Review and Appraisal. *Population and Development Review* 19 (3): 431–66.

Massey, D.S., L. Goldring and J. Durand. 1994. Continuities in Transnational Migration: An Analysis of Nineteen Mexican Communities. *American Journal of Sociology* 99 (6): 1492–1533.

Ministry of Foreign Affairs and Foreign Trade. 1993. Government of Jamaica, Ministry Paper 2 (Jan): 13.

Modood, T., et al. 1997. *Ethnic Minorities in Britain: Diversity and Disadvantage.* London: Policy Studies Institute.

National Association of Returning Residents (NARR). 2002. *NARR*, no. 4.

Nazaroo, J.Y. 1997. *Ethnicity and Mental Health*. London: Policy Studies Institute.

Peach, C. 1998. Trends in the Levels of Caribbean Segregation, Great Britain, 1961–91. In *Caribbean Migration*, ed. M. Chamberlain, 203–16. London: Routledge.

Planning Institute of Jamaica. 2002. *Economic and Social Survey, Jamaica*. Kingston: Planning Institute of Jamaica.

———. 2003. *Economic and Social Survey, Jamaica*. Kingston: Planning Institute of Jamaica.

Rose, E.J., N. Deakin and M. Abraham 1969. *Colour and Citizenship: A Report on British Race Relations*. London: Oxford University Press.

Salt, J. 1996. Immigration and Ethnic Group. In *Ethnicity in the 1991 Census*. Volume 1, *Demographic Characteristics of Ethnic Minority Population,* ed. D. Coleman and J. Salt. London: HMSO.

Small, J. 2002. Remittances as a Development Tool in Jamaica. Paper presented at Multilateral Investment Fund, Inter-American Development Bank Round Table, Kingston, Jamaica.

———. 2003. Return Migration and the Caribbean: Some Implications for the Jamaican Diaspora. Paper delivered at Jamaican Diaspora Reciprocal Relations: Way Forward Symposium, Mona School of Business, University of the West Indies, Mona, Jamaica.

Thomas-Hope, E. 1985. Return Migration and Its Implications for Caribbean Development. In *Migration and Development in the Caribbean,* ed. R.A. Pastor, 157–77. Boulder: Westview Press.

———. 1998. Globalization and the Development of Caribbean Migration Culture. In *Caribbean Migration: Globalised Identities,* ed. M. Chamberlain, 188–99. London: Routledge.

Tilly, C. 1990. Transplanted Networks. In *Immigration Reconsidered: History, Sociology and Politics,* ed. V. Yans-McLaughlin, 79–95. New York: Oxford University Press.

United Kingdom. Pensions and Overseas Benefits Directorate. 1999. Table of Retirement Pensions, Widows Benefits and Sickness and Invalidity Benefits Paid to Caribbean Territories. Newcastle: Department of Social Security.

Warnes, T. 1996. The Age Structure and Aging of the Ethnic Groups. In *Ethnicity in the 1991 Census*. Vol. 1, *Demographic Characteristics of Ethnic Minority Populations,* ed. D. Coleman and J. Salt, London: HMSO.

# "Return" Migration to Jamaica and Barbados from the United Kingdom in the 1990s

## Some Lessons

| Harry Goulbourne |

## Introduction

The decision to return to Jamaica had been made a long time ago, the third time I had been back to Jamaica was 1978. At that time, I was already sixty years old and I said to myself, if I am in England in the next ten years then something is wrong. I just thought that this is the place that I want to retire, return to my roots and make a comfortable life for myself. . . . To me the crime and social breakdown in Jamaica is the same as everywhere. I am aware of it. I just pray that it does not affect me personally. You are aware of the crime, poverty and violence, but it does not consume me. It happens in Britain, so it's nothing new. I do take precautions like not parking my car in a secluded place or checking my yard before opening the front door. One cannot be too lacks with those sorts of hit and run crimes in Jamaica which are common but at the same time one cannot run their life always in fear. I am glad that I did follow my dream and now live in Mandeville. (JR 38 1A)[1]

I find that most Jamaicans assume, if you're coming to Jamaica at our age, mid-thirties or whatever, then, somehow, you are either mad, which the English are supposed to be . . . or you come back and you have lots of money, otherwise, why would you come back to Jamaica? . . . You've got a visa, you've got a passport and you're young so what the hell are you doing in Jamaica? (JRRI 150A)

These statements indicate the complex lives which, arguably, are part of the movement into and from the Caribbean region since large-scale migration to Britain began in the late 1950s. This chapter focuses on an important and developing dimension of a continuous story by outlining aspects of the "return" migration of Caribbeans to Jamaica and Barbados in the 1990s. While the chapter draws on research conducted in the late 1990s, the general trends and patterns outlined are relevant during the first five years of the new century. It must also be noted that some relevant developments – not discussed in this chapter – have occurred since the first years of the present century including, for example, government upgrading of the units dealing with returnees and encouraging the establishment of "diasporic" organizations in Britain to facilitate return, investment, and so forth.

## Background

While the movement of people between the Caribbean and Britain has been continuous since at least the seventeenth century, large-scale migration from the region effectively started in 1948 with the arrival of 492 Jamaicans on the SS *Empire Windrush*. This peaked in 1961 and more or less ended by 1973. After the mid-1970s, the annual net-migration balance between the two countries amounted to only a few thousand people, and at the turn of the century a noticeable new wave of migration, mainly from Jamaica, recommenced. In the immediate post-war years, the pattern of emigration from the Caribbean to Britain was largely seen as a response to demand for labour in the mother country and the belief among West Indian sojourners that higher wages could be obtained for their labour. Prior to the 1950s, West Indians preferred to migrate to the United States because there was a large Caribbean population already settled there. The United States was also considered to be a wealthier country, but the McCarran Walter Act in 1952 detached the British West Indies from Britain and so reduced the number of West Indians who could migrate to the United States.

The decade of the 1990s is very important in the history of post-war Caribbean migration to Britain because the group who arrived in the 1950s and 1960s at nineteen to twenty-four years of age began reaching the age of retirement. The subgroup of the Caribbean population in Britain who are of pensionable age doubled between the census of 1981 and 1991 from less than

6 per cent to over 11 per cent of the total. By 2001, this age group will have increased in size to nearly 50 per cent of the Caribbean-born population (Byron and Condon 1996; Byron 1999), and an early analysis of the 2001 national census suggests that in general this pattern has continued into the present century (Owen 2005). In the 1990s, studies by Byron and Condon (1996) and Peach (1991) concentrated on the ageing Caribbean-born population and their return to the region and to a lesser extent to their possible re-migration (most likely to North America). Peach showed that from a high of over 330,000 in 1966, the Caribbean-born population declined to 233,000 in the period of 1986 to 1988 (1991, 2). After taking into account 1,457 deaths over the period, he concluded that re-migration to North America and return migration to the Caribbean must have accounted for the majority of the 97,000 decline in this element of the UK population. Drawing on the 1991 British national census and the regional census by the Commonwealth Caribbean Economic Community (CARICOM) of the same year, Byron and Condon (1996, 96) suggested that between 1981 and 1991 the Caribbean-born population in the United Kingdom declined by 26,988 persons, or approximately 9 per cent, after taking into account the deaths of 3,600 persons.

With respect to destination, Peach (1991, 12–14) speculated that during the two decades from 1966, over 50 per cent of returnees, or about 48,000, would be destined for Jamaica. Barbados received the next highest number of returnees at about 7,000. This was because over 50 per cent of Commonwealth Caribbean migrants to Britain came from Jamaica, with Barbados being the next largest sending country (see Peach 1968; Deakin 1970, chs. 3, 4) and the 1991 census returns confirmed a continuing predominance by people of Jamaican background in the Caribbean community in Britain (see Owen 1996). It is not surprising, therefore, that Jamaica is the destination of the vast majority of people returning to the region.

While the phenomenon of return migration is far from being new, it is suggested here that the volume and patterns of return in the 1990s creates new opportunities as well as raises problems for families and fresh social policy issues for relevant authorities in Britain and those Commonwealth Caribbean countries, such as Jamaica and Barbados, which are immediately affected.

# The Volume of Return Migrants to
# Jamaica and Barbados

Observing the trend of the increasing volume of return migration since the late 1980s, the government of Jamaica was the first in the region to provide a structure for the management of the process of returning citizens and residents through the establishment of the Returning Residents Facilitation Unit. Before considering the arrangements in place in Jamaica for returnees in the last decade, however, it is first relevant to indicate further the volume of return to Jamaica, the country with the largest migrant population and for which data were available by the end of the 1990s.

In the first instance, table 11.1 shows the obvious fact that the vast majority of people who returned to Jamaica were from North America and the United Kingdom. The table does not show the figure for 1992, but according to the Returning Residents Facilitation Unit, in that year 1,552 persons returned to Jamaica "who would have met the criteria of the Returning Residents Programme" (RRFU 1997) had it been in operation at the time. The numbers increased and remained at over 2,000 in the four years from 1993 to 1996, as table 11.1 shows.

The second characteristic to note from table 11.1 is that while the returnees from North America constituted a simple majority, the single largest contingent of Jamaicans returning to the island was from the United Kingdom. This difference may have been due to two important factors. First, sizeable post-war migration from Jamaica and the rest of then British

**Table 11.1**        Number of Returning Residents to Jamaica, 1993–1997

| Year | UK | USA | Canada | Other | Total |
|------|------|------|--------|-------|--------|
| 1993 | 919 | 988 | 278 | 174 | 2,359 |
| 1994 | 1,145 | 999 | 333 | 110 | 2,587 |
| 1995 | 1,007 | 905 | 288 | 153 | 2,353 |
| 1996 | 995 | 863 | 296 | 114 | 2,268 |
| 1997 | 995 | 762 | 244 | 91 | 2,092 |
| Total | 5,061 | 4,517 | 1,439 | 642 | 11,659 |

Source: *RRFU 1997*.

West Indies to North America occurred later than migration to the United Kingdom. Consequently, there may be proportionally more of this cohort of elderly Jamaican-born people in Britain than in North America. Second, the proximity of Caribbean points of departure and North American destinations facilitated greater frequency of visits and may have also meant that there was less of a feeling of need to return on a long-term or permanent basis.

In other words, regular and frequent contacts between North America and Jamaica far out distanced those between the island and the United Kingdom, and these contacts, along with the relative proximity, may partly explain the motivation to return on a long-term basis by UK residents.

There are, of course, important aspects of the return phenomenon which these figures do not tell. For example, it should be stressed that the return migration phenomenon was not simply a matter of migrants returning to the region after their sojourn in Britain. Many of those described as returnees were in fact migrants to the region, because they were born and brought up in the United Kingdom or they were spouses of individuals from, or with close links in, the region. These characteristics of the Caribbean communities in the United Kingdom were reflected in the difficulty officials in the

**Table 11.2**   Number of Returning Residents to Jamaica by Month 1996

| Month | UK | USA | Canada | Other | Total |
|---|---|---|---|---|---|
| January | 84 | 62 | 25 | 07 | 178 |
| February | 57 | 52 | 14 | 08 | 131 |
| March | 58 | 43 | 13 | 09 | 123 |
| April | 65 | 59 | 16 | 05 | 145 |
| May | 78 | 63 | 17 | 11 | 169 |
| June | 66 | 73 | 20 | 05 | 164 |
| July | 75 | 85 | 33 | 13 | 206 |
| August | 62 | 85 | 27 | 17 | 191 |
| September | 68 | 70 | 27 | 13 | 178 |
| October | 138 | 98 | 32 | 13 | 281 |
| November | 125 | 80 | 32 | 06 | 243 |
| December | 119 | 93 | 40 | 07 | 259 |
| Total | 995 | 863 | 296 | 114 | 2,268 |

*Source*: RRFU 1997.

**Table 11.3**    Number of Returning Residents to Jamaica 1997

| Month | UK | USA | Canada | Other | Total |
|---|---|---|---|---|---|
| January | 97 | 61 | 20 | 11 | 189 |
| February | 74 | 50 | 16 | 11 | 151 |
| March | 66 | 55 | 14 | 10 | 145 |
| April | 72 | 46 | 13 | 07 | 138 |
| May | 75 | 57 | 18 | 04 | 154 |
| June | 84 | 64 | 20 | 10 | 178 |
| July | 83 | 77 | 25 | 04 | 189 |
| August | 52 | 75 | 20 | 11 | 158 |
| September | 90 | 78 | 21 | 10 | 189 |
| October | 113 | 65 | 25 | 03 | 206 |
| November | 93 | 54 | 23 | 07 | 177 |
| December | 96 | 80 | 29 | 03 | 208 |
| Total | 995 | 762 | 244 | 91 | 2,082 |

*Source:* RRFU 1998.

Caribbean have in describing the status of returnees who are variously referred to as "returning residents", "returning citizens" and "returning nationals". However, none of these is an adequate description of all the people involved in the process, confirming King's (1986) observation that there are several models of return migration.

Three factors help to explain this situation. First, from at least the 1970s, the majority of people of Caribbean background in Britain were born in the United Kingdom but due to their well-documented unfavourable differential incorporation, many share the long-term aspiration of their parents to live in the Caribbean and a small minority take the step to fulfil this dream. Second, people of Caribbean backgrounds in Britain exhibit a strong tendency towards exogenous marriages and living companionships, with a significant percentage of children (over 20 per cent) in this segment of the community having both Caribbean and indigenous white parents (see Owen 1996). Third, there is no legal obstacle to the fulfilment of the desire to live in the region.

Another aspect of the return migration experience is that the return is not a permanent or static feature but is rather a recurring and dynamic process.

This is also no doubt an important difference from earlier experiences of migration and return (to Panama or Cuba, for instance) in the region (see, for example, Richardson 1985). In other words, the experiences of families reveal a fairly regular pattern of return to the Caribbean often followed by "return" to the United Kingdom. This is true both for elderly Caribbean-born returnees as well as young people who were born and brought up in the United Kingdom and who, on "returning" to the region with some members of their families, do not necessarily close off their options to find their way back to the United Kingdom.

## The Structure and Contents of Support for Return

Expectedly, the return phenomenon raises questions about the nature and structure of support for returning residents and their families. These include informal supports such as are provided by families themselves as well as the more formal public structures through which support is channelled. The latter includes the island associations and a variety of welfare bodies that Caribbean communities have established over the years in Britain and increasingly in Jamaica, facilitation units established by the Jamaican government (as mentioned earlier), and the formal structure of relations between Britain and Commonwealth Caribbean states.

Whatever the actual size of return migration during the years since the 1960s, it was not until the 1990s that governments in the Caribbean have been forced to take account of the volume and patterns of return of citizens and their families. Jamaica was the first to do so, followed by Barbados. St Lucia, which is also experiencing a significant volume of returning citizens and their families (Abenaty 2000, 2001), by 2000 was also set to follow the Jamaican and Barbadian lead. In contrast to Barbados and Jamaica, officials in Trinidad and Tobago in the late 1990s had not felt a need to establish any special unit to facilitate returnees, because the volume had not been significant.

In Jamaica, the Returning Residents Facilitation Unit was established under former Ambassador Don Brice in 1993 within the Ministry of Foreign Affairs and Foreign Trade. Brice had served in Barbados and had led the Jamaican team in the negotiations to extend membership of CARICOM beyond the Commonwealth Caribbean. The appointment of this senior diplomat would suggest that the Jamaican government was giving priority to this initiative.

Following suit, in 1996 the Barbadian government established the Facilitation Unit for Returning Nationals, also within the Ministry of Foreign Affairs under the co-ordination of Jeffrey Hunte, a senior foreign service official who had served in London and knew well the Barbadian community in the United Kingdom. Like the Jamaican Returning Residents Facilitation Unit, one of the first actions of the Facilitation Unit for Returning Nationals was to publish a booklet setting out the government's generous concessions to intending returnees. In the view of some Jamaicans in London, the Barbadian Charter for Returning and Overseas Nationals is much more generous than its Jamaican model, the Charter for Long-Term Returning Residents.

Consistent with the establishment of these bodies, the Jamaican and Barbadian governments took steps actively to provide relevant information to intending returnees, and their high commissions, embassies and consulates in the United Kingdom and North America have accessible facilities for families with such plans. In particular, coinciding with the promotion of Jamaica Expo exhibitions to the United Kingdom from the mid-1990s, Don Brice and Lloyd Wilkes at the high commission organized seminars in London to inform and advise potential returnees about the facilities, opportunities and difficulties in Jamaica. These meetings were usually well attended and lively. Well-informed discussions took place about the issues returnees and intending returnees raise. In addition, the *Jamaica Gleaner* newspaper, which is widely circulated in the Jamaican and Caribbean communities in Britain, from time-to-time published a returning residents supplement. Newspapers in Barbados also sometimes carried important news about returnees. The unit also established a website accessible by all who wished to consult it for information about the developing situation across the Atlantic.

The Barbadian and Jamaican facilitation units collected relevant data about returnees and their families from customs, embassies, high commissions, community associations and other relevant bodies. They provided information about the total process of return, including government concessions with respect to custom and excise duties, expected pitfalls of return and opportunities available to returnees. A data bank of the skills of returnees was created with the aim of facilitating the contribution of returnees to the Jamaican and Barbadian economies.

Returning nationals and their families as well as the governments of respective countries benefited from the activities of island and welfare associations on both sides of the Atlantic. The island associations were generally established during the period of entry and settlement in British cities, particularly from the mid-1950s (see Goulbourne 1990; Fitzgerald 1988; Heinemann 1972). But while it was generally thought that with time these organizations would atrophy through lack of support from migrants' children, many of these organizations have remained buoyant with the active support of retired migrants as well as younger people who wish to maintain and celebrate their parents' Caribbean heritage which is a living part of their present. For example, Hinds (1992) found that there were fifteen such associations operating in London and the twelve among which he conducted research had a total membership of 2,854 members. Of course memberships vary, but Hinds's figures suggested that each association had an average of 238 members. In other parts of the country, researchers have reported similar statistics (see, for example, Hylton 1997; Goulbourne 1990, 2003), suggesting that these bodies were very much alive and active in Caribbean communities.

In the main, these associations have been concerned with maintaining close links with their members' homelands, preserving of island cultures, helping members with welfare problems, providing assistance to nationals in Britain and the Caribbean and, on specific occasions, mobilizing around political or natural crises "back home". In the 1990s, the return migration process was another factor that gave new life to these bodies, because they were well placed to provide assistance to members planning to return or re-migrate. Along with their other functions, these associations served as forums for transmitting information about those who had taken the step to return and from time to time visit families and friends.

Just as Caribbean migrants to Britain formed associations to provide for their needs, so too when they returned to the region were they busy forming returning residents or nationals associations in the 1990s. There were associations in all the fourteen parishes in Jamaica and these associations are also widespread in Barbados. These bodies may have been seen as Caribbean extensions of their British counterpart, because they were inspired by much the same concerns about integration in the local community, defending their interests and bringing their comparative experience to bear on particular situations. Immigrants to Britain needed to protect themselves, as well as gather to provide companionship and help for each other in a less than friendly environment. On returning to the islands they soon found that the experiences during their sojourns had changed them, unaware, into English men and women. They were discovering that they spoke, walked, dressed, shopped and went about their daily routines in ways that were not merely "foreign", but peculiarly "English" in the eyes of their erstwhile country women and men. This change was also evident to those who had not travelled or whose sojourn had taken them to North America and elsewhere closer to home.

Of course, the situation in the 1990s was not helped by the fact that the returnee frequently decided to resettle in an area some distance from where they had close family connections, thereby realizing another aspect of the Caribbean migrant's dream, that is, self-improvement defined in terms of physical relocation or residential upward social mobility (see Thomas-Hope 1992). For example, in Jamaica the hill town of Mandeville has acquired the reputation of being a desirable destination for returnees who create a prosperous ghetto characterized by some English past-times: rounding off of the afternoon with English tea as well as the cultivation and display of well-manicured lawns and gardens ordered more for aesthetic satisfaction than for practical use. These gardens stand in sharp contrast with the utilitarian kitchen and fruit gardens of rural Jamaica.

It is significant that in Jamaica, returnees from North America did not feel the need to organize to promote or defend interests particular to themselves while the less numerous UK returnees have been compulsive organizers whose voices are now being heard, if only in a minor key, by policy makers. This suggests that the important differences in the British and North American migrant experiences that some commentators have pointed to (see, for example, Thomas-Hope 1992) remain and have significant implications in the return loop of the Caribbean diasporic experience.

## State-to-State Relations

There has, of course, been a well-established structure of relations between the British state and states in the Commonwealth Caribbean. This provided an overall context within which the process of return could be managed and made relatively easy. Commonwealth membership helps to ensure the enjoyment of dual citizenship status, residential and voting rights where local by-laws and regulations (such as residency or entry on the electoral roll) are met and the sharing of a number of judicial and political institutions, some of which are about to change.

One arrangement that is independent of Commonwealth membership and of paramount importance for the returnee or those migrating from the United Kingdom to the region concerns pensions and benefits. While there have long been provisions for a person to exercise their pension rights abroad, there are restrictions regarding the receipt of benefits and inflation rise. Specific bilateral agreements have had to be entered into with Britain. Barbados and Jamaica have agreements from which returnees can now benefit. Jamaica was one of the first countries in the 1970s to take advantage of this regime and in 1992 Barbados did the same.

There are, however, several kinds of benefits and each bilateral agreement has to specify which are covered. For example, in the case of Jamaica, only six benefits were covered (whereas a similar agreement with Cyprus covered nine); however, while the Jamaican agreement did not cover invalidity benefits at the time of the report, it now does. A report by the Commission for Racial Equality (1992) noted that there were three conditions which appeared to govern these agreements: reciprocity, that is, countries entering into such agreements with Britain should have similar systems in operation to that in the United Kingdom; substantial population exchange; and not a situation of Britain "exporting benefits" to another country. These and related issues remain to be further researched and their implications for transnational families considered, but at this point it is pertinent to turn to some of the problems and opportunities involved in the return phenomenon.

## Problems Returnees Face

There are several problems and opportunities generated by the process of return and resettlement. These include both psychological and practical difficulties involved in the decision to move from one physical and social location to another, and these are often compounded by the returnees' memories and expectations. Problems associated with custom and excise rules, health services, house price and residential choice and concentration as well as the less than professional behaviour of some lawyers have been at the root of the returnees' practical concerns and these have tended to influence not only the final decision to return but also the day-to-day struggles involved in the process of resettlement.

As noted earlier, the Jamaican Returning Residents Facilitation Unit and the Barbadian Facilitation Unit for Returning Nationals set out generous terms for returnees. In the first place, the returnee is generously defined with respect to nationality, law and the number of years spent abroad in order to qualify for the concessions offered. The Jamaican charter described a national as a person who had attained the age of eighteen and who had "been resident overseas for not less than the past three consecutive years" (RRFU 1995, 5); the Barbadian charter spoke of a "citizen by birth, descent, registration or naturalisation" returning to the island after ten years abroad (FURN 1996, 5). While Jamaica has been more lenient with the number of years spent abroad to qualify as a returning resident, Barbados was more generous about specific concessions regarding personal possessions and cars, but both charters were careful to set out, in considerable detail, the provisions for returning nationals about household and personal possessions, motor vehicles and tools of trade, each of which was carefully defined and described to avoid ambiguity and uncertainty.

Nonetheless, and as might be expected, intending and actual returnees complained about the restrictions imposed on items such as the number of televisions, pieces of furniture and so forth that they could take without charge into Barbados or Jamaica. There were also complaints about the level of tax placed on more expensive items such as cars. In Jamaica, returnees frequently complained about more day-to-day aspects of life such as the rough and ready or brusque manners of public functionaries such as custom officers, lawyers, secretaries and others with whom returnees come into close contact at the time of return and soon thereafter as they resettled.

In Barbados, there have been signs of a degree of resentment against returnees receiving differential treatment at excise and customs. Jamaicans were particularly vociferous about these issues, and they felt that since they had lived and worked hard for their possessions in a hostile British environment, they should be allowed to take them without too much hindrance back to a Jamaica which they had continued to regard as home during what many saw as their painful sojourn.

A long-standing issue faced by some returnees has been that of dishonest estate dealers and lawyers. There have been cases of individuals returning with their families to find that the properties they thought they had been paying for over several years from hard earned savings either do not exist or were owned by others. As regards Britain, while some elderly returnees tend to express the view that they had no desire to return to the United Kingdom, there was a general feeling that they might visit family members, especially their children and grandchildren who continued to live in England.

Many returnees were, as noted earlier, young people who may have been expected to be healthy and easily insurable by the many private companies active in the region. It may be supposed, however, that the vast majority of returnees were born in these countries and are now in their twilight years of retirement. In this period of life, these individuals look forward to reaping some of the small benefits of a life of hard work in a foreign land, even if that land was regarded by some as the mother country, in an imperial myth that was central to the colonial Caribbean they left four or five decades before. The age profile of the majority of returnees sets the framework for the kinds of health problems they were likely to face: high blood pressure, diabetes and other old age infirmities.

Returnees from the United Kingdom faced particular difficulties, and Jamaicans appeared to face greater problems than Barbadians. In Barbados, the health and social security systems were more comprehensive than in Jamaica and the less fortunate returnees were more likely to receive help than in Jamaica where assistance appeared to have been less progressive. For example, in Barbados it was possible for persons with pensions which fell below the national average to be topped up, and, as pointed out by officials, by 1996 there had been at least one such instance of assistance to a returnee from the United Kingdom.

In Jamaica, returnees appeared to be in need of state assistance in making adequate health arrangements for their later years. This problem may have stemmed from a widespread view in the United Kingdom that it is the state's responsibility to provide medical care for citizens who contributed their taxes to the public purse and, therefore, the individual need not enter into private arrangements with insurance companies or medical firms.

In contrast, people returning from the United States appeared not to have this problem, because in that country the general assumption is that the individual will see to his or her family's health needs through private arrangements. Jamaican returnees from the United Kingdom were therefore in need of the assistance of the UK and the Jamaican governments to establish schemes with medical insurance companies, and in the late 1990s there were discussions taking place along such lines between some leaders of returnees, the Jamaican government and the American company Blue Cross. Meanwhile, it appeared that for those who could afford it, one option was to visit the United Kingdom periodically for monitoring and treatment of health conditions and also to purchase drugs less expensively. Obviously, it is in situations such as this that family members still in the United Kingdom may provide assistance to those who have returned to the Caribbean.

## Opportunities for Returnees to Jamaica

There is no intention to leave the impression that returning to the Caribbean is nothing but a fraught business. It must now be obvious that while there were and are likely to be a number of problems facing many of those who decide to return and settle in Jamaica, there have also been many opportunities for those seeking to make or re-establish their homes in these countries. In the first place, in both Barbados and Jamaica, there appeared in the 1990s to have been little difficulty in securing employment by individuals who returned with skills varying from secretarial to legal work, small-scale farming, as well as employment in the manufacturing, tourist and other industries.

One obvious and significant opportunity that arises from the return phenomenon is the considerable financial contribution made to the economy of Jamaica. Such financial contributions include the transfer of savings, investments, gifts and other contributions from family members in the United Kingdom. It is not possible to quantify family contributions and gifts but it is relatively easy to quantify the transfer of pensions and benefits from the United Kingdom to the Caribbean. Since June 1994, the Pensions and Overseas Benefits Directorate in Newcastle Upon Tyne has kept information on the number of beneficiaries abroad and the amount paid. They do not, however, keep statistics on beneficiaries' age or gender, nor do they have projections for future years. Another drawback with the data is that by the very nature of pensions and benefits, the directorate is not able to have exact figures about the numbers of beneficiaries and instead concentrates on taking a "snapshot" once in the year to determine the numbers of persons receiving pensions.

**Table 11.4** Pensions and Benefits from the United Kingdom to Selected Caribbean Countries, 1995–1997

| | January–December 1995[a] | | | January–December 1996[b] | | | January–August 1997[c] | | |
|---|---|---|---|---|---|---|---|---|---|
| | RP | WB | STB | RP | WB | STB | RP | WB | STB |
| **Barbados** | | | | | | | | | |
| £ | 04,261,576.78 | 052,950.45 | 039,893.49 | 05,474,839.54 | 068,321.25 | 05,360.31 | 03,567,776.08 | 030,503.81 | 09,620.47 |
| No. | 02,499 | 30 | NA | 2,805 | 35 | NA | NA | NA | NA |
| £ | 38,005,476.97 | 785,992.55 | 411,157.06 | 45,072,245.90 | 927,987.30 | 29,746.15 | 27,739,071.10 | 560,307.78 | 24,976.23 |
| **Jamaica** | | | | | | | | | |
| No. | 20,044 | 370 | NA | 21,192 | 367 | NA | NA | NA | NA |
| £ | 00,768,601.63 | 013,169.82 | 003,158.42 | 00,851,636.49 | 015,749.67 | 00 | 00,568,544.61 | 008,739.44 | 00 |
| **Trinidad** | | | | | | | | | |
| No. | 553 | 11 | NA | 644 | 12 | NA | NA | NA | NA |

*Note:* RP = retirement pensions; WB = widows= benefits; STB = short-term benefits; NA = not available

[a]February excluded; data not available.
[b]March excluded; data not available.
[c]Data not available for the remainder of 1997.

*Source:* Pensions and Overseas Benefits Directorate, Department of Social Security, 1997.

**Table 11.5** Pensions and Benefits from the United Kingdom to Selected Caribbean Countries, 1998–1999

|  | January–December 1998 | | | January–December 1999 | | |
|---|---|---|---|---|---|---|
|  | RP | WB | STB | RP | WB | STB |
| £ | 07, 233, 480.94 | 070, 312.74 | 01, 635.82 | 08, 206,532.31 | 079, 092.66 | 00, 119. 03 |
| **Barbados** | | | | | | |
| No. | 3, 406 | 41 | NA | 03, 695 | 35 | NA |
| £ | 52, 776, 732.73 | 893, 181.36 | 16, 875.14 | 56, 287, 200.98 | 958, 338.61341 | 49, 870.32 |
| **Jamaica** | | | | | | |
| No. | 22, 966 | 340 | NA | 23, 589 | 341 | NA |
| £ | 01, 041, 284.68 | 012, 930. 41 | 00 | 01, 106, 644. 46 | 014, 758.99 | 00 |
| **Trinidad** | | | | | | |
| No. | 790 | 15 | NA | 833 | 16 | NA |

*Note:* RP = retirement pensions; WB = widows= benefits; STB = short-term benefits; NA = not available

*Source:* Pensions and Overseas Benefits Directorate, Department of Social Security, 2001.

Table 11.5 shows the continuing patterns of flows of returnees' pensions and benefits, particularly to Jamaica and Barbados, at the turn of the century. The importance of this contribution to the national economies is being recognized, but there is still more than a lingering unwillingness to give this the status it deserves in public policy. What is true for Jamaica is also true for some of the smaller islands, such as St Lucia and Grenada, but it is more difficult to locate specific figures for these islands, because of their relative small sizes. The figures for 2000 should indicate a continuing trend, but officials at the Department of Social Security were not able to supply figures at the time of writing.

Of course, it is a matter of speculation whether the number of pensioners will continue to increase or will decline or remain stable in the years ahead. What may be more likely is the steady decline of retired persons and perhaps increases in early retirees and those who are seeking to take advantage of employment opportunities, particularly skilled. The return of elderly people to the Caribbean is no doubt an advantage to those societies, but may be a loss to their families in the United Kingdom who continue to do without their full complement of relatives who made up the traditional extended family and household during the period of entry and settlement (Barrow 1982). In other words, as Nutter suggested in his study of returnees in Kingston in the mid 1980s, some of the benefits associated with returnees are limited, despite the benefits brought to the society of resettlement (see, for example, Chevannes and Ricketts 1997; Brown 1997). This may be particularly so when we consider the vulnerability of the Caribbean communities in the United Kingdom and the possible loss of social resources through the return process.

## Conclusion

These observations about the return phenomenon in the 1990s have implications for both policy and research in the United Kingdom and the Caribbean. These would include the relevance and impact of age and gender in the return migration process and resettlement; reassessment of the present and potential skills and financial contribution of returnees to Caribbean economies; the impact of returnees on family members who remain in the United Kingdom, in particular the absence of grandparents in the development of the young; audit of the needs of elderly returnees and what the UK and Caribbean governments can do to help a remarkably resilient and self-reliant element of the population to help themselves and make a worthwhile contribution to civil society; and the impact of returnees on housing, local communities and medical facilities. By the beginning of the new millennium the British media were covering a number of occasions when returnees to the region, particularly Jamaica, were being targeted by robbers as part of the apparent anomic violence that is becoming characteristic of the region.

These are issues for the research community to address and they provide a basis for overcoming the great divide between those scholars who see themselves concerned with race relations matters in Britain and those who are concerned with migration and Caribbean societies. The discussion here suggests that we need to recognize more clearly the unified field in which these matters are actually enacted. After all, for the individuals and the families involved in the transatlantic world, bordered by the British Isles, North America and the Caribbean, migration is a unified experience and family networks are only temporarily fractured in the crossings of the waters.

## Acknowledgements

A similar version of this chapter was published by Harry Goulborne in a self-authored book entitled *Caribbean Transnational Experience* (London: Pluto, 2002).

## Note

1. All primary references, unless otherwise stated, are interview data collected in the Economic and Social Research Council research programme on Population and Household Change. The project is entitled "Family Structure and Social Change of Caribbeans in Britain". The data tapes are deposited with the Economic and Social Research Council Qualidata Resource Centre at the University of Essex. The tape reference is divided into three parts. First, the letter refers to the place of origin of the respondent: J is for Jamaican and B is for Barbados; second, the num-

ber refers to the family code; and third, the last numbers are the tape number and the side (A or B) of the tape where the quote was taken.

# References

Abenaty, F. 2000. St Lucians and Migration: Migrant Returnees, their Families and St Lucian Society. PhD thesis, London South Bank University, London.

————. 2001. The Dynamics of Return Migration to St Lucia. In *Caribbean Families in Britain and the Trans-Atlantic World,* ed. H. Goulbourne and M. Chamberlain, 131–51. London: Macmillan.

Barrow, J. 1982. West Indian Families: An Insider's Perspective. In *Families in Britain,* ed. R.N. Rapoport, M.P. Fogerty and R. Rapoport, 52–69. London: Routledge and Kegan Paul.

Brown, D. 1997. Workforce Losses and Return Migration to the Caribbean: A Case Study of Jamaican Nurses. In *Caribbean Circuits: New Directions in the Study of Caribbean Migration,* ed. P.R. Pessar, 197–223. New York: Center for Migration Studies.

Byron, M. 1999. The Caribbean-Born Population in 1990s Britain: Who Will Return? *Journal of Ethnic and Migration Studies* 25 (2): 285–301.

Byron, M., and S. Condon. 1996. A Comparative Study of Caribbean Return Migration from Britain and France: Towards a Context-Dependent Explanation. *Transaction, Institute of British Geographers* 21 (1): 91–104.

Chevannes, B., and R. Ricketts. 1997. Return Migration and Small Business Development in Jamaica. In *Caribbean Circuits: New Directions in the Study of Caribbean Migration,* ed. P.R. Pessar, 161–95. New York: Center for Migration Studies.

Commission for Racial Equality. 1992. *The Social Security Persons Abroad Regulations: An Analysis of the Conditions Governing Continued Entitlement to Disability Benefits of Persons Going Abroad and their Implications for Ethnic Minorities.* London: Commission for Racial Equality.

Deakin, N. 1970. *Colour, Citizenship and British Society.* London: Panther Modern Society.

Facilitation Unit for Returning Nationals/Ministry of Foreign Affairs (FURN). 1996. *Returning Nationals Booklet.* Bridgetown, Barbados: Facilitation Unit for Returning Nationals/Ministry of Foreign Affairs.

Fitzgerald, M. 1988. African Caribbean Involvement in British politics. In *Lost Illusions: Caribbean Minorities in Britain and the Netherlands,* ed. M. Cross and H. Entzinger, 127–49. London: Routledge.

Goulbourne, H. 2002. *Caribbean Transnational Experience.* London: Pluto Press.

———. 2003. Editorial: Caribbean Families and Communities. *Community, Work and Family* 6 (1): 3–16.

———, ed. 1990. *Black Politics in Britain.* Aldershot: Avebury.

Heinemann, B. 1972. *The Politics of the Powerless.* Oxford: Oxford University Press.

Hinds, A. 1992. *Report on Organizations Serving the Afro-Caribbean Community.* London: West Indian Standing Conference.

Hylton, C. 1997. Caribbean Community Organisations in Leeds. PhD Thesis, Department of Sociology, University of Leeds.

International Office, Pensions and Overseas Benefits Directorate, Department of Social Security. 2001. Comission Regulation (EC) No 89/2001 of 17 January 2001 amending Council Regulation (EEC) No 574/72 laying down the procedure for implementing Regulation (EEC) No 1408/71. Newcastle upon Tyne: HMSO.

King, R. 1986. Return Migration and Regional Economic Development: An Overview. In *Return Migration and Regional Economic Problems,* ed. R. King, 9–25 . London: Croom Helm.

Owen, D. 1996. Size, Structure and Growth of the Ethnic Minority Populations. In *Ethnicity in the 1991 Census: Demographic Characteristics of the Ethnic Minority Populations,* ed. D. Coleman and J. Salt. London: HMSO.

———. 2005. Demographic Profiles and Social Cohesion of Minority Ethnic Communities in Britain. Paper presented at Families, Minority Ethnic Communities and Social Capital seminar, London, South Bank University, 14 January.

Peach, C. 1968. *West Indian Migration to Britain: A Social Geography.* London: Oxford University Press.

———. 1991. *The Caribbean in Europe: Contrasting Patterns of Migration and Settlement in Britain, France and the Netherlands.* Research Paper in Ethnic Relations, no. 15. Coventry: Centre for Research in Ethnic Relations, Warwick University.

Pensions and Overseas Benefits Directorate, Department of Social Security, Commission Regulations. 1997. (EC) No 89/2001. Newcastle upon Tyne: HMSO.

Returning Residents Facilitation Unit/Ministry of Foreign Affairs and Foreign Trade (RRFU). 1995. *Numbers of Returning Residents.* Kingston: Returning Residents Facilitation Unit/Ministry of Foreign Affairs and Foreign Trade.

———. 1997. *Numbers of Returning Residents.* Kingston: Returning Residents Facilitation Unit/Ministry of Foreign Affairs and Foreign Trade.

———. 1998. *Numbers of Returning Residents.* Kingston: Returning Residents Facilitation Unit/Ministry of Foreign Affairs and Foreign Trade.

Richardson, B. 1985. *Panana Money in Barbados, 1900–1920,* Knoxville: University of Tennessee Press.

Thomas-Hope, E. 1992. *Explanation in Caribbean Migration.* London: Macmillan.

# Contributors

**Dwaine E. Plaza** is Associate Professor, Department of Sociology, Oregon State University. His teaching interests are in race and ethnic relations, research methods, and cross-cultural issues. He completed a doctorate at York University in 1996, which focused on the mobility strategies used by African-Caribbean men in Canada. His current research interests are on the settlement and acculturation issues facing second-generation Caribbeans in the international diaspora.

**Frances Henry** is Professor Emerita, York University, Canada, but she continues an active research and writing career both in Canada and the Caribbean. Dr Henry has been a member of the prestigious Royal Society of Canada since 1989. Since the mid-1970s, she has consistently pioneered research in the field of attitudes towards people of colour. She has had a continuing interest in migration and return. Her publications include *The Colour of Democracy: Racism in Canadian Society*; *Challenging Racism in the Arts*; and *Discourses of Domination: Racial Bias in the Canadian English Language Press; The Caribbean Diaspora in Toronto: Learning to Live with Racism;* and *Reclaiming African Religions in Trinidad: The Socio-Political Legitimation of the Orisha and Spiritual Baptist Faiths.*

**Francis K. Abenaty** was for many years Senior Lecturer at the Birmingham College of Food, Tourism and Creative Studies. He retired to resettle in St Lucia. In 2000, he completed his doctorate on the return of St Lucian families from Britain, and he is presently developing and extending his interest in return migration. Abenaty was born and raised in St Lucia.

**Dennis A.V. Brown** is Lecturer, Department of Behavioural Sciences, University of the West Indies, St Augustine. His main area of interest is development studies, with a focus on poverty and international migration. His most recent publications include "Listening to the 'Youthman': Structure, Meaning and Identity in the Explanation of Male Juvenile

Delinquency among Poor Youth in Trinidad and Tobago" and "Inbetween-ity: Marginalization, Migration and Poverty among Haitians in the Turks and Caicos Islands".

**Roger-Mark De Souza** is Technical Director of the Population, Health and Environment Programme at the Population Reference Bureau, a research organization that examines the policy implications of population trends. For more than a decade, De Souza has conducted policy analysis on a wide range of development issues internationally and within the United States. He holds a master's in development policy from George Washington University and a post-graduate degree in international relations from the University of the West Indies.

**George Gmelch** is Roger Thayer Stone Professor of Anthropology at Union College. He is the author of nine books on topics ranging from Irish travellers to urban anthropology to American professional baseball. His most recent writing has been on tourism, notably *Behind the Smile: The Working Lives of Caribbean Tourism*. He is currently editing a book on the globalization of baseball.

**Harry Goulbourne** is Professor of Sociology, London South Bank University. He has taught sociology and politics at the universities of Gloucestershire and Warwick (United Kingdom), West Indies (Jamaica) and Dar es Salaam (Tanzania), and he has published extensively on a range of subjects including nationalism, race and ethnicity, development politics and, more recently, family studies. His present work focuses on families, social capital, society and change in post-imperial Britain.

**Heather A. Horst** is an honorary research fellow in the Department of Anthropology at University College London. Her publications include "A Pilgrimage Home: Tombs, Burial and Belonging in Jamaica" in the Journal of Material Culture and "Landscaping Englishness: The Postcolonial Predicaments of Returnees in Mandeville, Jamaica", in *The Experience of Return Migration: Caribbean Perspectives,* edited by Rob Potter, Dennis Conway and Joan Phillips. She is currently preparing a manuscript with Daniel Miller about the appropriation of the cellular phones among low-income Jamaicans.

**Godfrey C. St Bernard** is a research fellow at the Sir Arthur Lewis Institute of Social and Economic Studies, University of the West Indies, St Augustine, Trinidad and Tobago. His publications cover a range of issues including population and development, Caribbean family structures, adult literacy, social measurement, ethnicity and youth. He is also the co-author of a book entitled *Behind the Bridge: Politics, Power and Patronage in Laventille, Trinidad.*

**John Small** is Lecturer in Human Service Management and Coordinator of the Management concentration of the Master of Social Work programme, University of the West Indies, Mona. He has published several papers in social work and human services in international journals, and is co-author of *Social Work with Black Children and their Families.* His current research includes international migration, return migration, transnational families and dual heritage.

**Elizabeth Thomas-Hope** is the James Seivright Moss-Solomon (Snr.) Professor of Environmental Management and head of the Department of Geography and Geology, University of the West Indies, Mona. Her publications include *Explanation in Caribbean Migration,* reprinted as *Caribbean Migration*; *Geography of the Third World* (co-author); *Solid Waste Management: Critical Issues for Developing Countries; Natural Resource Management for Sustainable Development in the Caribbean* (co-editor); as well as other works on migration, Caribbean social issues and the environment.